# DATE DUE

# Journalists under Fire

# Journalists under Fire:
# The Psychological Hazards of Covering War

Anthony Feinstein, M.Phil., Ph.D., F.R.C.P.(C)

Professor, Department of Psychiatry
University of Toronto

Foreword by Chris Hedges

THE JOHNS HOPKINS UNIVERSITY PRESS    BALTIMORE

The Johns Hopkins University Press
2715 North Charles Street
Baltimore, Maryland 21218-4363
www.press.jhu.edu

An earlier version of portions of this book was published in 2003 as
*Dangerous Lives: War and the Men and Women Who Report It.*

Library of Congress Cataloging-in-Publication Data

Feinstein, A. (Anthony), 1956–
  Journalists under fire : the psychological hazards of covering war /
Anthony Feinstein.
    p. ; cm.
  Includes bibliographical references and index.
    ISBN 0-8018-8441-1 (hardcover : alk. paper)
    1. Neuroses — Case studies. 2. Post-traumatic stress disorder — Case
studies. 3. War correspondents — Mental health — Case studies. 4. War —
Psychological aspects. I. Title.
  [DNLM: 1. Stress Disorders, Post-Traumatic — psychology — Case Reports.
2. Journalism — Case Reports. 3. War — Case Reports.
WM 170 F299j 2006]
RC361.F45 2006
616.85′21 — dc22        2006002415

A catalog record for this book is available from the British Library.

To John Owen and Chris Cramer

# Contents

# Foreword

When it is all over, when the emotional and physical exhaustion have left war journalists depleted and broken, their personal lives often in shambles, their sleep plagued by images of carnage and death, and their careers at times in tatters, they come home to their news organizations, or, in the slang of the profession, to the beast. The beast, which for years they fed with exotic news stories, photographs, and video footage, loomed over them as they filed from dismal and depressing towns and cities, wracked by violence and fear, in Africa, Latin America, the Middle East, and the Balkans. The beast was rarely satiated, always looking for a new angle, a new variant on the killing and the mayhem. The names of these obscure, far-flung conflicts become dusty and vague with time to those who were not there. But these same names, and the pain and misery the names evoke, wind themselves slowly like a huge coil around the hearts of survivors. The beast moves on, swallowing new news, consuming different lives and passions. This is the nature of beasts. But those who were in the war cannot forget. They become frozen in time, walking around newsrooms years later with eyes that see things others do not see, haunted by graphic memories of human cruelty and depravity, no longer sure what life is about or what it means, wondering if they can ever connect with those around them. I have watched some fall, like high-flying aircraft that burst suddenly into flames, to earth, where the twisted wreckage of their lives lies in pathetic heaps. The beast moves on. It leaves them behind. It consumes new fodder, those young idealists who go to war to change the world and come home betrayed, bearing the awful mark of Cain.

*Journalists under Fire* is not simply about the trauma of covering war. It is also, although this is often unstated, about the callousness and cruelty of news organizations, which crumple up and discard those who return to them in pieces. It is about a news culture that does not take care of its own. And no organization, as Dr. Anthony Feinstein observes, is exempt: "Not only had most of the news organizations neglected to provide for the psychological welfare of their war reporters, but trauma researchers had ignored them too." Feinstein writes, "Trawling through the literature, I could not find a single reference to the subject—no articles, chapters, or abstracts. I had stumbled on a virgin topic, lying unrecognized within a larger literature devoted to the emotional consequences of traumatic events." As much as this book is a chronicle of the trauma of war journalists, it is also a searing indictment of the beast, which even now feeds off of the emotional and physical shattering of those it sends to war, many of them freelance journalists and so more easily neglected by the beast because of a lack of formal institutional ties. But the beast is not solely to blame.

"To a degree," Dr. Feinstein notes correctly, "the profession itself has helped foster this silence. Embedded within the persona of the war journalist is an element of self-deception: the idea that he is someone who can confront war with impunity. It could be argued that this is a necessary prerequisite that allows war journalists to practice their profession. The news bosses are not immune to this way of thinking either, for it affords them a degree of comfort when dispatching journalists to wherever the latest conflagration erupts. The profession has been so effective in fortifying these constructs and perpetuating a very public myth that researchers in the field of psychological stress have, to date, passed them by."

War is a potent narcotic. Like any narcotic, it is highly addictive. In large doses, it can kill you. Once you sink into the weird subculture of war, it is hard to return home, where all seems banal and trivial. In war the polarities of life and death are laid bare. In war your senses are heightened. Colors are brighter. You are aware in ways you never were before. There is no past or future. All is one intense, overpowering rush, something soldiers call a "combat high." And those who can control their fear go back to seek these experiences again, seek them in strange, twisted landscapes of human depravity. "For many war journalists, particularly when young and starting out on their careers, it is not just the risk of novelty that drives them, but also the risk of danger," Dr. Feinstein writes. "And because the latter is the more intense experience, it often becomes the defining one. Placing your life on the line by venturing into the front lines of conflict zones cannot be surpassed."

But war perverts and destroys you. It pushes you closer and closer to your own annihilation—spiritual, emotional, and finally physical. And those who practice the trade of war reporting with a relentless intensity over many years flirt with their self-destruction. Greg Marinovich, João Silva, Ken Oosterbroek, and Kevin Carter were four South African photographers who chronicled the implosion of violence that swept across South Africa in the 1990s: "the rampaging mobs, the murder by stabbing or necklacing, the panic of crowds fired upon by the security police, the summary roadside execution of white supremacists by a black soldier." They were known as the "Bang Bang Club." By the time of South Africa's multi-racial election, Oosterbroek had been killed, Carter had committed suicide, and Marinovich had been shot. Their story is a microcosm of the cost.

Weaning yourself from this addiction is difficult. It took me three years to return to a place where I could reconnect with those around me. As Dr. Feinstein observes, "Once you have viewed the world through the prism of war, your perspective on life invariably alters." I slowly willed myself away from the poisonous elixir of war, refusing to go back to combat zones and then confronting the demons war had left behind. I carried with me strange residues of war. Red meat, after seeing what huge explosive shells did to human flesh in Sarajevo, disgusted me. I could barely look at it, much less eat it. I helped my small son on Christmas make a gingerbread house and found myself saying, as soon as we were finished, "and now let's play Bosnia and burn it down." I refused for a year to drink even one glass of wine because of alcohol's ability, in large enough quantities, to make me forget the nightmares that dredged up some of the hundreds of traumatic memories most of us carry. The decision to stop drinking meant that on many nights I had to do battle, like Job, with my trauma. I would wake with a sudden gasp, a racing heartbeat, and powerful, disturbing visions that would linger in toxic doses until dawn. When these traumatic visions came in waves over successive nights, my days were shattered. My waking hours were filled with alienation and exhaustion. I was plunged into a state of profound despair. Shaving and getting my kids to school was a Herculean task. These small acts became my victories, however pitiful, against the forces that tried to pull me back into the pit. And one always does this alone. Someone can help you on with your coat, but you must walk out the door by yourself.

When my friends Kurt Schork and Miguel Gil Moreno were killed in Sierra Leone in May 2000, I was in Queens covering a massacre at a Wendy's for the *New York Times*. Two gunmen had walked into the fast food restaurant and herded five of the workers into the basement freezer, wrapped plastic bags around the victims' heads, and shot them at point-blank range. The barbarity of the crime was perfectly tailored to rekindle a past I wanted to tame. And it was part of the obliviousness of the beast that its editors sent me to the scene. Serif Turgut, a Turkish reporter who worked with me during the wars in Bosnia and Kosovo, called me on my cell phone in tears from Istanbul. She told me that Kurt and Miguel had been killed in an ambush. I fell into a stupor. I dropped my notebook. A friend, a Swiss reporter who had been in Kosovo with me during the war and who happened to be visiting me in New York, picked up the notebook. I remember her sitting me down on a bench. I believe it was in a pizza parlor. I don't remember much else. I did not talk. She did the interviews with the survivors and witnesses. She typed the notes into my computer. She sent it to the paper, where the quotations and facts were filtered into other stories, none of which would carry my byline. She took my car keys from me and drove me home. For three days I could barely function. I sat mute and in pain, a passenger in Charon's boat on the river Lethe. I longed to drink the waters of the Lethe, which the ancient Greeks believed obliterates all memory.

I avoid all stimulants, including violent films, which can retrigger my trauma. I do not go to war, but more importantly, I do not want to go to war. I can drink a glass of wine. The dreams are less frequent now, although they return, and can even return over successive nights. On those days, I sit in my garden with my dog or walk along the Delaware River. I carry within me the ghosts of my friends and colleagues, now gone. I remember their courage and their passion. I remember how funny they were. The brave are often funny. I reach out to those who have not been as fortunate in their efforts to recover, sitting in silence, neither of us saying anything, the solidarity of our unspoken pain enough. I try to do for them the simple tasks they sometimes cannot accomplish. I do not regret going to war. Suffering brings with it knowledge. I use this knowledge, this rage, to dismantle the myth of war, the lies told to us about heroism and glory and honor. I endure. I only wish the beast had understood.

CHRIS HEDGES
former *New York Times* war correspondent
and author of *War Is a Force That Gives Us Meaning*

# Acknowledgments

This book owes much to the journalists who made time in busy, often hectic schedules to fill out questionnaires and meet with me. Of those I interviewed, all were prepared to be quoted, although some preferred anonymity. I have respected this need for confidentiality, which in rare instances meant that I had to alter some personal identifying characteristics. I have not, however, changed the content of what any journalist had to say.

My first study was funded by the Freedom Forum in those halcyon pre–September 11 days when the world seemed safe and life less fraught. John Owen was then the European director of the Freedom Forum and ran what can be best described as a journalist's salon in a beautiful set of offices overlooking the greenery of London's Hyde Park. It was John who persuaded the Freedom Forum in Washington, D.C., to fund my study, and it was John who opened the doors to many of the news organizations. Without his enthusiasm and good offices, I doubt whether a lot of hard-boiled news bosses would have entertained a visit from a Canadian psychiatrist asking to explore the emotional lives of their employees. The London offices of the Freedom Forum are, sadly, no more. I, like many others, benefited from the rich cultural and academic milieu that John created.

Funding for my second study, which focused on the war in Iraq, came from CNN and, in particular, Chris Cramer, managing director of CNN International. Over the years, Chris has established a remarkable reputation as a champion of good, safe journalism, and his unwavering commitment to this project and others is gratefully acknowledged.

My thanks go to Stephen Jukes, formerly of Reuters; Dave Modrowski, of Associated Press Television News; Vin Ray, of the British Broadcasting Corporation; Tony Burman, of the Canadian Broadcasting Corporation; and Michael Jermey, of Independent Television News. They all helped by opening their staff rosters of war journalists to me, allowing me to enroll a large and representative sample to study. In addition, Tina Carr, of the

Rory Peck Trust, was instrumental in helping recruit freelance journalists, and I thank her for this.

I would like to acknowledge colleagues at the Dart Center for Journalism and Trauma, including Frank Ochberg, Mark Brayne, Elana Newman, Roger Simpson, Bruce Shapiro, Jonathan Shay, and others, who generously invited me onto their Advisory Committee, where I can always find a stimulating debate about many issues relating to the emotional health of journalists.

I approached every journalist wearing my research hat. But by the time the interview had ended, or my questionnaires had been completed, or my email correspondence had concluded, my role had not infrequently changed to that of clinician. Ethical considerations dictated that I could not walk away from a journalist in distress. The more prolonged contact that subsequently ensued between us allowed me to dispense therapy and advice, and when that was not possible for reasons of geography and time, I arranged for assistance to be given elsewhere by others. I hope my interventions were helpful. I know that, for me, what I learned in the process deepened my understanding of the profession.

My thanks go to Wendy Harris and Brendan Coyne at the Johns Hopkins University Press. I was also most fortunate in having Susan Lantz as my editor. Her attention to detail and the fresh insights she provided have done much to enhance the text.

This book was written on weekends, evenings, and holidays. It was written in the bedroom, the dining room, and hotel rooms on four continents. During this time, I have had the support of a wonderful family. To my wife, Karen, and children, Pippa, Saul, and Clarrie, I add love to my thanks.

# Journalists under Fire

# 1

# A Hazardous Profession

* * *

Meanwhile, all across Rwanda murder, murder, murder,
murder, murder, murder, murder, murder, murder.

Philip Gourevitch

The patient who entered my office on a frigid December morning came with an interesting history. The referral note from the hospital's senior neurologist laid out the clinical details. The woman suddenly took ill in a restaurant while dining with family and friends. Her husband noticed her ashen appearance and the beads of sweat on her brow and nose. When asked what was the matter, she was unable to reply coherently. Alarmed by his wife's garbled speech, he called for an ambulance.

En route to the hospital, the woman lapsed in and out of consciousness, and by the time she arrived in the emergency room it was feared she'd had a stroke. The neurology service was consulted and the patient sent for a brain CT scan. To the surprise of the medical staff, no abnormality was seen, despite the persistence of her moribund state. She was admitted to the hospital for further tests, but by the following morning had made a spontaneous and complete recovery. At her own request, she was discharged. She left the hospital smiling and in good spirits.

A week later, before she could keep her first outpatient appointment, the symptoms returned, suddenly and dramatically. One moment she was fine, calm, and intelligible; the next, agitated, tremulous, and incoherent. She was again rushed to the hospital, where she was readmitted for more tests: scans that revealed the cerebral anatomy with postmortem-like clarity and showed how much blood was flowing to individual brain areas, electrodes that picked up the intensity and frequency of brain waves, multiple tubes of blood drawn. All test results were normal. With methodical tenacity, the neurologist-in-chief worked his way through a long list of possible

1

neurological causes for his patient's symptoms. Each was definitively ruled out. This done, he called in a cardiologist for an opinion. If there was nothing wrong with her brain, perhaps the problem lay with her heart and its ability to keep sufficient blood flowing to the brain. More tests followed. A mountain of computer printouts representing thousands of health care dollars were distilled into a terse comment, scrawled in the patient's chart: "No abnormalities found." By this time, the patient had, as before, made a full recovery.

At this point, the woman was referred to my neuropsychiatric service. The typed letter from the neurologist-in-chief echoed Conan Doyle, whose lucid, deceptively simple prose and keen analytic mind he had long admired: "The physical examination is normal, the laboratory results are normal," he wrote. "When we have excluded the possible, whatever remains, however improbable, is the answer to the diagnostic riddle. I have therefore concluded there is nothing physically wrong with the patient." And then, almost as an afterthought, he penned below his signature, in a beautiful flowing cursive, the following: "I wonder if it all has anything to do with her work? You may recognise the name. She's a war reporter."

It is not uncommon for patients to present with neurological symptoms with no obvious physiological cause. Neurologists see many thousands of such patients a year. These patients are said, in psychiatric parlance, to have a *conversion disorder.* This is, in effect, a rerouting of emotional distress into physical symptoms, an unconscious process that changes, or *converts*, emotional dysfunction into any of a variety of neurological abnormalities. Patients with conversion disorder may be unable to speak, move limbs, or experience sensations such as touch and pain. What they all have in common, despite the disparate set of complaints, is the absence of a neurological disorder that could account for their condition.

In the past, these patients were given a diagnosis of hysteria. The sometimes bizarre and florid nature of their symptoms would seize the physician's attention and even make for good theater. The great nineteenth-century French behavioral neurologist Jean-Martin Charcot routinely displayed such cases before a rapt audience at the Salpetriere Hospital in Paris. A famous painting by Pierre Andre Brouillet, exhibited at the Salon de Paris in 1887, shows Charcot and a swooning patient surrounded by an assortment of onlookers: physicians, students, journalists, artists, and even Charcot's twenty-year-old son.

The often dramatic presentation, coupled with the neurologist's sense that he may be missing some underlying disorder, frequently leads to a slew of unnecessary investigations. Test after test is ordered, cementing in the patient's mind a belief that she is afflicted with a serious physical illness. And there is a compelling, albeit false, logic to that belief, often unwittingly reinforced by the medical profession. "Why do so many tests if you do not suspect something is seriously wrong?" reasons the patient. If symptoms begin suddenly, if there is a clearly identifiable stressor, and if the patient is open to psychological explanations, the prognosis is improved.

In the case of the female journalist, the neurologist-in-chief made the correct diagnosis. By the time she came to see me, there was no trace of any language impediment and the history I obtained was an articulate, compelling narrative of a career spent in war zones. For years, I learned, this woman led an itinerant lifestyle, following in the wake of armies and relief organizations, recording events that were for the most part brutal and desperately sad. A decade of cumulative stress, which included a number of near-death experiences, reached an apogee when, in the span of a few days, her cameraman was killed while on assignment with her and, in a separate incident, a close colleague was badly wounded in an assassination attempt. Deeply shaken by these experiences, she took to medicating herself with tranquilizers and alcohol, two drugs that were readily available on the black market in war zones. She thought this would calm her nerves and give her a few hours of peaceful sleep, but instead her anxiety became acute; it was soon accompanied by a host of physical symptoms such as uncontrollable fits of shaking, sweating, a rapidly beating pulse, and tightness in her chest. Frightened by these attacks, which she attributed to heart problems, she consulted a physician in Khartoum, who advised her to return to Canada for treatment. When she got back to her family in Toronto, however, some of her symptoms spontaneously disappeared. Buoyed by this improvement, she never went to see a physician. It was a week after her return that she took ill in the restaurant.

It soon became clear in our conversations that while she loved her work as a war journalist, she found the job stressful and at times terrifying. The death of her cameraman and the shooting of a close friend were not isolated events; she had seen colleagues killed and wounded at depressingly frequent intervals over the years. Still, although she counted many of those colleagues as friends, death had until recently bypassed her own immediate circle. She saw it as something that happened to others, never to her. This charmed belief system suddenly disintegrated with the mortar shell that fell out of a clear blue African sky and took the life of her cameraman, someone with whom she had worked closely for five years.

As I gained more insights into her profession, I began to realize that the tragedy that overtook my patient was not unusual for a war reporter. So I was surprised when she told me that psychiatric help, even in the form of basic counseling, was not readily available to her. She was employed by one of the world's major news organizations, but she had no access to this type of assistance.

"There is an unspoken view within the profession that you either cut it or else get out," she told me. "There are no half measures. Reporting war is all about having the 'right stuff.' Sure we know that we drink too much and at times our emotions are all screwed up, but that comes with the turf and if you find that hard to deal with, then there is always the royal family to follow or a Wimbledon to report on, heavens forbid." She shuddered. She had by that time made the decision to give up working in conflict zones, but it was clear that domestic reporting had little appeal for her.

In the months after her first visit to the emergency room, I persuaded her to cut back significantly on her alcohol consumption and begin exercising. These two measures — coupled with medication to alleviate residual, at times intense, symptoms of anxiety — brought about a considerable improvement in her mental state. She judged herself almost back to her old normal self, and her husband concurred.

But despite deciding not to return to front-line reporting, she remained haunted by her past and revisited these events in her therapy sessions with an obsessional regularity. The more I listened, the more I came to realize that her profession, for all its allure and excitement, was practiced at a cost to both emotional equilibrium and physical health. After a session in which she recalled, in moving terms, the famine in Sudan and how the images of that disaster refused to leave her, I turned to the medical literature to see what had been written about war journalists and their particular susceptibility to psychiatric distress. I imagined that a subject of such descriptive power would surely have stimulated a considerable body of work. No doubt I would be able to find some guidelines to long-term management and outcome, two variables that were of interest to me given my patient's good early response to treatment.

A second surprise was in store, however. Not only had most of the news organizations neglected to provide for the psychological welfare of their war reporters, but trauma researchers had ignored them too. Trawling through the literature, I could not find a single reference to the subject — no articles, chapters, or abstracts. I had stumbled on a virgin topic, lying unrecognized within a larger literature devoted to the emotional consequences of traumatic events.

Matters could have been left, quite satisfactorily, at that. After all, the patient had recovered, and I had learned from an interesting case. But the stories and images my patient conveyed to me over the course of six months had more than piqued my curiosity. They'd instilled within my researcher's mind a need to know more about this group of individuals — journalists who, if my patient was any yardstick, chased wars, revolutions, and famines with a tenacity both impressive and alarming. My contact with her stimulated a host of questions. What kind of people choose war journalism as a career? What motivating factors make them decide on such a dangerous profession? What are their backgrounds? What are their family lives like? Why had no one researched this area before? And, central to the whole topic, how do war journalists react psychologically to the stresses and dangers of the job? In the case of my patient, the presentation was florid; work-related stress masqueraded as a constellation of neurological symptoms suggesting a stroke. Such a reaction struck me as extreme. But was it? I had no way of knowing. There were no data out there.

War journalists loom large in the public's consciousness. These intrepid men and women appear on prime-time television news against a backdrop of conflict and mayhem. The locations are frequently exotic and the visual images imbued with all the tension and drama that accompanies war. Any recent major conflict — Kosovo, Bosnia, the West Bank and the Gaza Strip, the Gulf War — brings to mind images of flak-jacketed, helmeted reporters clutching microphones, while all around smoke billows, buildings lie in ruins, and explosions punctuate the dispatches. Their faces disappear and reappear as the media focus shifts from one part of the globe to another. But despite all the uncertainty and danger associated with war, their familiar presence remains one of the few constants. Somehow, they appear untouched by the death and destruction that surrounds them and forms the heart of their métier.

This belief that war journalists are removed from the events they report on is captured perfectly by Jules Verne. His richly imagined novel *Mysterious Island* begins with the escape of four Union soldiers by balloon from a military prison in Richmond, Virginia, during the American Civil War. After surmounting many hazards, the men find themselves marooned on an island, where their fight for survival is aided by Captain Nemo of the submarine *Nautilus*. On meeting the group for the first time, the mysterious captain tells one of the escapees, Gideon Spillet, a war correspondent with the *New York Herald*, "I know you. You specialize in war news. You supply the ink, the soldiers supply the blood." Spillet does not challenge the captain's opinion, and his silence may be construed as tacit agreement that this is, indeed, how his profession operates. Soldiers may bleed and die, but journalists emerge unscathed. And is this not how it should be? After all, war journalists are not combatants — the conflict is not theirs and they do not bear arms. They simply have a job to do, which is to report the news. Night after night their presence in millions of homes is testimony to Nemo's trenchant opinion.

Jules Verne is not alone in his view. Over the past twenty years, a burgeoning literature has focused on how individuals deal with potentially life-threatening stressors. A formidable psychological trauma industry has been spawned, leaving few traumas unexplored. Researchers have examined how veterans respond to the dangers of combat and how civilians cope with man-made and natural disasters. Rape victims, assault victims, refugees, policemen, firemen, abused spouses and children, survivors of motor vehicle and industrial accidents — all have been studied in depth and their psychological response to trauma documented. Yet, as I discovered, nowhere in the countless pages of journals devoted to psychological trauma is there a single piece of research on war journalists.

To a degree, the profession itself has helped foster this silence. Embedded within the persona of the war journalist is an element of self-deception: the idea that he is someone who can confront war with impunity. It could be argued that this is a necessary prerequisite that allows war journalists to practice their profession. The news bosses are not immune to this way of thinking either, for it affords them a degree of comfort when dispatching journalists to wherever the latest conflagration erupts.* The profession has been so effective in fortifying these constructs and perpetuating a very public myth that researchers in the field of psychological stress have, to date, passed them by.

---

*There has been a concern on the part of journalists that, although assignments are in theory voluntary, refusal to accept a dangerous posting could have a negative impact on their career.

But cracks have started to appear in the well-constructed defenses. Organizations such as Reporters sans frontières and the Canadian-based International Freedom of Expression Exchange now keep statistics on the number of journalists arrested, tortured, wounded, and killed. Their communiqué for 2000 lists sixty-two journalists who were assassinated that year. (Sixty-three journalists were killed in 2005.) Although most of these were local reporters killed for exposing crime and corruption, the names of war journalists also figure prominently. The deaths in Sierra Leone of two celebrated and very experienced journalists, Kurt Schork of Reuters and Miguel Gil Moreno of Associated Press Television News, have helped dent the myth of invulnerability that has so tightly enveloped the profession.

* * *

Chris Cramer is just one journalist who has suffered work-related psychological trauma. What makes him different is that he has written with candor about his experience. In 1980, when he was a reporter with the BBC, Cramer went to the Iranian Embassy in London to apply for a visa. He wanted to go to Tehran to report on the American hostage drama that was then unfolding. He had been standing in line for only a few minutes when six terrorists stormed the embassy and took him and others hostage. Held for thirty-six hours, he escaped by faking a heart attack. The remaining hostages were freed by the Special Air Services six days later. After the siege ended, Cramer was offered stress counseling by the BBC and the United Kingdom's Home Office. He rejected both, a decision he later came to regret. "It wasn't the done thing, but I think if I knew then what I know now I would have taken myself off to a shrink."

Like many individuals exposed to hazardous situations, Cramer found that the event lived on in his mind in the weeks, months, and years that followed, not only influencing his emotions and behavior but also serving as a catalyst for life-changing decisions. "It fundamentally changed my ability to do my job," he recalled. "In other words, I lost my bottle. I did not want to be knowingly anywhere that was unsafe — at one point that could even be a restaurant or the underground. I didn't want to be anywhere that put things outside my control." Six months after the siege, he moved from reporting the news into a management position at the BBC.

Today Cramer is managing director of CNN International. Sensitized by his own experience, he uses his present position to facilitate debate on what can be done to help war journalists traumatized by their work. He is not alone in his concern. The BBC established a policy of offering counseling to employees in the 1990s, and other news organizations are starting to follow suit. An overall concern for journalists' physical safety seems to have led to a newfound willingness to discuss their psychological safety as well.

The time seemed right to initiate the first organized study of the effects of stress and trauma on war journalists. Before I could even begin to assess the extent of the problem — if indeed there was one — I needed to develop an understanding of what war journalists experience in bringing the news to the public. Many in the profession are wordsmiths, and their accounts of what they have endured are frequently articulate and imbued with all the passion of the events witnessed. Accordingly, letting them speak in their own words has certain important advantages: better to hear this direct than have it filtered through the word processor of the researcher.

As an aside, I was initially uncertain what to call the study's participants. The terms *foreign correspondents* and *war correspondents*, while widely used, do not capture the stills photographers, television cameramen and camerawomen, and producers covering conflict. For similar reasons, the label *war reporter* seems too limiting. In the end, I opted for *war journalists*, but I recognize that journalists such as John Simpson dislike the term. In his memoirs, he describes an episode in which, in the presence of Martha Gelhorn, he berated his colleague Max Hastings for using the words. Simpson's objection is that some journalists may use the "war" descriptor as a means to self-aggrandizement. In certain cases he is probably correct, although none of the journalists in my study used the term this way. And while the journalists I studied did not confine their work to war zones, war and conflict formed such a large and defining part of their careers that the term seems appropriate.

\* \* \*

Anthony Loyd is a journalist working for the London *Times*. He is the author of a painfully candid memoir, *My War Gone By. I Miss It So*, and his career has taken him to Bosnia, Croatia, Albania, Kosovo, Afghanistan, Nigeria, Ethiopia, and Syria. But the conflict that stands out for him as the most dangerous was Chechnya.

"Chechnya was the most shocking because the violence was so intense and the war so encompassing," he told me. "There was a guarantee that if you scrambled out of your basement and went out in the day in the city center, you either saw people getting killed or people who had just been killed or were terribly wounded. Or you would have a near-death experience yourself."

Loyd arrived in Chechnya in the winter of 1994 and stayed for six weeks. The level of violence in Russia's breakaway republic was so extreme that many journalists opted to stay away. In besieged Grozny, he found a city under such intense bombardment that there was no place for journalists to hunker down and wait out the danger. Loyd explained:

> I can generally expose myself to violence for a period of time if I want to and then go back to some place safe at the end of the day. Once you were in Grozny, however, there was none of that, and the image I have taken away is one of the sudden explosion of shells and then people sprayed all over the walls.
>
> One experience particularly sticks with me. There was a heavy barrage going on outside the basement I was holed up in with four or five colleagues and then it stopped and this young Russian girl came rushing in and was shouting in her broken English, "Help us, help us." We ran off with her into the snow and not very far away we run smack into this woman, a big woman covered in blood and wearing a fur coat — I don't know if it is her blood or not — and she is dragging a sledge and on the sledge was, I don't know who, her husband or brother or whatever. He was dead, in bloody shreds, twisted torso — with one leg dragging off it. They must have been walking along and must have had the sledge with something else on it and then he must have been killed by the shelling and she must have just rolled him on to the sledge and in her hand she had his leg — a big leg — with the boot right on the side and she was completely unhinged by what had happened maybe half a minute before and she was screaming at us, as close as I am to you, with this leg going back and forth, this big fucking leg — and you could just see in the gap between her gloves and coat, her skin, taut with the effort from the weight of the leg, and she was screaming at us. We were transfixed and just behind her where this barrage of shells had landed there were about six or seven people — her own people actually — who were just blown into bits lying around with bits of head and limb and everything.

*Groznaya.* The word in Russian means "terrible." And terrible indeed were the sights that Loyd confronted. Amid the carnage an old man lay facedown, covered in dust. Both legs had been severed, one above the knee, the other below. As Loyd walked past the stricken man, a hand reached out and grabbed his ankle. "He was still alive! The heat of the blast had actually cauterized his wounds. He was not even bleeding. I was just in shock," recalled Loyd.

> What the fuck to do? I mean you are in this place where there is no hospital and there is no car, there is heavy fighting everywhere, there were no people on the streets that you can see because of the fighting and even the fighters are inside taking shelter and then you confront this horrible mutilation and this one old guy is still alive without his legs! We could hear the raining barrage of shells which were sort of fixed in lines to fire and were going off all over the place. Maybe there were thirty shells which were suddenly exploding all over the place and which might be coming closer to us . . . or might not, it was impossible to gauge.
>
> There was this really heavy fear between me and these other three guys and we just looked at each other and this old man could tell what was happening. I can speak a bit of Russian and could understand what he was saying. He kept grabbing at my legs, saying, "My legs, my legs, please don't leave me, please don't leave me," and we ran because we were fucking frightened. I think we were really shell shocked and mutilation itself is really distressing to witness — so we ran back to our cellar and a couple of the other journalists were trying to say that the Russian girl had come because she wanted us to film what had happened because she felt that it was bad and wanted journalists to show the world what was happening. I am fucking sure that she did not come for that reason. I am sure she came because she wanted us to help.

For Anthony Loyd, six years later, the memories of that terrible scene in Grozny remained vivid. He had seen many people killed in conflict before, but that day, and particularly the image of the woman waving the leg, was engraved in his memory. "It is like looking at a light bulb and then looking at the imprint. Days after it, I could still see that woman. Literally for several days after it, there was this serum of an imprint. I still think of it very often. I certainly have not forgotten it."

One of the other journalists who was in Grozny on that fateful winter's day was Jon Jones. A veteran of photographing conflict over a fifteen-year period, Jones, too, regarded Grozny as his most dangerous assignment, but it was not the actual fighting or even his own near-death experiences that disturbed him the most. Rather, what moved Jones was the fallout of the fighting — that is, the effects of war on the local population and the destruction it brings to their lives.

On one occasion, Jones and some other journalists were taken to a hospital to view the victims of a Russian bombing attack on a Chechen farm.

There he met two sisters. The older one, who was about nine, was badly wounded, but it was the younger one, about eight, who really affected him.

> She was unscathed, covered in mud, but she was crying blood. She had blood running down her cheeks from the concussion effects of the bombs. After that visit, we were taken to the farm [where the bombing had occurred] and it had been devastated. They took us into this little room and there was this bed just full of dismembered children. There were about eight or nine of them under these blankets. They were in pieces, literally in pieces. You can't shoot it. You can't. What I used to do was shoot a frame or two in acknowledgment that I had been there and had seen it and as a way of showing my editors I had been there. But I knew it wasn't going to go anywhere. Nobody is going to publish it. So you do it because you are there to record it, but you don't make a thing of it . . . the picture I have is of a child's head and just a blanket, but they took the blanket off and it's like . . . you can't do that, put the blanket back on. That and the image of the girl crying blood stay with me.

Why repeat stories like these? What is there to be achieved by describing the minutiae of a massacre? Is it not sufficient to state that war journalists are exposed to danger and see gruesome sights? After all, a degree of self-imposed media censorship is already taking place, as alluded to by Jon Jones. Even as he focused his lens on the bed of dismembered children, he knew the few frames he shot were going nowhere. The images were simply unprintable, the horror of the episode deemed beyond the threshold of what the public could stomach. However, when news organizations sanitize the content of news, pandering to their viewers' sensitivities, they also inadvertently cleanse the image of the working lives of war journalists, obscuring the many risks and dangers they confront.

The experience of war defines the profession and the very essence of those who practice it. This is what captures the public's imagination so vividly, but also what drives the symptoms that live on for journalists long after the events they documented. However, maintaining a balance between factual description on the one hand and sensationalism on the other demands vigilance. Fascination with what the war journalist endures in war zones can very easily slip into voyeurism. This does the profession and any study of it a disservice. Conversely, to back off from describing the full magnitude and breadth of the dangers confronted by war journalists would leave the impression that ink was more likely to be spilled than blood. Extending an anodyne to the lives of war journalists would also make any meaningful psychological study of the profession impossible. For the reader to discern the significance of war journalists' dreams or flashbacks — to comprehend the strains placed on their relationships and the difficulties many have in adjusting to life back in a society not racked by conflict — war, and the "pity of war," in Wilfred Owen's memorable words, must be laid bare. It is a theme that will reappear throughout this book; to understand what war journalists do, the sanitized wrapping placed around war must be stripped away.

The lives of war journalists are, to varying degrees, bound to the lives of the perpetrators and, especially, to the victims of war. And being war's amanuensis can come at a cost. In Bosnia in 1989, Jon Jones experienced firsthand the terror of being cast as a target by Serbian paramilitary forces.

On a number of occasions I was taken into the wood at midnight and had a mock execution. On two occasions I was dragged out of a car and put up against a wall. I thought that was it. They stripped me of all identification. You can tell, you know, that you are in trouble when you hand over your passport and a guy spits on it and throws it into the bushes. We couldn't speak Serb or Croat and they thought we were spies. They were hassling us, intimidating us, trying to force us into speaking Serb or Croat, which you would do the more scared you got [when people tend to revert to their mother tongue]. But we couldn't speak the language, so in the end they let us go and I remember climbing into the car and I was shaking. I couldn't drive. It was a real effort.

It happened in Grozny as well. Pro-Russian rebels took me into a wood in a car and I tried to get out and they kicked the door shut. I thought, this is it. They'll just waste me in the car. They didn't. I was there for about an hour. They put me into the car and made me drive to the frontline at two o'clock in the morning, which is even more dangerous, and luckily I was fine. Those kind of things would just happen.

While there is an element of brinkmanship on the part of these rogue militia, at times, threats translate into action. The case of Fred Cuny is a tragic example of this. William Shawcross, in his book *Deliver Us from Evil*, calls Cuny a "great American — a sort of universal Schindler, a man with lists of millions of people . . . whose lives he succoured and saved." Cuny combined his technical expertise in urban planning with a remarkable gift for improvisation and force of character to spearhead humanitarian relief operations, first in Biafra and thereafter wherever conflict or disaster demanded the attention of the world's non-governmental organizations: Bangladesh, Cambodia, Guatemala, Armenia, the Gulf War, Kuwait, Somalia, Bosnia, Albania, and finally Chechnya, where he went missing with two Russian Red Cross doctors and an interpreter. Despite the efforts of many, from President Clinton down, he was not found until years later some Chechens claiming to have his body offered it as ransom to his family. Such is the randomness of war. On a whim, on a callous and, to us, inexplicable impulse of a bandit warlord or one of his minions, a life embracing a quarter-century of the most remarkable humanitarianism can be snuffed out.

Sitting captive in his car in the Chechen woods, Jon Jones knew this. Those who kill so easily seldom weigh the scales of justice. "Where there is anarchy you can do anything you want," he said in an interview with me. "That's why soldiers just go berserk. If soldiers take a town they don't stop killing. Once all the defenders have gone they kill everything, you know, birds, dogs, cows, chickens. They don't stop until it's all gone."

We paused in the interview and Jones lit a cigarette. Having listened to him relate several other harrowing escapes, I asked an obvious question: Had experiences like these ever made him think of doing something else for a living? In response, he got up from the kitchen table and walked over to a notice board, removed a pin, and handed me a photograph that showed a room with a hole in the wall, the faint pattern of wallpaper, smashed furniture at the head of a bed. He told me quietly:

> The only time I thought of that was when I had a shell in my bed. I was lying in bed at night — this is Sarajevo — and a mortar tank from the local army pulled up outside my front door and started firing at the Serbs. This is a regular thing they do. But normally they fire four or five rounds and then run. This time it was kind of eight, nine, ten, eleven rounds. The first round of returning fire hits the building next to me . . . and the second round comes through my wall. It is an artillery round, it comes through the wall into a chest of drawers that my bed is up against and explodes and blows me right across the room into another wall. And I haven't got a mark on me, not a scratch. But I am wet. I started panicking because I thought it was blood. A friend of mine ran in from the next room with a torch. It was milk. A big carton of milk had exploded. So I was covered in milk, covered in plaster dust, just standing there.

**\*    \*    \***

I came to observe that the violence inflicted on war journalists, by either accident or intent, was at times of a level indistinguishable from that endured by the civilian population in the areas of conflict. What befell the photographer John Liebenberg on the battlefields of northern Namibia and Angola in the late 1980s and 1990s illustrates both the randomness and the premeditated nature of this threat. Liebenberg was on the staff of the *Namibian* newspaper, a vocal and barely tolerated opponent of South African occupation. His photographs of atrocities committed against SWAPO (the South West Africa People's Organisation) fighters by members of Koevoet, a lawless Namibian police group closely allied to South Africa, led to his frequent arrest and maltreatment. On one occasion he was incarcerated in a room with a wild baboon. "The animal was really savage," he recalled. "It had bitten people and sat there snarling at me . . . and that fear . . . that sweat . . . it is still with me." Despite such intimidation, he persisted in his work, even after a bounty was placed on his head. When independence finally came to Namibia, Liebenberg turned his attention to the civil war in neighboring Angola. His personal archive of horror accumulated in Portugal's erstwhile colonial jewel is of an extraordinary magnitude and unsettling to record.

> I was very fortunate to have known some of the generals in Luanda who gave me access to the front lines. One day I flew into an area recently captured from UNITA [National Union for the Total Independence of Angola] and the MPLA [Popular Movement for the Liberation of Angola] general gave an order that looters would be shot. That afternoon two boys were brought to him. They had been caught raping some women. They were angry that UNITA people had been living in their house. The general just took out his pistol and shot one of the youngsters in the groin and the other in the stomach and then he sat back in his chair. The boys were in agony, asking for water, crying "oh my God," and the commander looked over at me and said, if you give these guys water, my friend, I will fucking kill you now.

A shocked Liebenberg ignored the threat. He was fortunate. The general did not shoot him too. His penalty was to be placed back on the helicopter and banished from the front lines for a week. But the episode, like many others, stayed with him. "Instead of trying to describe how I feel about it today, let me just say I don't photograph weddings and I won't photograph baptisms, because I cry," he confided.

In Liebenberg's tortured Angolan narrative, there is a hurried sense of the inevitability of future calamity.

In 1997, the plane I was traveling in crashed near Huambo, one of the districts in central Angola . . . we were coming in to land, in a tight spiral. UNITA had just left the fringes of the city, but elements had stayed behind and a group fired a missile at the plane. It hit a wing . . . the plane crashed quite badly . . . the pilots were killed and some of my colleagues were really badly injured . . . after the crash, the plane exploded . . . it was quite close to a battalion of young MPLA soldiers, tank soldiers and they immediately started looting the plane . . . and there I was with a serious bang on the head, trying to get my equipment and stuff out.

The events that befell Anthony Loyd, Jon Jones, and John Liebenberg are not unusual. They are repeated time and again for war journalists, with a relentless intensity over the course of many years. Greg Marinovich, João Silva, Ken Oosterbroek, and Kevin Carter were four South African photographers who experienced just that. Traveling the unpaved streets and alleys of the sprawling black ghettoes of Johannesburg, they produced a series of shocking, startling images documenting their country's transition from shame-faced polecat to regional powerhouse. "The time of greatest danger is when a bad regime starts to reform," observed Alexis de Tocqueville. South Africa in the early 1990s was the perfect affirmation of this. Rampaging mobs, murder by stabbing or necklacing, the panic of crowds fired upon by the security police, the summary roadside execution of white supremacists by a black soldier: these images gained the photographers national and international prominence. Awards followed, including a Pulitzer for Marinovich for an image of a man stabbed and set alight by a crazed mob. The four photographers quickly became known as the "Bang Bang Club" and were the subject of articles and photographs that recorded their hazardous lives. By the time South Africa limped into her first multiracial general election, the toll exerted by the unremitting violence on the Bang Bang Club was appalling. Oosterbroek had been killed, Carter had committed suicide, Marinovich had been shot. Only Silva emerged physically unscathed. Adding to the attrition, an unofficial fifth member of the group, the photographer Gary Bernard, also committed suicide. The two surviving members told their story in a book that became the vehicle for a cathartic outpouring of pent-up grief and anger.

Marinovich's career is an example of the risks war journalists encounter.

He has been wounded four different times, once during the same confrontation that claimed the life of Oosterbroek. On that fateful day, the Bang Bang Club had gone to Thakosa to photograph a looming showdown between rival militia. Members of the National Peacekeeping Force, a conglomeration of troops from the South African police, apartheid homeland armies, and the South African Defence Force, were meant to storm a hostel occupied by Inkatha fighters. But the poorly trained peacekeepers panicked, firing their weapons indiscriminately, killing Oosterbroek and seriously wounding Marinovich.

It was a day Marinovich would never forget, but his initial reaction was not what we might expect. "The most interesting sensation was, after the pain and the shock of those first few minutes, when I thought I was going to die, there was this massive relief. Because of all these feelings I was telling you about, this guilt, this voyeurism, this profiting through the whole thing. Always escaping unhurt, having covered various conflicts, not just South Africa, by then, and with varying degrees of caring about what you're doing. So there was this relief of having finally paid my dues, making up for what I've photographed. Scared was no longer there. It wasn't there."

Marinovich was rushed to the hospital where his condition deteriorated and fear returned, intermingled with grief for his dead friend who was lying nearby: "My pulse was dropping, and I couldn't breathe properly because the lung had collapsed. Some friends came into the hospital ER with TV cameras and they just, instead of rolling, they were just looking at me. Very experienced people and I thought, 'Fuck, I'm going to die.'"

When we met, I encountered a large, pleasantly disheveled man with an open forthright manner. His answers came quickly, emotionally. There was a no-nonsense warmth to him. Like many of the journalists I interviewed, his descriptions of events were often scatological. Marinovich liked the word *fuck:* fuck this, fuck that, racist fucks. We chatted on the rooftop of a Johannesburg hotel. After the trauma of the past decade, it was an exciting, happy time for him and João Silva. Their photographic skills had received international acclaim, their book, *The Bang Bang Club*, was about to be launched, and there was talk of a movie. His cell phone rang constantly. After he spoke to his fiancée, who phoned from Switzerland, he turned the phone off and we resumed talking.

Three months after he was shot, financial pressures pushed Marinovich into an ill-timed assignment, and he developed a series of lung infections and gout, all complications of his initial surgery. He needed almost a year to recover fully. Another shooting followed five months after the first. ("The police opened up with birdshot and I was wounded all over. Not traumatic.") Marinovich was shot a third time three years after that, during the South African invasion of Lesotho. This injury was more serious.

> That was terrifying. João [Silva] plus myself and Suzanne [Daley, the chief correspondent from the *New York Times*] got caught in ambush after ambush with these South African soldiers. We got Suzanne into a safe spot and we went up to the armored vehicles that were pinned down under ambush. We were doing very good pictures. There's bullets around and it's quite scary, but there was this excitement because they were soldiers, not civilians. There's a difference, you know what I mean? Then we got out of that situation and parked the car quite a distance away and decided not to take further chances, just wait for the South Africans to finish mopping up and then go in. And a machine gun opened up on us where we were parked. So I started the car, drove off, and stalled, or the anti-hijack device kicked in. And we just kept taking this machine-gun fire. As I stalled I got hit in the leg, [but] . . . I didn't say anything as I had to keep the car going. We drove another kilometer under constant fire, completely terrified, and that magic bubble had disappeared yet again, that bubble of invincibility. 'Cause until you're hit, you're immortal, right? That's what happened in the first shooting. Once you're hit, you feel very vulnerable to this kind of stuff. That magic bubble is gone.

Listening to Greg Marinovich, I discerned a common thread linking his thinking to that of Loyd, Jones, Liebenberg, and almost all of the other war journalists who spoke to me of their experiences. They operate within a unique belief system, one that defines the concepts of threat and danger quite differently from any other group of subjects I have studied. It is not that their appreciation of what constitutes danger is absent, but rather that their threshold of what defines risk has been shifted so far along the continuum of our shared beliefs as to make it difficult to detect. How else to interpret what João Silva had to tell me? "I've been injured. Twice in fact. But all minor details. I've never been shot. I was injured in a grenade explosion and took a bit of shrapnel in my lower elbow. The second incident was during a riot. I got smashed in the face with a brick. It took me out of commission for a couple of days. I've never been injured in the sense that I've been hospitalized for months, so it doesn't really count." Or the immediate reaction of Jon Jones to the mortar shell that smashed through his wall: "I was furious, really kind of angry about the whole thing, you know. Saturday night. Midnight. I don't mind it during the day when I'm looking for it."

*   *   *

Fergal Keane was one of forty war journalists whose names were given to me by the BBC. My initial contacts with him had been via email, and in those brief exchanges, as we passed messages back and forth trying to set up a date and time for an interview, I became aware of his articulate, eager voice. He was impatient to share his thoughts on why journalists choose war as their subject and the consequences of that choice on their psyche. We finally met in his west London home on a blustery, wet, and cold winter's morning. My first impressions of the man were confirmed. He brought an intensity and energy to the discussion that demanded attention. We spoke of many topics pertaining to war journalists, including the physical dangers they confront; their relationships with family, friends, and news bosses; the question of whether the profession is becoming more dangerous over time; the difficulty of maintaining journalistic neutrality in a conflict; and the problem of substance abuse within the profession. For the most part, the conversation flowed easily, but whenever it derailed, the reason inevitably was Rwanda.

Keane had already covered several African conflicts, including the war between Ethiopia and Eritrea and the run-up to the first multiracial general election in South Africa, by the time he went to Rwanda in 1994. But nothing could have prepared him for the genocide he encountered there. It was clear to me, almost eight years later, that his Rwandan experiences had left an indelible impression. Even for Fergal Keane, the most articulate of men, the horror was on a scale that made it ineffable.

> We lived out in the field. There was no hotel to go back to at the end of the day. So, we lived with them, the victims, in abandoned villages with the smell of the corpses around you. And I suppose I found it incredibly frightening because half the journey [from the border to the town of Butari] was through areas controlled by the genocidal forces, the Interahamwe [the Hutu militia responsible for the genocide], and that was the kind of fear I've never experienced before . . . it was more than just personally dangerous. The tensions were frightening, but this was a level beyond. There was a degree to which the whole moral order was gone, so killing was the right thing to do. There were no boundaries and everyone around you had this

kind of blood frenzy . . . We felt very threatened. There were like thirty roadblocks between the Burundi border and Butari and negotiating those roadblocks was just petrifying. The [Interahamwe] would come up and hold grenades in the window, by the pin, and you were trying to persuade them you weren't Belgian because they wanted to kill any Belgians. That was terrifying.

Keane's first Rwandan visit lasted three weeks. He came to look back on it as the most difficult and frightening period of his career. When he returned to the country soon after the slaughter had abated, the emotional residue of that first experience clung tenaciously.

When I was first in the country we saw a group of Tutsis, survivors who had not been killed, outside the mayor's office. We went and we filmed, and then we went back again that night to try and film them again. [But] we were turned away at gunpoint. We were told by a priest that these people had been taken and killed that night, and we were too scared to go back and do anything about it. I felt a lot of guilt about that.

On the last day of my second trip, we met a woman who had been in Butari at the time, a Tutsi survivor. She turned out to be one of those people who was in front of the mayor's office and she said that she remembered us coming. She then said something that was really devastating. She said, "we thought you were with the militia because you did nothing to help us. We thought you must be with them." And she said that three busloads of them were taken away and the militia killed two busloads and then they ran out of energy for killing. I said to her, "Look, I want you to know I'm sorry, but I was too afraid at the time." We were too afraid to do anything. I mean it's hard to convey to you the level of fear in a situation like that.

I had completed twenty-six interviews with war journalists by the time I interviewed Mr. Keane. For the most part, the interviews took place in the journalists' homes or a local café. There had been no prior contact between my subjects and me, other than an exchange of letters, faxes, or emails. To begin my study, I collected detailed questionnaires from 140 war journalists, out of 170 names given to me by respected news organizations including CNN, the BBC, Reuters, the Associated Press Television News, NBC, ITN (Independent Television News), and the Rory Peck Trust (an organization of freelance camerapeople named for one of the most admired freelancers of his generation, a man killed in crossfire while covering the October coup and demonstrations outside Moscow's television center in 1993).

The thirty journalists who did not respond to the questionnaire either could not be traced or politely refused, save one who wrote:

> I happen to be just amazed about the questionnaire I found in my mail. The first sheet happened to ask me how much beer cans I could drink in a week and if I was a cocaine addict.* You might know we are a very small community of war correspondents, and my friends might have the same feeling: are we all supposed to be neurotic, alcoholic, overstressed depressed jerks, permanently flirting with suicidal ideas? Should I rush to a psychoanalyst's couch if I consider myself—and am widely considered—a well balanced father of two, normally stressed in a stressful profession, enjoying parties like any average 36 years old human being? Anyway, I am retired from the job now, being a correspondent in Washington. So you won't be offended if I don't answer your questionnaire. At least it did have a positive impact on my depression: a huge laugh. Respectfully yours.

The second phase of my study involved face-to-face interviews with a random sample of one in five of the war journalists who returned the questionnaires.† These twenty-eight interviews took place in London, New York, Paris, Madrid, Barcelona, and Johannesburg, and together with the information from the questionnaires they form the basis of this book. To control for the stressors generic to journalism, such as getting the scoop and pressured deadlines, a group of 107 domestic journalists who had never been to war or disaster zones underwent the same assessment procedure (questionnaires for all and interviews for one in five). When discussing the findings reference will be made to this group as well.

Most of the journalists who took part in my study were male (more than 70 percent) and in their late thirties or early forties. Those in the "war group" were also experienced, having spent, on average, fifteen years covering wars. Between them, they had written about or filmed every late-twentieth-century conflagration, big and small. More than 70 percent had been to the Balkans, making this region the most widely covered of the many conflict zones listed. (Contrast this with the 33 percent who went to Rwanda, the less than 20 percent who covered Sierra Leone, or the single photojournalist who found his way to Angola, Africa's longest running war. Clearly, reporting on Africa was not a top priority for news organizations and their journalists.) Other trouble spots visited by the journalists

---

*The questionnaire did neither of these things.
†The data from questionnaires and interviews were collected in 2000 and 2001.

included Lebanon during the civil war of the early 1980s, Iraq during the Gulf War of the early 1990s, Chechnya, Nagorno-Karabakh, East Timor, Israel, the Gaza Strip and the West Bank, Afghanistan, the Congo, Ethiopia, Eritrea, Sudan, South Africa, Namibia, and El Salvador.

All the war journalists contacted for interviews were willing to speak with me. After a decade or more in combat zones there was much to tell, but every journalist had, in his repository of literally hundreds of traumatic memories, a particular event that stood out with an eidetic quality. Most of these fell into one of two categories. The first, applicable to the majority, involved near-death experiences: getting wounded, or being shot at, or having their plane shot down. What intrigued me, however, was the second type of response. Here the event (and it was seldom more than a single event), did not necessarily involve anything life-threatening. Nor did it involve witnessing scenes of mutilation or wide-scale destruction. Rather, it centered on the survivors of war, the victims who, through some peculiar twist in fate, had been spared death only to confront a shattered existence. It was the plight of the distraught — people who had lost their children, families, livelihood, homes, and communities, overtaken by events often not of their making, devastated by the magnitude of their loss — that shocked the journalists' sensibilities, outraged their morality, and triggered compassion and pity. And it was one or any combination of these reactions that coalesced around the image and seared it into their consciousness.

Thus, for some of these men and women who had witnessed death and dying of almost biblical proportions, it was not death itself but the consequences of death on those who lived that provided the most memorable and troubling recollections. Jeremy Bowen, the BBC's Middle East correspondent, told me:

> At times I felt like an undertaker seeing the number of bodies. After having seen [a body] for the first time in El Salvador, going from that to the ridiculous, with piles of corpses, terribly mangled. I remember an event, the missile attack on the Amiriya shelter in Baghdad during the Gulf War, the so-called Command Bunker . . . We got to the site a couple of hours after it happened. They were pulling out the most horrendous bits of bodies, not just bodies, but bits of bodies, and later we went to the morgue where they had taken them. You walked into the building, the corridors were full of bodies. There was a big lecture room, which was a pathology lecture theater, with two slabs at the bottom and tiered seating, like in a university. The slabs had bodies on them, the floors and the tiered seating of the lecture

theater had bodies on them. We were literally walking around like this [and here Jeremy Bowen rose on his toes to demonstrate the absence of floor space], picking our way around the things. So going from not seeing bodies at all to that place and watching the cameraman trying to put his tripod up, trying to find place on the floor for his tripod, and literally between the legs of the tripod was a corpse. And you know, horrible things! They were terribly mangled a lot of them, but what was worse was the grief of the survivors. I always find that is the case. Death is nasty, but it ends there for the dead.

When sympathy for the survivors merges into personal identification with them, the resultant image assumes a different emotional valence, becoming even more moving, disturbing, and, thus, unforgettable. It often takes very little to bring this about. "Dead is dead. It's all the same really," confided Jon Jones. "Sometimes the worst things aren't the carnage. The worst things are people you can relate to, people who look like your mother or sister."

Having to varying degrees become habituated to death and the misery of whole populations displaced, journalists may find that suddenly confronting something familiar in one of the bereaved or dispossessed — and it may be no more than the shape of a mouth or nose, a particular tilt to the head, or some subtle, idiosyncratic mannerism — is enough to shatter the cocoon of detachment and force the tragedy of some nameless victim into that well-defended, inviolable frame of personal reference. With the wall breached, an array of fears and anxieties, previously held at bay by fortified psychological defenses, may be let in, further magnifying the emotional impact of the image. This, then, is the memory that some war journalists select, with little hesitation, from a decade-long catalog of traumatic experiences as the one that stands out the most. And the speed with which they make their choice, coupled with the clarity of their recall, highlights the power of the personalized image to capture their imagination.

There is also a third type of experience, one that I have touched on only briefly thus far. It concerns loss — the death of a colleague who also may have been a close friend. It is the most emotive of topics, and it has affected every war journalist I interviewed. No one has escaped it, everyone is conscious of it, and the threat posed by it hovers over them all, introducing an additional tension to the work they do. In this small, tightly knit group of men and women, the death of one is felt collectively. The loss of colleagues, introducing as it does guilt and self-reappraisal, is a theme central to the profession, one linked inextricably to the nature of the war journalist's experience.

In time, I also came to realize that the experience helps explain who war journalists are as people. In my correspondence and in the many hours of taped interviews, the drama of lives devoted to recording war, with all its excitement and wonder, tragedy and pathos, was laid bare. What a heady concoction it is. An unknown source sums it up well: "Call war damnable — there is nothing too bad that can be said about it — and yet, it has a knack, which peace never learned, of uncovering the splendour in commonplace persons."

That insight is applicable, in varying measures, to both war's combatants and victims. It holds true also for war journalists; their anecdotes are testimony to the extraordinary lengths to which they go to document the news. Therein lies their paradox: war is the catalyst, not the nemesis, to their creativity. In this chapter, I have relayed but few of the many experiences conveyed to me. For the men and women of my study have not only led dangerous lives, they have been busy, too, in a decade (the 1990s) that, according to the International Red Cross, saw over fifty-six wars, resulting in 17 million refugees and 26 million people left homeless.

# 2

# Danger's Troubled Legacy:
# Post-traumatic Stress Disorder

The dangers war journalists work under were exposed, tragically, early on in my study. With the questionnaires en route to him, Miguel Gil Moreno, one of the most respected cameramen in the profession, was killed while covering the civil war in Sierra Leone. Shock, disbelief, outrage, anguish — I would witness these emotions time and again when war journalists were killed or wounded. That Moreno had intimations of his own mortality was revealed in a haunting segment of video interview. "The last six years of my life [have been] the most incredible experience a single human being can have," he divulged in a BBC documentary. "But I cannot see the picture of my family the day they get the phone call saying I have been killed in a war."

Moreno's work as a cameraman had an emotional intensity he was unlikely to experience elsewhere. This explains his relentless desire to return to areas he knew were hazardous. And, though he wanted to avoid these issues, in the few lines of that interview he disclosed that he had thought of his demise. No doubt he did so often, given the frequency with which he would have seen death come to others in his six-year tenure as cameraman to the world's misery. Feted with a Rory Peck Award for freelance cameraperson of the year, Moreno specialized in the visual image, yet, ironically, the one picture that eluded his imagination was that of his family receiving notification of his death. And that image proved elusive because he could not quite bring himself to believe in it. From this brief insight into his emotional life, we see two competing forces at play. On one hand, the images Moreno had seen of death and dying begged the question, When is it my turn? a thought so distressing it could be contemplated only in the abstract. On the other hand, he avoided this thought's logical conclusion, the effect of his death on his shocked and grieving family. Moreno stopped short of being able to see this tragic denouement, the image was effectively suppressed, albeit unconsciously, and as a result he avoided witnessing (and experiencing) the pain and hurt his death would bring to loved ones.

I never met Miguel Gil Moreno and must therefore draw back from the temptation of letting an analysis of just two sentences generate an all-embracing clinical opinion. I cannot say whether this intrepid cameraman ever suffered psychologically from what he had seen and experienced, but in that brief, prescient comment captured on film, I find evidence of intrusion and avoidance, two of the three central tenets underpinning a syndrome known as *post-traumatic stress disorder (PTSD)*.

*  *  *

Much has been written about PTSD, a diagnosis that first appeared in 1980 when the American Psychiatric Association revised its classification system for mental illness. It was not, however, a "new" diagnosis, appearing *de novo*. For much of the twentieth century, psychiatrists had recognized that individuals who were subjected to life-threatening stressors could suffer psychologically. What had been contentious was how this suffering manifested, and there began a vigorous discussion on the type of signs and symptoms that typically arose in traumatized people. The debate continues to this day, albeit less intensely, with the majority of psychiatrists who believe in the validity of PTSD at loggerheads with a skeptical minority who feel the condition has more to do with post-Vietnam psychosocial forces within American society than empirical science. Notwithstanding these rumblings of disquiet, the disorder has been accepted by both the World Health Organization and the American Psychiatric Association as a valid set of symptoms that may follow exposure to a life-threatening stressor.

According to diagnostic criteria, to suffer from PTSD an individual must have experienced or witnessed an event that involved actual or threatened death or serious injury. The person's response to this must involve fear, helplessness, or horror. A specified number of symptoms from each of three categories, intrusion, avoidance, and arousal, must also be present before the diagnosis can be made. These three categories make up the PTSD triad.

Re-experienced or intrusive symptoms include recurrent and involuntary distressing images, thoughts, dreams, and flashbacks of the traumatic event. Examples of persistent avoidant symptoms are efforts to ward off thoughts, feelings, or conversations associated with the trauma, efforts to stay away from activities, places, or people that prompt recollections of the trauma, a restricted range of emotions, a feeling of detachment or estrangement from others, and an inability to recall an important aspect of the trauma. Arousal symptoms refer to difficulties with sleep, anger control, concentration, an exaggerated startle response, and hypervigilance (such as being wary of potential dangers even when away from a war zone).

There is a consistency to the way individuals react to catastrophic trauma, irrespective of what the trauma entails. To varying degrees, they will persistently re-experience the traumatic event, make attempts at avoiding the distressing nature of this involuntary recall, and display levels of arousal that affect functions such as sleep and concentration. I assumed the responses the war journalists gave on their questionnaires would show they weren't any different. What I didn't know, however, were the frequency and extent to which they would endorse symptoms of PTSD.

A shared set of symptoms should not, however, obscure the manner in which they are acquired by journalists. What sets the war journalist apart is a constant need to seek out the conflict, violence, and destruction that generate international headlines. If the threat of peace hangs over every war journalist, however, it is unlikely to occasion little more than temporary disappointment. In a world that has consistently shown a rapacious appetite for violence combined with a diabolical ingenuity for manufacturing it, sustainable peace proves the most illusive of chimeras. There are always opportunities for war journalists to live willingly in cities under siege, at times subject to the same privations and dangers as the beleaguered residents, getting shot at or wounded, losing friends and colleagues. These experiences play themselves out day after day, the weeks stretching into months and then years. Even soldiers and policemen, to mention two other hazardous professions, operate under a different set of constructs, trying to resolve conflict, not live off its escalation. But events that fizzle out quietly and characters who go peacefully into the night make for dull news. Steve Northup, who photographed the Vietnam War in the mid-1960s for United Press International, said it well when he observed, "When you started out on the day's march, one thing weighed on your mind. If you were going to make really good images that day, something would have to happen; people would have to be hurt or killed. Otherwise it was just another long, hot walk."

*  *  *

We sat in a small café in the old quarter of Barcelona. It was a winter's afternoon and darkness had come early. I was listening to the odyssey of a journalist unfold. In the background the hiss of an espresso machine, the dulcet adagio from a Vivaldi lute concerto and the intermittent staccato of rain on the windowpanes. The man I was interviewing heard none of this. Overwhelmed by memory, he was reliving his years spent in Bosnia. That period in time had never left him. It defined his life, gave him a career, awards, recognition, a livelihood. But there were other things on his mind.

> There are a lot of situations that stay with you. Nightmares. I find myself abusing alcohol and drugs in order not to remember my dreams. In other words, the dreams are there and if I am on a trip someplace, or go for a week or so without smoking dope or drinking a lot, I find the dreams come back and can be quite disturbing. They are not always there, not like it's every night, but out of a given four or five nights, I might get two or three days of bad sleep and nightmares. And I find that if I go to bed completely stoned and drunk, I can't remember my dreams, so I wake up without having to worry about them. And that, for me, in the last few years, has worked, but it's not good, it's not healthy. It screws up many things, your short-term memory, your concentration. I wonder if certain anti-social attitudes that I'm going through over the last few years are related to what's on my mind and how much of those are related to the various drugs and whatnot I am putting into myself to deal with that?

He paused and looked up, eyes moist, focusing on a point behind me. I was nearing the end of my series of interviews, and few war journalists had managed to keep their equanimity throughout their discussions with me. I came to anticipate these moments, a period when the vividness and pain of recall overwhelmed speech. I waited patiently for him to go on, for I had also learned that, difficult as it is to recollect the past, the need to talk about it is greater by far.

> I was not feeling well. I wasn't sure of what was wrong with me. I knew it was work related and I knew it was specifically conflict related. So I went to see this fellow for about an hour, in London, and we basically went through everything step by step and he said, "Well, there is no doubt in my mind you are suffering from PTSD." And I was quite relieved that somebody had diagnosed what was wrong with me. He gave me some exercises to do, which involved recording the most disturbing episodes in my career, writing them down in a very detailed fashion and then listening to the recordings.

He described it as phobia therapy. I did that a few times and found it to be quite effective immediately, but because the therapy wasn't sustained I never got better. I was still having nightmares. I remember at the time being sent to a morgue in Egypt to try and find the bodies of some fundamentalists who had been executed. And I remember the smell of the morgue, this disinfectant, this body smell that provoked a very physical reaction in me. I was shaking. I was very emotional, partly because back in Bosnia, I spent a lot of time in the morgue. The smell of morgues was bad news.

A long pause. The rain had stopped and Vivaldi made way for Mozart, the cheerful finale of his Fifth Violin Concerto, "The Turkish." The coffee was replenished. I used the break to summarize what had been said: nightmares, alcohol, cannabis, and cocaine to still the dreams, a diagnosis of PTSD, a failure to follow through with therapy, an inability to tolerate the smell of a morgue. I wondered aloud how much more this man had to confide. He told me, with a bitter laugh, that all that was but a prelude.

I got a bit disgusted with myself. I felt that I was just feeling sorry for myself and that I had to get on with things. So I went to do this war in Yemen followed by some domestic stories here in Spain, before deciding in early 1995 that I had to go back to Bosnia. I felt it was very important for me to go back to Bosnia. So I did. I had no desire to at all, but felt it was an obligation that I had imposed on myself. I felt I had to get back on the horse. I lasted about ten days and I got blown up. A mortar fell fairly close, put a piece of shrapnel into my leg. My flak jacket and equipment stopped other shrapnel. I was operated on in Sarajevo; they gave me an epidural, pulled out the metal, kept me in hospital for four or five days and then I was evacuated. Well, can you imagine! In a sense I had conquered my ghosts, I had gone back, I had overcome my fear, but I had lasted only ten days before I got blown up. I came back here to recuperate and all my friends were saying to me, "Okay, don't you think that is enough? You've seen this through, that's enough." And it was the opposite, I was angry. I was furious. I had made such a big effort to get back to Sarajevo, such a big effort to overcome my fears and now I am out of the game because some Serb, a few kilometers away, pops a mortar in on us. Screw that. I'll carry on. I figured I had invested enough and put enough time and effort into this at that point, I'd be damned if I was going to stop. So I carried on.

I was aware that there was a war going on, but the battle being fought was between a man and his personal demons, not between opposing armies.

His fierce determination to use war as a means to conquer fear drove this journalist back to the front lines. The desire to report the news, to get the breaking story, was still there, but for the moment it had been displaced as a priority. The challenge was vintage Hemingway, and it seemed apt that this self-administered test was being discussed in the land that was home to the bullfight. But comparisons between a matador sweating the big drop and war journalism are of course specious, for the outcome in war is far less certain than the one handed out in the late afternoon corrida. The man sitting in front of me giving vent to his frustrations, fears, and anger had lost his way in a dangerous profession. War had sapped his emotional and physical resources, and yet it was to war that he went looking to replenish them. By now my curiosity as a researcher had given way to the concerns of a clinician. The odyssey was not yet complete, but the ending was disturbingly predictable.

"It has come to the point where I no longer want to go out. I do not want to meet people. If my partner goes away for a weekend, I lock myself up in the house and order in food and just stay drunk and stoned. I have become a recluse. I do not want to deal with people. I have become hyperaware, hyperalert to noises and other such things that bother me. But on a social level, I do not want any new experiences."

In this vignette are to be found all the cardinal features of post-traumatic stress disorder. There are the unwanted, traumatic memories that return as nightmares or are triggered by a certain smell. There is the hypervigilance and difficulty concentrating. And, finally, there is reclusive behavior and substance abuse, both attempts at numbing or damping down the painful recollections. In my interviews with war journalists, I found that 29 percent of the group had met the diagnostic criteria for PTSD over the course of long careers.

A notable observation here was that PTSD symptoms were differentially distributed according to the type of journalism practiced. Symptoms were more frequent and intense in stills photographers, followed by cameramen, and then print reporters and producers. The necessity for proximity to an event, encapsulated in Robert Capa's famous dictum, "If your photographs are not good enough, you are not close enough," offers the simplest, most eloquent explanation for these findings. Across all domains of war journalism, the overall PTSD lifetime rate of 29 percent well exceeds the rate of 5 percent in the general population and 7 percent to 13 percent for traumatized police officers. (None of the domestic journalists in the control group were diagnosed with PTSD.) It comes close to the rate reported in combat veterans in general and, depending on the veterans' degree of combat exposure, may in certain cases exceed it.

While these comparisons are informative, they obscure another fundamental difference between war journalism and other hazardous professions: policemen, firefighters, and soldiers are schooled in violence and danger. They enter their professions with the expectation of encountering it and are trained over months or years to learn how to deal with it. Journalists have little of this preparation. The typical war journalist is someone who, after leaving college or university, drifts into conflict zones either by design or, more often, by chance, unprepared for the dangers ahead. For some, the harsh realities of war prove too unsettling. After covering one or two conflicts, they move on to other work. Those who stay are exposed to repetitive cycles of danger while working and safety when back home, and so extreme are the differences between these states that, for some, both may prove psychologically enervating.

Even among the more than 70 percent of journalists who do not have the full syndrome, isolated intrusive symptoms persist and prove troubling. One journalist who had covered the wars in Bosnia and Chechnya and who felt he had coped well with both, nevertheless found his behavior changed on his return to London. "Coming back from Bosnia, I had a funny feeling every time I walked on grass. I just avoided grass for fear of landmines in Bosnia. I still have that feeling. If I am walking on the pavement and have to step off onto some grass, I become a little agitated."

For a journalist who had reported on the genocide in Rwanda, the slaughter and mounds of corpses lived with him seven years later, intruding into his consciousness with a disconcerting unpredictability. "I think the images and smells and experiences stayed with me for months because of their intensity," he told me. "Remember, I had been through a lot of conflicts before that, but this was on a dramatically different scale. I was back about a week and my wife and I were invited to a friend's house in north London. As I lifted a drink to my lips, there was the smell of corpses from the glass of champagne. I just had to put it down. That has happened a lot, the sense that the smell was all over you, that no matter how many times you washed your clothes, it would not go away."

For this journalist, therapy helped with some of the more troubling recollections, but it had been unable to halt the demons that came intermittently with sleep, stealing into his dreams when his guard was down: "The most common dream I had was being trapped under a mound of bodies and not being able to get out. And then there was another variation to this, in which I was trapped under this mound of bodies and there was a guy above with a machete who was trying to get down to kill me."

For another journalist, the dreams seldom came while he was working: "If I have been on a hard job and have seen a lot of violence, as in Chechnya for example, I won't usually have any dreams. It seems that when I get back home, I start having two or three a week. In these dreams there is a lot of mutilation, a lot of darkness and a lot of fear, but they are not direct replicas of what I have seen. They are more abstract and might be of dismembered bodies and disemboweled bodies, but not actually replicas of the ones I have seen."

While intrusive symptoms tend to decrease over time, for the majority of the 140 war journalists studied, they never disappeared entirely. During the period I collected my data, the first Chechen war was already over, the Balkans had gone quiet, and the Middle East had yet to erupt. Only regional African conflicts, such as those in Sierra Leone, the Congo, and Angola, continued their unrelenting pattern of massacre and mutilation. Most war journalists were between traumas, with many weeks, if not months, since their last exposure to danger. Yet, despite this lull in hostilities, 62 percent still reported unwanted recollections of traumatic events, 77 percent described flashbacks, and a similar percentage experienced strong and unpleasant waves of emotion associated with these involuntarily recollections. Thus, even those journalists without PTSD experienced isolated, persistent, and at times disturbing intrusive symptoms.

Experience offers little protection from these symptoms. Whether a neophyte or veteran, the price paid by a journalist in search of a conflict's defining image can be devastating. Dan Eldon was a twenty-two-year-old photojournalist on his first assignment for Reuters when he was stoned to death by an enraged mob in Somalia. Two of his Reuters colleagues, Anthony Macharia and Hos Maina, and a colleague from Associated Press, Hansi Kraus, suffered the same fate. Eldon kept a series of journals, which were documented after his death in *Dying to Tell the Story*, a film by his sister. In one, Eldon wrote, "The terror of being surrounded by violence and the horrors of the famine threw me into a dark depression. Even journalists who had covered many conflicts were moved to tears. But for me, this was my first experience with war. Before Somalia, I had only seen two dead bodies in my life. Now I have seen hundreds, tossed into ditches like sacks. The worse things I could not photograph." After one particularly difficult stint he confided, "It was a horrible and terrifying experience . . . being in a place like that really eats away at the mind . . . when I left I had gone a little nuts . . . I don't know how these experiences have changed me, but I feel different."

In her quest to find out what happened to her brother on that hot, violent afternoon in Mogadishu, Amy Eldon sought out others in the profession, including Don McCullin, one of the great war photojournalists. For her film, she interviewed him in a gallery exhibiting his work. The black-and-white prints are startling, the faces and bodies of soldiers, civilians, children saturated with anguish. It is unsettling to see these images, for they force us to open our eyes and minds and confront a nightmare existence. What, then, of the man who has taken the pictures? For decades, Don McCullin has pushed his lens into the face of grief, despair, hopelessness, and misery. He may have been able to return to the comfort of his home in England at periodic intervals, but it is clear that this buffer has not kept the demons at bay. The cumulative weight of all that sadness has left its psychological imprint. In *Dying to Tell the Story*, Don McCullin appears melancholic, a recluse haunted by the images lining the walls of the gallery. He tells Amy Eldon, "emotionally I was like a destroyed person." Those images that have brought him fame will not let him be, their memory is a constant companion. A collection of his most famous photographs is entitled *Sleeping with Ghosts: A Life's Work in Photography*, and the title speaks to the repetitive, intrusive nature of his traumatic memories. He imagines a ghoulish spectacle unfolding each night in his home, a morbid variant of the ballet *Coppélia* in which the ghosts of the victims he has photographed come together in a macabre meeting of departed souls.

Amy Eldon also filmed an interview with Mohammed Shaffi, a Reuters cameraman who accompanied her brother that fateful afternoon. Although badly beaten, he alone survived the mob's frenzied attack, and his account is central to understanding the events surrounding his colleagues' deaths. Four years have passed since the stoning, and he has returned to the scene of the killing accompanied by Amy Eldon. "I can't forget what has happened," he confides emotionally into the camera. Tears come easily and, like Don McCullin, he seems subdued by the weight of cumulative memory.

A few years after *Dying to Tell the Story* aired, Mohammed Shaffi wrote to me. "My big problem is I cannot sleep," he confided. "I still get flashbacks of the stories I had covered, people being killed in front of my eyes in [the] hundreds. I can see myself running while bullets are flying over my head. The truth is I am afraid to sleep. I talk a lot in my sleep. The next morning I can remember everything I had gone through last night. I love my work and nothing will or can stop me covering hard news stories. When

I am alone my mind goes back to what I have gone through. I feel sick and very tired. I have never spoken to my family about this because I don't want them to worry."

His reference to his family reminded me of something else he had said in Eldon's film. "The work I was doing was more important than my family," he admitted. "I have the rest of my life to make it up to them." In that, however, he was mistaken. Six months after I received his letter, Mohammed Shaffi was found dead in a hotel room in Jerusalem. He had had a heart attack. He was fifty years old.

The florid nature of the dreams, the eidetic quality of recall, and the power of the past to intrude repetitively into the present or constantly, involuntarily reinvent itself make for dramatic narrative. These symptoms come to define whether an individual is psychologically distressed, and while they may be considered the quintessential feature of PTSD, they may not prove the most disabling. Time may diminish their frequency and intensity, but for many war journalists, they never completely disappear, insinuating themselves into the mental fabric of their existence, disconcerting, albeit no longer terrifying.

Not so the avoidance phenomena, the second group of symptoms that make up the PTSD triad. These occur frequently in war journalists, and the most prevalent of all is a feeling of detachment or estrangement from other people. Not surprisingly, the effect on relationships is often destructive. One camerawoman echoed the sentiments of many of her colleagues when she said:

> While I was doing the Croatia-Bosnia stuff, I was out in the field all the time. And I was moving around, I'd be one of the guys. I'd be living in army barracks and stuff like that. Then I'd get back home and someone would invite me to a dinner party and people would be talking about Bernie's car or skiing holidays in Switzerland and I'd feel like I was not fitting in. I would sit there thinking, you guys don't know anything about the real world. It got so that I did not want to see these people, and they had been my friends, you know. I do that even now. Last weekend, I didn't go out at all. I just did not feel like it.

War journalists are acutely aware of the contrast between the intensity of living and working in a war zone and the mundaneness of life in a society at peace. No matter the conflict, a couple of hours in a plane will have you back in London or Paris in a comfortable bed in a quiet apartment, the stores stocked with every imaginable item, people laughing, carefree, and caught up in the rhythm of life in a civil society. Details like paying the electricity bill or getting the lawn cut, when placed alongside death and survival, heroism and cowardice, can seem annoyingly trivial. A wedge is inserted between two disparate realities: the world inhabited by war journalists and their coterie of soldiers, refugees, mercenaries, informants, and fixers, and that occupied by the journalists' families with their shopkeepers, schoolteachers, appliance repairmen, and garage attendants. The adjustment for journalists when they re-enter this orbit poses a challenge, and it can test their emotional maturity and the strength of their relationships.

The French photojournalist Jerome Delay told me the story of coming home from his first trip to Sarajevo.

> We had difficulty getting out of the city. I was with a *Washington Post* correspondent. There was a lot of fighting going on and we waited for an hour, two hours, three hours. Then at one point we said, "Okay, let's go for it." So I put on two flak jackets and drove up to the Bosnian checkpoint. "Is the road okay?" I asked, and the soldier says, "Well, it might be." So we hit it. There's a stretch of road about three kilometers long. We picked up speed, passed a burned-out truck, took a sharp right turn, came under fire, but made it through. I spent the night in Split, got drunk, got on a plane to Frankfurt, got drunk in Frankfurt at nine in the morning. Then I flew to London. All of a sudden I was alone in this plane and then in Heathrow, I took a cab to a hotel. The cab driver wanted to talk and I told her, "Listen, I'm sorry, but I don't want to talk, so just shut up." And we drive through these London suburbs to go downtown and I see people who are not running. There are all these . . . all these shops . . . It was dark. It was raining. Food everywhere. Food. It is overwhelming, the quantity of things. It is almost . . . not insane; it was disgusting and there is one thing I want to do from then on. It is just to go back. Because I felt . . . it was not normal. My normalcy was no running water, people running, and shelling. That was where I had become comfortable. That was my reality. Then I went to this hotel and spent two days there, just doing nothing, not seeing anybody and then I came home. I have learnt not to come straight home. Because every time I have done it, it is not good.

Delay even came up against the everyday challenges of life away from a war zone while he was in Bosnia.

I remember talking to my wife on my cell phone while I was in Sarajevo and she tells me, "Oh, we've got a big problem. The washing machine is not working properly." I go, "Honey, excuse me, but we have not had running water here for two-and-a-half months, okay! So, I don't know . . . buy a new machine, have it fixed. I really don't care." Later I realized that was really the wrong thing to say, because their world is very important. They have their parameters and I have mine too, when I'm away on assignment. We each have our markers and one thing I've learned over the years is to respect those markers. And yes, to my wife and two little girls, the fact the washing machine was not working was as important to them as the absence of running water was to me in Sarajevo. My wife respected me more than I respected her in that regard.

For journalists based in Europe, the Bosnian war was literally on their doorstep. They could spend the morning under siege in Sarajevo and the afternoon taking a stroll in the Ramblas or Tuilleries. The temporal proximity of London, Paris, and Madrid to war heightened the sense of unreality attached to the whole conflict. To the incredulity that a war accompanied by ethnic cleansing and concentration camps could take root on European soil yet again was added the befuddlement induced by technology. During a lull in the shelling, a journalist could easily phone an editor, a spouse, friend, or lover. Hunkered down in some ruined church or deserted basement, journalists would run up against the blandness of domestic life back home. Not all welcomed such reminders.

Finding a middle ground that acknowledges two distinct lifestyles often proves elusive. When journalists return home from war, their sense of estrangement may be matched by their partner's trouble fathoming what life is like in a conflict zone. An effort to appear understanding, to shield the war journalist from events that are perceived as trivial, may upset the equilibrium within a relationship. The partner who stays home can abrogate his or her sense of identity, subscribing to a view of life that equates war with meaning and relegates everything outside of war to the boring and mundane. This *folie à deux* becomes, in time, untenable. Relationships wither.

Few have made the transition from a conflict zone to civil society more often than James Nachtwey. The celebrated photographer has not missed a war in twenty years, his longevity a source of admiration and wonder to colleagues who see him as the standard-bearer of a tradition in war photography going back to such icons as Larry Burrows, Robert Capa, and

Eugene Smith. Nachtwey, the subject of an Academy Award–nominated documentary, *War Photographer,* was not an easy man to get hold of. For more than half the year he is away from home, mostly working in war zones or areas of conflict. When we did finally meet, I found observing the man to be almost as interesting as listening to what he had to say. Of slight build, he had an immaculate appearance but dressed very simply. The fastidiousness reflected an understated persona: precise, neat, unruffled, no stray lock of hair or trace of stubble. His apartment, restrained, orderly, and elegant, mirrored his personal appearance. His voice, too, was revealing — a quiet, measured monotone with minimal emotional inflection or what neurologists term *prosody.* A temperate manner of speaking, without mannerism or gesture, matched the delivery. The overall impression was of an aesthete — the tranquility, orderliness, and restraint a foil to the inferno captured by his camera.

When he was younger, Nachtwey's sense of disconnection from life back home matched that of his colleagues. "At first I thought people were spoiled and they had too much, and how could they possibly be concerned about such petty things," he told me. But in time, these views underwent a metamorphosis, and what emerged in their place was a unique perception of life in the affluent developed world, a view that took the angry denouncements and turned them inside out. He explained:

> I think my early views were immature and inexperienced, because after a couple of years I actually was glad that those petty things were all that people had to be concerned about. I was very happy for them. I'm really happy that's what they have to deal with. That they don't have to deal with having family members killed in front of their eyes, and having their houses destroyed and their culture destroyed and being oppressed. This is what normal life is and people do get worried about things, which compared to the enormity of where I have just been, can seem petty and foolish. But I actually feel fine, and I hope it's the worst thing that ever happens to them — that their cab didn't show up on time or something. And I am actually grateful that's the case.

But Nachtwey is the exception. The sense of estrangement many journalists feel on their return from war, and the difficulties this introduces into relationships, translates into a high percentage of unmarried war journalists. Of those I studied, over half were either single or divorced. The comparable figure for domestic journalists who have never been to war is one-third, a difference that is statistically highly significant. Even more illuminating are the statistics from the population at large; by the fifth decade of life (remember that the average age of the war journalists interviewed approached forty), a large majority of people are married.

A feeling of emotional detachment from those around them affected half the war journalists I studied. While psychologically crippling for some, it was not the most striking symptom of avoidant behavior that I encountered. More dramatic was the inability to remember an important aspect of the traumatic event, evidence of the power of the mind to censor memory. One television cameraman displayed just this kind of behavior when he related to me an event he had experienced in Somalia in 1993.

> One day we were in Mogadishu — in one of those communication vehicles with a driver and two armed guards in the back — in the midst of a very large crowd outside the American embassy. They started to drag me out of the car. There were all going mad. A lot of gunmen were around us, and we drove right through the crowd. Then I'm not sure what happened, but there was gunfire — we were shooting all over the place and I was being pulled out of the car. My only memory I really have of that time is seeing a marine behind the gates of the embassy just looking away and not doing anything. I also vaguely remember trying to get my sunglasses back from some guy. So I am not sure how many people we killed, if we killed any, that is, and how many we ran over. I have no real memory of that.

Detachment, estrangement, amnesia — all are common symptoms of avoidance reported by the war journalists. However, one symptom seldom gets mentioned, and that is the effort to evade thoughts, feelings, or conversations associated with the trauma. Here the war journalists are in a unique bind, for that central traumatic event often constitutes the news. The print reporter, in preparing her story, will have to revisit in her mind what has occurred. Memory is essential to the process; without it there is no story. Similarly, the television reporter or cameraman will have to pour over the images captured on film until the visual story has been conveyed to his satisfaction. The demands of the profession are at odds with how an individual may respond to overwhelming stressors. This tension may not necessarily be a bad thing, however, for in being forced to confront the traumatic event, repeatedly if necessary, the war journalists are given a cathartic outlet, an opportunity to work through and process on both a cognitive and an emotional level what has befallen them. To the less resilient among them, however, this constant revisiting of past traumas may upset an already fragile emotional equilibrium, driving them further into a tightly cocooned, emotionally constricted existence. "It slowly takes away your smile," is the way João Silva describes it.

* * *

The final part of the PTSD triad is symptoms of arousal, which include difficulties with sleep, irritability or temper outbursts, and poor concentration. These symptoms are not necessarily specific to those with PTSD, for they are found in many people with psychiatric disorders and, to lesser degrees, in the population at large. Nevertheless, their presence is a sign of emotional distress, and they are required for a diagnosis of PTSD. Of all the arousal symptoms, the two most significant are hypervigilance and an exaggerated startle response. Both were frequently reported by the war journalists in my study.

The following anecdote, given to me by a BBC reporter, illustrates how the threat of danger in a war zone follows the journalist home.

> Once, when I was in the middle of covering the Bosnian war, I went down to visit a good friend of mine who happens to be a journalist as well as a political correspondent in London. He lives in a village in Hampshire and we went out for a walk on a beautiful, crisp Sunday morning. He has a little boy, about four years old at the time, and he went with us. We were walking along a tarmac road, thinking or talking about nothing connected with work . . . Suddenly the little boy spotted something and he ran up a grassy verge and my heart leapt. I ran after him and shouted, "no, no, no, don't go there," and I was thinking of landmines, just coming off the tarmac. It was absurd.

A cameraman just returned from the charnel house of Grozny reported a similar experience. "You'd have the twitches, you know," he confided, "and I could never forget it. Shortly after coming back to England, I was filming at the Paddington Green Police Station. The police had a couple of suspects and the press wanted to film them. I was just standing there and a lorry drove over a plastic bottle and it sort of exploded, and you have never seen anyone hit the deck so quickly. And everyone just looked at me and said, 'God, what's wrong with you?' "

The startle response is often accompanied by other symptoms of arousal, most often irritability. One journalist told me the story of a going-away party he attended soon after returning from what was then Zaire.

> I had come straight from the airport, dumped my bags and gone off to have this drink session. Literally within a day, you come back from a war zone to

London and you are off to a TGIF place where they had all these balloons for the party. Somebody popped a balloon and I was down on the floor before I realized it. The people around me knew I had been out in the field. But the waiter thought it would be funny to pop some more balloons and see my reaction. As I said, my aggression levels were right up there, and it's like whew! I was on my way to him and the waiter wasn't too sure what was going on and I was diverted by three of four of my mates, straight out the door. Yeah, it's important to have friends who understand the situation.

Despite reactions like these and the others I have described, it would be misleading to convey the impression that war journalists are riddled with PTSD-type psychopathology. There is no doubt that the risks they expose themselves to are astonishing by any standard, for at times, in their eagerness to capture the news of war, they place themselves in the vanguard of armies. But what is perhaps more extraordinary is that more than 70 percent of them do not have PTSD. Every account of unwanted intrusive thoughts, nightmares, startle responses, and emotional withdrawal was matched by stories of journalists taken to the brink of death in the most perverse and sadistic fashion, yet reacting with an equanimity that rivets the attention. Certain individuals appear immune to the long-term adverse psychological consequences of repeated exposure to life-threatening danger. This is not to say they never experience fear, but rather that their threshold for it is raised. When crossed, their emotional responses are more circumscribed and transient. One photographer told me of his Balkan experiences:

A colleague and I were covering an offensive. We were arrested by the Serbs. It seemed initially like a routine arrest—I didn't think much of it. Then something must have happened, because the tension level went up much higher. We got handcuffed, thrown into a car, driven off to some remote location, and there we were interrogated, separated, beaten, hoods were placed over our heads, and we were subjected to mock executions. I was being held in a wooden shed. They left me in there, but took my colleague out. A gun went off and a few minutes later they came back and took me into another room where there was this commander, and they told me they had just executed my friend, and that if I did not confess to being a spy in the next hour, they would execute me too.

While he talked, I observed this man closely. There were no outward signs of emotion. He paused, took a sip from a Diet Coke, and resumed his dispassionate account.

I had nothing to confess, so I did not do anything. I said I was a photographer and stuck to the story. The hood was placed over my head again, my hands, which were now uncuffed, were tied behind my back, and I was taken into another room. They asked me, "What is your mission here?" I said I was a photographer. This went on for about fifteen minutes or so. Each time I answered they would punch me in the face. They accused us of being spies and said we were there illegally, which we were not. It was very cold and they had doused us with water, so it was very uncomfortable and my main thought was to keep warm, and all the while I was replaying things in my mind, trying to figure out whether what they had said was true. I had not heard my colleague call out after the shot had gone off, I had not heard a body fall, so had they really shot him?

I had this man's questionnaires in front of me, and I glanced again at his PTSD responses. For each question the respondent can choose one of five options: not at all, a little bit, moderately, quite a bit, and extremely. In this case, a neat tick had been placed in the "not at all" column for twenty of the twenty-two PTSD questions. The remaining two were rated "a little bit."

He continued, "I had become very calm and very clear headed and also very accepting of the inevitable — that I was ready for them. Whether I would have felt that way when they put the gun to my head, I don't know, but I really felt I was ready to accept my fate."

He took another sip of Diet Coke. I commented on what an ordeal it must have been and asked whether he felt fear at any point. "Yeah, yeah, I was scared, but I was not scared in a hysterical way. One thing that I did do, that I had learned, I guess, from previous experience, was that it was not wise to be completely calm in front of them because they would think you were a real professional spy, as it were. So I kind of acted more outwardly scared when I was with them, hoping to make them feel sorry for me, or something like that."

As I listened to this account of horrendous maltreatment, I was reminded of two researchers, Holmes and Rahe, who in the 1980s devised a rating scale that quantified life events. Points were assigned to changing a job, getting married, the death of a family member, moving house, and so on. The more stressful the event, the more points awarded. The aim was to show that if an individual's points exceeded a certain threshold within a finite period, say six months or a year, their chances of developing a psychiatric illness would significantly increase. What, I wondered, would Holmes and Rahe have made of this man's experience? Held captive, isolated, freezing, wet, hooded, handcuffed, repeatedly punched, his colleague presumably executed, and facing a similar fate himself within the hour. His score would be off the chart. It could not be quantified. And what was his response? Of all things, he had to simulate fear, not control it.

The story did not, however, end there, for there was an addendum that shifted a remarkable narrative into the realm of the fantastic. The war journalist waited to the very end of his story to reveal that he had an even more alarming reason to be terrified of his captors. "Everybody has gone through this type of thing, to varying degrees, all the way to actually getting killed. But I had seen a number of executions in front of me, by Serbs against Croatians and Bosnians, and I had photographed some of them, which caused more trouble for me with them. Some people were looking for me. A price had been placed on my head by a paramilitary-mafia guy, and I was very worried that the Serbs holding me would make the connection between me and this warlord."

There were multiple layers of trauma to be peeled away here, and like an archeologist seeking the primal source, I went looking for the individual submerged within. One by one, traumatic events were revealed, carefully defined, and their essential characteristics clarified before they were put to one side and we moved on to the next layer. Eventually, all the threats, dousings, humiliations, beatings, and mock executions administered over the course of a five-year conflict were cataloged. And when all this had been done, what emotional residue was left? The answer was, very little. The man did not have PTSD. He was not depressed. He did not drink excessively. He did not use drugs. He loved his work. Yes, at times he had been frightened, but never for long.

Are we to express incredulity or admiration? Are the responses of this journalist no more than those of a naysayer unable to disentangle himself from the macho image of his profession? Would an admission of fearful nightmares or startle responses shatter a carefully constructed persona? In the end, I came to reject this assessment. The relative absence of psychological distress was not unique to him. Others responded in a similar fashion to stressors equally severe. One was Elizabeth Jones, a Canadian freelance camerawoman.

The worst situation I had was in Kisangani, in the north of the Congo, in 1997. There were a lot of Interahamwe around Kisangani because the Rwandan refugee camps were being broken up. There were a few journalists in town. We all knew each other and were staying at the same hotel. There was a guy I knew from other stories; he is a cameraman at one of the big news agencies, and he was collecting all of our tapes to take them to the airport and ship them out. What happened was that he got to the airport and somebody recognized him from an earlier episode in the war and thought he was a Belgian mercenary because he had a crew cut and did look like one. The airport was absolutely full, with hundreds, no, thousands of soldiers who were retreating. And they just opened fire on him — he survived actually, but a number of people around him were killed. I was not actually there for any of this. He was rescued from this hail of bullets by a couple of guys who threw him into their car and drove him to the edge of the airport where they stuck a gun to his head and said, "Give us everything you've got. How much money do you have?" And he had like ten dollars. So he said he did not have much, but a friend of mine who is over at the mission — I know because I just saw her there — she has a lot of money. That was me, and so at this point I was completely oblivious to what was going on.

What happened next was that I was at the mission and these nutty guys with guns came raging into the room, with a gun to the head of this guy and other guns blazing away. It was very scary and they said, "Who is the woman with the money? Which one? Is that you?" and pointed at me. I leapt behind a door. I thought they were going to shoot me. It was a very ugly moment . . . I do not know how long it lasted for, but they were really threatening everybody else at the mission as well, pointing guns, and then they just grabbed my camera and gear and I threw the money out of my wallet and gave them all I had, which was quite a lot, and they stormed out with this guy and I assumed they had taken him off to be shot. We did not know what to do. I was with a colleague of that cameraman and he just collapsed really. He completely broke down. He did not know what to do.

It was interesting to observe the war journalists during their interviews. The notes I made about their appearance and demeanor, essentially a record of their mental state at the time, were often as informative as what they had to say. During our interview, Jones sat on a lounge settee with her feet drawn up under her. She was attractive, relaxed, and calm; her brow unfurrowed, she seemed at ease with herself and the story she related. To me, the outside observer, there was an incongruence between her exterior equanimity and the turbulent events of her narrative. I reminded myself that the Congo was this woman's passion, a land she returned to many times, always alone, to make critically acclaimed, self-financed, money-losing documentaries about a country the size of France, Germany, Italy, Britain, and Spain combined, a country that few in the West are interested in.

Congo. There is no country in Africa with a more evocative name. Africa's impenetrable, ungovernable heart, dark, foreboding, a metaphor for chaos. It is this unstable cauldron that the woman I was interviewing chose as her workplace. Every day she rubbed shoulders with genocidal Interahamwe, rogue militia, ill-disciplined armies, mercenaries, and displaced millions, while confronting the risk of cholera, AIDS, yellow fever, and malaria, among the more pernicious health hazards. In this malignant climate of death and disease, events unfolded at speed and with unpredictability. Her story was testimony to that. It also demonstrated a temperament that soaks up adversity. Picking up the threads of her story, she said:

> I was feeling fine, actually, although I knew I was really being tested. It was a most frightening moment and these guys were ready to kill. They were pointing their guns up your nose and were very threatening in a loud, aggressive, blow-your-brains-out kind of way. It was really horrible. They had disappeared with the cameraman and we did not now if they were going to shoot him and then come back for us. His colleague just freaked out—he was in tears, a real basket case. I was thinking to myself that I feel quite okay, I am thinking very clearly. I was really quite conscious of the fact that I was able to make decisions. When I have been put into that sort of situation I often think that I am more calm than the other people around me. So it must be something within me.

This last statement was said in the most matter-of-fact kind of way, without a trace of bravura. She had been in tough situations, seen the reactions of some of her male colleagues, and judged her responses against theirs. She was unable to articulate these differences, other than to say there was something within her, some poorly understood characteristic that allowed her to deal calmly with terror. But this is no foolhardy trait, as the ending to her story showed.

> I went outside the mission to see if the militia were going to shoot this cameraman, and at that moment a truck full of soldiers pulled up and arrested me and the other guy, who was still crying. They then went around the town picking up all the journalists they could find and threw us all into, not a prison, but some kind of holding room. The whole episode lasted twenty-four hours. I was separated from the men as I was the only woman, and some of the men were beaten. I was just kept alone. I did not know

whether they were planning to rape me. I had no idea what was going on [but] I was thinking clearly and one thing that I had done at the mission was rather clever, for I had found a priest and told him to phone the British consulate, which he did. That had been a good thing to do, because there was no other opportunity to tell people what had happened to us. The twenty-four hours passed slowly. I was just bored and hungry and thirsty... Eventually we were taken to the secret service headquarters and given a long lecture in the middle of the night. We were then given a car with a driver who was supposed to take us back to the hotel, but it all ended rather comically, as it can in the Congo, when the car ran out of gas. We were all dispatched to find some petrol in the middle of the night, so we all ended [up] walking back to our hotel.

Shaken up by this episode, she took a break from Africa. A year later, however, she was back in the Congo.

There is a clearly discernable thread that runs through all of the war journalists' responses. Whether they reported symptoms of PTSD or not, they share a belief that their work has changed them as individuals. This is evident in Chris Hedges's book, *War Is a Force That Gives Us Meaning*. After three harrowing trips to the civil war in El Salvador, the manner in which Hedges finally left the country was testimony to the considerable emotional strain he was under: "My last act was, in a frenzy of rage and anguish, to leap over the KLM counter in the airport in Costa Rica because of a perceived slight by a hapless airline clerk. I beat him to the floor as his bewildered colleagues locked themselves in the room behind the counter. Blood streamed down his face and mine. I refused to wipe the dried stains off my cheeks on the flight to Madrid, and I carry a scar on my face from where he thrust his pen into my cheek. War's sickness had become mine." This overwrought behavior came not from some paparazzo with psychopathic tendencies, but from a respected journalist with a stellar pedigree: foreign correspondent to the *New York Times* for over a decade, part of a Pulitzer-winning team, adjunct professor of journalism at New York University, holder of a bachelor of arts degree from Colgate University, a master's in divinity from Harvard University, and a Nieman Fellowship at Harvard. The jarring dissonance of a divinity major hurdling the check-in counter to assault an airline attendant is matched by the very public emotional disintegration of ITN cameraman Jon Steele at Heathrow's Terminal 4. His memoir, *War Junkie*, opens with savage self-deprecation: "Attention, Club World and World Traveller passengers. British Airways is happy to announce the nervous breakdown of Jon Denis Steele, at check-in counter twenty."

If such public manifestations of distress are uncommon, the underlying emotions are not. The many personal anecdotes given to me demonstrate that. When I looked beyond the scotomatous domain of symptom checklists and structured psychiatric interviews, to a man and woman, the war journalists I met spoke about the ability of remarkable events to move them to tears, anger, rage, euphoria, frustration, hatred, and love. Such were the magnitude of these events and the intensities of emotions generated that they would never again view their world as before. To varying degrees, this translated into an awakened or bolstered social conscience mixed, at times, with embitterment and deep cynicism. Once you have viewed the world through the prism of war, your perspective on life invariably alters.

Throughout this chapter, voices of the journalists have given testimony to the ways in which war has profoundly affected them. It is therefore fitting that I end with the words of one of their most articulate spokesmen, the BBC's Allan Little, who reported in the *Evening Standard* that a feisty exchange among war journalists took place in London at a meeting in which I presented my data to the profession. Little wrote:

> The historian Philip Knightley, who has written a brilliant book on war correspondents, was also there on Thursday night. He recited, with some condescension, a canon of war correspondent "greats" such as Alexander Clifford, Alan Whitehead, Martha Gelhorn and Ernest Hemingway. What, he mused, would they have made of all this self-indulgent talk of trauma? I think this question was designed to intimidate or shame us. Well, I am neither intimidated nor shamed. For I have seen a lot of war and I think I know what it can do. Do you not think Hemingway broached this subject? Why do we do this? Why do we love it? What are we obsessed with, living so dangerously, drinking so heavily, bursting into tears so easily? Oh yes [he] did!

After urging his fellow war journalists to take responsibility for their actions and avoid a compensation culture, reminding them that, in relation to the victims of war, their difficulties are insignificant, Little ended with this simple caution: "Do not delude yourself into thinking that you can swan in and out of other people's wars year after year and not be affected in some way."

# 3

# Why Take the Risks?

"WAR IN EUROPE OVER. There is absolutely no reason to get up in the
mornings any more." So ends the memoir of Robert Capa, the great war
photographer. It is a revealing final statement and encapsulates a philosophy to life shared by many of his colleagues. War may be "that stupid crime,
that devil's madness," yet for a small group of men and women — and they
number no more than a couple of hundred — it acts as a magnet, attracting
them to environs often far flung and always dangerous, and in the process
conferring meaning on their lives and making it that much easier to get up
in the morning and face each day.

Why should this be? Why is it that war journalists return repeatedly to
scenes of carnage and suffering, placing themselves at great personal risk,
venturing into areas that have regularly and disturbingly claimed the lives
of colleagues and friends? Perhaps in the case of those journalists who are
untroubled psychologically by their work, such behavior is a little easier to
fathom. But what they all share, irrespective of whether they have one or
two symptoms of PTSD or the full-blown disorder, is a relentless drive to
tell the story of war. For many of the veterans, those who have been in
the field for a decade or more, the intermittent nightmares, flashbacks,
and moodiness are seldom deterrents. Colleagues are buried, friends are
mourned, and still they return to the fray. Even the death of eight journalists in Afghanistan in little over a week failed to drive them from the battlefield. At times, this tenacity in the face of so much horror and personal
loss perplexes the journalists themselves. Fergal Keane, mourning the loss
of his BBC colleague John Harrison in the Bantustans of South Africa,

wrote bitterly, "Journalists race around in search of civil war, secretly happiest when they sign off from some hell hole where the bodies are stacking up and the omens of apocalypse are most vivid. I am sick to the teeth of war stories, the flak jackets and all the attendant bullshit. Why did we do it all? Why do people like John and me and countless others race around townships and battle zones? I am still searching for the answer, but I know that pursuit of the truth is only one part of the equation."

Even before I began my interviews with war journalists, I often heard the term "adrenaline junkie" bandied about by those who were acquainted with the profession. The difficulty with the term, however, is that while it has some biochemical legitimacy, it also has pejorative, demeaning undertones. Still, not everyone is sensitive to the connotations. The ITN cameraman Jon Steele openly acknowledged the addictive quality of danger in the provocative title of his memoir, *War Junkie*. Notwithstanding Steele's *cri de couer* account, many war journalists find the term offensive because it conjures up an image of behavior enslaved to violence, of a base craving for a fix, devoid of personal choice, intellectual curiosity, or morality. In this light, their actions appear inherently selfish, as if the journalists use war and the catastrophic misery of others as a vehicle for fulfilling their own egotistic needs.

Many war journalists have looked inward and readily admit to the high that comes from experiencing and surviving combat, for even if their role on the battlefield is that of observer, the dangers they face are often no different from those confronted by combatants. Although the majority admitted to a rush of excitement that buoys them during or following combat, they all insisted that their motivation extended beyond attaining a state of exhilarated physiological arousal.

Yet despite these disclaimers, war as a stimulant was one of the themes that ran through the interviews I obtained. Fergal Keane recalled that "what I got out of war was a buzz. You don't ever feel more alive. You know the shelling is going on and you are exposed to this intense experience and at the time it seems like the most important thing in the world. It's just so addictive. So addictive."

Jeremy Bowen spoke of going to "places I knew would be dangerous and it troubled me at the time. I had several, probably half a dozen experiences when I thought, I am going to die, fucking hell, I have really had it. And there were many, many other times where the bullets were whizzing all over the place and I suddenly got this feeling, what have I done? What have I done? What the hell am I doing here? But that feeling would subside when we got the story. Yet again I wasn't dead. I was alive and that was for a while, in a strange way, exhilarating." Bowen perfectly captured the invigorating effects of life in a war zone. "It was a very intense experience," he explained to me. "After a day in Sarajevo, or one of the other places, the colors would seem brighter, drink would taste better, you would get excited." With this account of heightened visual and gustatory sensations, it is not difficult to understand that for Bowen, life away from a war zone was at times difficult. "In the mid-90s, when Sarajevo was going on, I loved it and hated not being there. I was having terrible withdrawal symptoms when I left there." The challenges of readjusting to life back in peaceful England became even more difficult when he decided to leave war journalism. "It has actually been a very difficult transition for me, really difficult," he explained.

> I still have many doubts. Eight days after I left the Middle East, the current cycle of violence kicked off in Jerusalem and I wasn't there . . . I had feelings akin to bereavement, I think . . . I felt terrible on every level: selfishly, professionally, in terms of my friends over there from both sides, Israelis and Palestinians who I wanted to be with. My drug had been taken away from me. For a period of five or six weeks, I could not even bring myself to watch the news. I remember where I was when I finally made my decision to take up the BBC offer of the morning show. I was filming a documentary about Jesus. We were filming in Petra, Jordan, and I was thinking about the new job, thinking and thinking. I had worked for the BBC for seventeen years and I didn't want to be just a one-trick guy, I suppose. Well, when I finally called them and said I am going to do it, I put the phone down and burst into tears. I could not bear the thought . . . I thought, what have I done?

Bowen's choice of language is noteworthy. He uses the same descriptors employed by substance abusers to depict their highs and periods of abstinence: exhilaration, brighter colors, "my drug had been taken away from me," withdrawal symptoms. Once hooked on a drug, addicts may require escalating doses to achieve the same effect, a phenomenon termed tolerance. Reading what Don McCullin had to say about his need for war, the analogy is once again striking: "I used to be a war-a-year man, but now that is not enough. I need two a year now. When it gets to be three or four, then I'll start to be worried." And Chris Dobson of the *Daily Mail* sealed the association: "When I'm actually taking part in an action, it's always as though I'm three martinis up. I'm in another, a higher, gear and it's marvelous."

Comments such as these resonate with those of a cameraman I interviewed, who introduced a novel twist to the repertoire of sensation-seeking experiences. "There's nothing like getting shot at or shelled," he told me. "It's very exciting. Very frightening, very terrifying, but there is an awful lot of adrenaline running around. And adrenaline, as you probably know, is a very powerful drug. You live life with a much greater intensity. Everything is that much more intense. I remember having the experience, for example, of making love to a woman while being shelled. That's very intense. They're trying to extinguish life and you're trying, in theory, to create it. That's very strange. Everything would be that much more intense."

This drive for intensity, this need for new experiences, has been well documented in the behavioral sciences literature. Pivotal work has been done by Marvin Zuckerman and colleagues at the University of Delaware, who in the early 1960s developed a rating scale to measure what they termed sensation-seeking behavior. They defined this as the search for varied, novel, and intense sensations and experiences, and the willingness to take physical, social, legal, and financial risks to get them. Over a number of decades, various forms of the scale were developed and refined, and in the process, four cardinal features of sensation-seeking behavior were identified: thrill and adventure seeking, experience seeking, disinhibition, and boredom susceptibility. Although in certain individuals these four factors may coexist, the data from field studies suggested independent properties for each subscale.

Before proceeding further with a discussion of motivation, it should be noted that some war journalists take exception to terms such as *sensation seeking*. James Nachtwey was one who peremptorily dismissed them as inaccurate: "I would reject the term *novelty seeker*. That is definitely not the way I would describe myself or my colleagues. I think that I'm someone who did not want to lead a conventional life, but it wasn't novelty I was seeking, it was experience. Seeking some meaning in life, not novelty. I just think that it's not the right way of looking at it." While I am sensitive to the concerns of Nachtwey and those who share his opinion, I do not believe that words like *sensation, novelty*, and *adventure* diminish in any way the motives of journalists who may see themselves as visual historians or the voice of the oppressed. By using these words, I am simply tapping into terminology that is well established in the behavioral sciences and that comes without judgmental labels. No matter how jarring the semantics, to

shy away from an impressive body of research because of a reluctance to
offend does any discussion of motivation a disservice.

The Sensation Seeking Scale (SSS) has been widely used by investiga-
tors searching for a better understanding of this aspect to human behavior.
Some demographic trends have been identified, and they relate to the
profile of war journalists. For example, data from the general population
have consistently shown that men have higher scores than women. This
helps explain my finding that three-quarters of all war journalists are male.
There is also a clear relationship between SSS scores and age, although
here the association is largely inverse. SSS scores start rising between nine
and fourteen years of age (around puberty), peak in late adolescence and the
early twenties, and thereafter decline steadily. Bringing this observation
back to my data, the match is again readily apparent. The mean age of my
sample of 140 war journalists was the late thirties, with only 7 percent of
active war journalists over fifty years of age.

A third demographic variable that deserves closer scrutiny is marital
status. We've seen that less than 45 percent of war journalists are married,
which compares with a figure of greater than 80 percent in the age-matched
general population. Zuckerman and colleagues found an association between high SSS scores and divorce in both genders, but the etiological
inferences are unclear. Do high SSS scores lead to divorce, or does the
breakup of a marriage lead to high SSS scores by forcing divorcés to adopt a
more sensation-seeking lifestyle? Zuckerman's data do not let him answer
the question, but in war journalists, for whom the case for sensation seeking
predivorce is irrefutable, it is tempting to suggest that this type of behavior
leads to marriages unraveling.

But although it is informative to extrapolate findings from the SSS
literature to my data and observe the close mesh, the fact that war journalists, like most sensation seekers, are predominantly young, male, and single
(or divorced), tells us nothing about why this should be so. To explore
etiology, we need to look elsewhere, at heredity and neurophysiology in
particular, for there is compelling evidence that war journalists are geneti-
cally and biologically primed to pursue their particular type of work.

Studies of identical and fraternal twins have proved that well over 50
percent of the sensation-seeking trait is heritable, a figure that puts it at the
upper end of the heritability range for most personality traits. But while
these genetic findings are compelling, they cannot stand alone. Other factors such as environmental influences and error in measuring the sensation-
seeking trait must be considered too. Yet even in a study of identical twins

reared apart, the heritability rate for sensation-seeking behavior was 59 percent, powerful evidence that shared family environment does not necessarily affect this particular personality trait.

Genes, however, do not directly control behavior. Rather, they determine an individual's neurophysiological makeup; it is at this level that a few key neurotransmitters and hormones modulate novelty-driven behavior. Neurotransmitters are chemical messengers that carry information from one nerve (neuron) to another. Neurotransmission underlies every aspect of behavior, from gross movement to the subtlest thought. Hormones, in turn, are chemical messengers produced by a tissue or an organ. Unlike neurotransmitters, they travel in the bloodstream to exert effects on other tissues or organs, in the process also modifying behavior.

When war journalists speak of getting their adrenaline surge in combat zones, they are identifying one neurotransmitter that in popular imagination is the archetypal behavioral stimulant. Adrenaline (also called *epinephrine*) is an important agent released by the adrenal medulla in response to stress; it speeds up the heart rate, increasing the rate of breathing and inducing sweating, among other familiar reactions. But it is not the neurotransmitter that controls sensation-seeking behavior. That role falls to a distant relative, two steps removed, called dopamine.

The body manufactures dopamine from an amino acid, tyrosine, found in dietary protein. Tyrosine is converted to a chemical L-dopa, a precursor to dopamine which in turn is converted to noradrenaline by the enzyme dopamine β-hydroxylase. Noradrenaline may then be transformed into adrenaline. Dopamine may also be broken down by the enzyme monoamine oxidase (MAO). With this basic knowledge we can see that dopamine, once formed, can be depleted by two routes, namely degradation via MAO or conversion to noradrenaline. And it is the influence of the MAO enzyme that has provided the most convincing evidence linking the seemingly disparate clinical, demographic, genetic, and biochemical correlates of risk-taking behavior.

MAO, which is under tight genetic control, exists in two forms, A and B. It is the latter that is active in the brain, where it breaks down dopamine. While it is not possible to directly measure brain MAO, an analogous form in blood platelets is quantifiable simply by taking a sample of blood. Many studies have explored the relationship between sensation-seeking behavior, as measured by Zuckerman's scale (SSS), and levels of MAO, and the consensus is that high SSS scores are associated with low MAO levels. This inverse relationship has been consistently noted for both genders. The inference is that low levels of MAO lead to high levels of dopamine, and that in turn manifests as pronounced sensation-seeking behavior. The converse is also true. MAO levels are higher in women and increase with age in both genders, which once again helps explain the war journalists' demographic profile.

*　*　*

The need for new sensations is, however, only one possible motivating factor. The journalists who spoke to me all offered theories of personal motivation, of which the buzz of war was but a part. The photographer Gary Knight's perception is that a multiplicity of factors are to be found among his colleagues.

> The Kosovo conflict is a very good example. You would have a group of people working there who I would say were very, very, very finely tuned in to the political issues involved [in] what was at stake and in some way were addressing these issues. That is a very small number of people. Then you would have a really large number of people who were just there because CNN or the BBC sent them there and maybe the correspondent is driven by the same motives found in the small clique I have just mentioned, but the crew are there just because they are the crew. That is the largest group of news people who just happen to find themselves there. Maybe they have some experience in that area, but that's it. I am not being derogatory when I say this. They are not people for whom this life is a mission. For this group, it is a job, no more than that. Then you have a smaller number than that who are war junkies who completely get off on the adrenaline flying around. And then you have people within all those groups who have that as well. But the pure adrenaline junkie, and certainly there a number of them, don't care what they are doing, who they are photographing. They don't give a shit about people being killed, about the trauma, they just care about the adventure. They are usually the guys you find walking over the mountains looking for the guerilla groups, like I did when I was young.

Like Knight, all veteran war journalists I interviewed regarded these thrill seekers with contempt, even while many acknowledged they too were galvanized by danger and threat. What in their minds distinguishes them from the self-serving, heedless adrenaline junkie is that they care passionately about those imperiled by conflict, the traumatized, dispossessed, bereaved victims that war spews forth with such disregard. "This life is a mission," is the credo by which Knight and his colleagues live and without which they too would be reduced to what the *Times* correspondent Janine di Giovanni calls "the whackoes, the adrenaline freaks, working for weird magazines like *Soldier of Fortune*, wearing khakis or soldier stuff and getting really excited by it all."

It is not just a sense of moral responsibility that keeps the war journalists I spoke with aloof from the thrill-seeking buccaneer types. It is also a sense of personal preservation. There are dangers enough in war zones without getting too close to those whose actions are swashbuckling and irresponsible. Veteran war journalists have accumulated a considerable knowledge of survival techniques over the course of a decade or more of working in zones of conflict, learned behaviors that contribute in no small measure to their longevity. The adventurer masquerading as a war journalist knows little, if any of this. Prey to impulsivity, imbued with narcissism and with a penchant for daredevil antics, they are attracted to trouble like moths to a flame. In turn, they can quickly bring trouble down on their own heads. The case of Ken Hechtman illustrates the point.

"Kidnapped Journalist a Rookie with a Reckless Past: Once Stole Lab Uranium," ran a headline in Canada's *National Post* newspaper at the height of the American-led war on the Taliban regime in Afghanistan. Described by an acquaintance as a "freelance everything, a jack-of-all-trades," the thirty-three-year-old Hechtman decided, just before the commencement of American bombing, to become a journalist. Paying his own way to Pakistan, he crossed the border into Afghanistan where he was quickly arrested by the Taliban, prompting efforts by Reporters without Borders and the Canadian government to procure his release. While he was in captivity, some colorful episodes in Hechtman's past came to light. As a student in New York, he had stolen a small quantity of uranium from an unlocked physics laboratory "because it seemed like a neat thing to have," and because he wanted to do "neat things with chemicals, simple experiments, minor pyrotechnics, that sort of thing." The deans, who placed Hechtman on disciplinary probation and ordered him out of student residence, also found him guilty of stealing a bathroom door and writing graffiti on a volunteer ambulance, among other offenses.

While Hechtman may have been looking for trouble, other journalists are in thrall to wanderlust, a hankering for distant, exotic lands that often takes root in childhood. Peter Arnett gives voice to this beautifully. He became known to millions of viewers as the Associated Press journalist who remained behind in Saigon in 1975, following the American pullout. More than a decade later, this time as the CNN man in Baghdad, he again stayed on while most of the networks left, and reported the dramatic opening shots of the Gulf War. In his memoir, *Live from the Battlefield*, he recalls a childhood growing up in Bluff, a small fishing town at the bottom end of New Zealand's south island. "I was thrilled that it was home to the southernmost lamppost in the world, so certified by a sign at Stirling Point, where the waters of the Pacific Ocean and Tasman Sea met, crashing against the worn-smooth rocks. Nailed to the lamppost were distance and directional signs to the rest of the world painted in black on yellow wood: London, 12,608; New York, 10,005; Hamburg, 12,198; Tokyo, 6,389. Those signs mesmerised me as the Pied Piper bewitched the children of Hamelin. I would follow those signs and my dreams to the far reaches of the world."

Jeremy Bowen also retains this strong childhood memory. "I always wanted to be a foreign correspondent even before I knew what it was," he told me. "I remember as a kid in school, when they went around the class and said, what do you want to be, people would say astronaut, footballer, and I would say foreign correspondent, and they would say, what is a foreign correspondent and I didn't honestly know, but I had this vision of a newspaperman in a white suit with a fan going in the roof."

Several of the interviewees told of similar recollections, some no more than a fleeting, albeit never forgotten, memory. The photographer Santiago Lyon remembers walking in Ireland with his father as a youngster and coming across a political demonstration. "There were a couple of photographers running around and my father said, 'Wow, look at those guys. Do you want to be like one of them, wearing a leather jacket and traveling the world?' And I thought, that sounds alright." Janine di Giovanni knew as a child that she "never wanted to marry a doctor and play tennis. I wanted to be in the middle of the world." Fergal Keane recalled "just escaping into books about foreign places, far away places, fantasyland."

In the case of one war journalist, wanderlust combined with family discord, magnifying the impetus to seek out foreign wars.

> My father had a regular job working nine to five, and until a certain point in my life, I thought everybody did that. Then I saw a book by a photographer on the Vietnam War and I bought it with my pocket money. When I read it I didn't understand how the book had come about. The interaction between the storytelling and the author didn't connect, and I couldn't understand how this person had gone off to this fantastic place and done this work. Yet it must be a job, so there must be things out there other than working nine to five. It was an adventurous, romantic notion. My parents divorced and I was

fed up at home. I was frustrated. I wanted to be a photojournalist ever since I read that book at fourteen. I wanted even more to escape my home at seventeen, when my parents' acrimonious divorce reached a peak. For me, becoming what was in that book on Vietnam was a form of adventure and self-exploration. It was also a form of escapism, and I guess it was a form of punishment for my parents. I think it was many things.

Being smitten in one's youth with a desire for adventure and travel does not, by itself, translate into a career as a war journalist. But for some, it does furnish one piece in a complex, multidimensional puzzle, linked as travel, war, and journalism are by unpredictability and risk. One of the great latter-day adventurers, Bruce Chatwin, addresses this very point in a collection of essays, *Anatomy of Restlessness*. "Travel must be adventurous," he writes. "The bumps are vital. They keep the adrenaline pumping around . . . We all have adrenaline. We cannot drain it from our system or pray it will evaporate. Deprived of danger we invent artificial enemies, psychosomatic illnesses, tax-collectors and worst of all, ourselves, if we are left alone in the single room. Adrenaline is our travel allowance. We might just as well use it up in a harmless way."

Interspersed among Chatwin's essays on travels to well-worn byways in France and Italy are expeditions to Timbuktu and Patagonia, and references to Bedouins and the Bushmen of the Kalahari. Chatwin, quoting from Robert Burton's seventeenth-century *Anatomy of Melancholy*, asserts that movement is the best cure for melancholy. It is no coincidence that the title of his essay collection paraphrases Burton's, the one's restlessness and the other's melancholia intricately fused, sharing an anatomical substrate rendered functional or dysfunctional by opportunity and the concentrations of pivotal neurotransmitters coursing through their central nervous system. Burton yearned to travel, but circumstances thwarted his desire. Chatwin was more fortunate, and so their names became forever linked with melancholy and adventure, respectively. Yet their shared insights, three centuries apart, highlight the biological drives underpinning motivation. For Chatwin, travel into the hinterland of Mali in search of Timbuktu, navigating the Sahel and blistering heat of Saharan Africa, was not without risk, for he writes, "It has been claiming European victims and luring many to their deaths, since it first appeared on a Catalan map of the fourteenth century." This evocative city got his adrenaline going, spurring him on to new experiences and to witness wondrous sights that stimulated an outpouring of remarkable prose. Sated, he returned home, his self-professed *horreur du domicile* in temporary abeyance, to a place where depleted resources could be replenished before restlessness again sent him on his way.

What sufficed for Chatwin, however, in terms of risk and novel experience, is unlikely to satisfy the biological and psychological makeup of many war journalists. For them, travel probably does little more than tickle abundant, dormant reserves of neurotransmitters, but by itself is hardly likely to send levels ratcheting upward as an impetus to action. The inveterate traveler and war journalist may therefore share certain character attributes, but they do so differentially. For many war journalists, particularly when young and starting out on their careers, it is not just the risk of novelty that drives them, but also the risk of danger. And because the latter is the more intense experience, it often becomes the defining one. Placing your life on the line by venturing into the front lines of conflict zones cannot be surpassed.

Or can it? If getting mortared, bombed, and shot at gives extreme risk takers that sought-after buzz, what do the perpetrators of violence experience? What kinds of emotions are they prey to as they inflict death on others? This question is not applicable to war journalists, for they are not combatants, but is relevant when addressing the addictive qualities of violence. Evidence suggests that, for some, the taking of life, given legitimacy in warfare, can prove an extraordinarily satisfying experience. Joanna Bourke's *An Intimate History of Killing* provides good evidence of this. She quotes the thoughts of Captain Julian Henry Frances Grenfell, a World War I combatant responsible for sniping and killing a number of Germans over the course of many months, actions that in part earned him a Distinguished Service Order. "It is all the most wonderful fun; better fun than one could ever imagine. I hope it goes on a nice long time; but pigsticking will be the only tolerable pursuit after this one or one will die of sheer ennui." For Grenfell, life without license to kill man (preferably) or beast (second best), would be intolerably boring, yet despite the callousness of these remarks, there is no other evidence indicating he was some raging psychopath, devoid of the vestiges of compassion. At times he admitted to feeling "terribly ashamed," and regarded his enemies as "poor, dead Huns." Captain Grenfell, in the unabashed honesty of his writings, reveals himself to be an intense sensation seeker who would have difficulty assuaging his desires even within the shifted spectrum of behavior followed by war journalists. War provided the outlet for this extreme drive, just as it unmasks similar traits in individuals who delight in its dark pleasures.

The examples given thus far clearly show that risk-taking behavior lies along a continuum. At the sedate end are found those individuals who hold down the nine to five job, varying little in their daily routine. Shift the gauge away from this secure zone of predictability and you start to encounter individuals whose behavior introduces a greater degree of uncertainty into their lives. Where you actually cross the threshold of what determines an adventurous life is arbitrary and subjective, but few would quibble that for someone like Bruce Chatwin, risk, adventure, and novelty are well-ensconced lifestyle attributes. Shift the gauge further upward and you meet the war journalist, encamped a little below the summit of extreme risk-taking behavior occupied by the inveterate adrenaline junkie, whose life is governed by that perpetual search for the ultimate thrill.

\*   \*   \*

Biological reductionism thus goes some way toward explaining why certain individuals choose war journalism as a profession and are prepared to take considerable risks over the course of a couple decades to pursue it. However, genes and biochemistry alone cannot furnish the complete picture. We also need to look anew at environmental influences. Here the search is no longer empirically focused, but it may help elucidate why some people choose a career as a war journalist as opposed to one as a policeman or extreme athlete, to give but two examples of high-risk occupations.

Notwithstanding the miscellaneous nature of this search, some discernable threads begin to emerge. Anthony Loyd, in his memoir of wars in Bosnia and Chechnya, has disclosed details of his family's military background. Loyd's father was a military man, and he had a poor relationship with him, a situation common to other war journalists. Of the twenty-two male war journalists I interviewed, five had fathers in the military or police force, and without exception all harbored unfilial feelings ranging from indifference to loathing at some point in their relationships. For some, rapprochement came with age, while for others antipathy endured. In all but one case, the son joined the military too as a way of invoking or redeeming a father's affection and esteem. The depth of the relationship malaise, however, defied such cosmetic remedying, and the son remained emotionally bereft of a father, but now with the added difficulty of finding himself adrift in an institution with tightly defined rules and regulations, intolerant of individuality and punitive towards dissenters.

Stifled by the rigidity of army life, yet captive to early family influences that had steered them in that direction, these men resigned from the mili-

tary and gravitated towards zones of conflict, where something as simple as
a camera or notepad gained them entry. Here they quickly realized they had
found their true calling — ready access to war largely on their own terms
and an opportunity to unleash a creativity they never knew they possessed.
The work not only forced them to confront danger, as their fathers had
done, but stimulated them to create remarkable images, in word and print,
of remarkable events. In the process they received the respect and accolades
of news agencies that were perennially on the lookout for talented young-
sters prepared to risk war and bring back a good story. The prestigious
awards that soon followed were powerful affirmations of their newfound
worth and confidence. They were finally able to confront their absentee
military fathers, either consciously or unconsciously, with the fact they too
had seen war, survived its horrors, and made something positive of the
experience.

*   *   *

Zones of conflict, with their loosely defined physical and personal bounda-
ries, are attractive places for some people who are searching not only for
meaning in life, but also for a personal identity. One photojournalist saw it
as "a form of escapism, an adventure, where you can create your own
persona. You can reinvent yourself. The job comes with all kinds of precon-
ceptions as far as people on the outside world are concerned, something
perhaps heroic about it, or romantic, that you can hide behind if you want
to. It is a great place to disappear into and experience some very extreme
sensations and punish people, find new people, punish yourself."

Time and again, my interviews unearthed evidence of family discord and
a troubled upbringing. These journalists did not need cajoling to share their
intimate recollections with me. Just the contrary. No sooner had I asked
why they chose this career than they launched into emotional recollections
of their childhoods and what dysfunctional parents they had. They talked of
role models who couldn't sustain a marriage and were often absent, drunk,
verbally abusive, and indifferent to the havoc they brought down on their
children's heads. Many of these journalists shared the conviction that their
painful, lonely, and at times violent childhoods had been powerful, sub-
conscious factors influencing career choice. Perspicacity, however, invariably arrived late. It was only when they were well entrenched in their careers
that they made any connection between their past and present lives. Such
was the case for one well-known reporter who, early in my study, shared
with me his insights on motivation.

I know that for a long time I tended to see the distress caused by my war experience in isolation, i.e., they were the direct consequences of witnessing traumatic events. It took some time for me to begin to look at the inner turmoil which propelled me towards war zones. They were comfortable, they were "home," a replay of the tension and fear with which I had grown up. War reporting allows you to remain in that place, to avoid the pain that comes with trying to accept yourself and your past. So many of the colleagues I met in war zones were the children of fractured or unhappy homes. No wonder we recognized each other, felt good together. And what value did we place on the sweetness of our own lives when we willingly, almost joyously, risked them every day?

Only after seeking and receiving psychotherapy was this man able to draw an analogy between the family battles of his youth and the later conflict he would witness as a war journalist.

It was what I was used to. I grew up in it, you know, but I didn't understand this at the time. There was no way I could have understood this as a child, but I was reading something recently and it just jumped out of the bloody page at me. It is possible to have post-traumatic stress disorder from your childhood. I grew up in a war zone. It was just madness. My father would break furniture and all the stuff that goes with that. I learned at a very early age these kinds of coping strategies, and this could explain why I now believe passionately in bearing witness to war, which is not unrelated to my sense as a kid that nobody bloody well heard me. Nobody ever heard.

A photojournalist, whose career before she took up a camera perhaps facilitated a quicker and more penetrating insight, sent me this email comment from a distant, all but forgotten hellhole: "I worked as a psychiatric social worker prior to becoming a journalist and have always analyzed our little clan with a lot of interest. I think we are all rather self destructive." These comments interleave with those of *Observer* journalist Emma Daly. When we met for an interview in Madrid, she was pregnant and had taken a break from war reporting. Her memories of the war in Bosnia remained vivid, however, including one particular set of exchanges with colleagues.

It was one night, after dinner at the Holiday Inn, where we were all staying in 1994. Because of the shelling and sniping we couldn't go anywhere or do anything. We were sitting around this big table and there were about fifteen of us present and we took turns speaking about our childhoods. One of the female journalists was fifteen years old when her mother died and her father did not want to set up home for her or her sister, so they were sent away to boarding school and would spend the holidays with a different set of relatives. Then there was another journalist whose father was this big shot Hollywood agent who ran out on him and his mother and their lifestyle changed from a big opulent mansion in Hollywood to living in a car. They were left destitute, and he did not see his father again until he was eighteen years old. And so it went on. When one of the journalists blurted out, "My brother killed himself," everybody burst out laughing because it was like some pathetic movie script, with the confessions getting more and more ridiculous. As everyone went around the table it just got sadder and sadder and, you know, more dramatic. There was only one man who had had a normal childhood, and he was like, "Gee guys, sorry, but my story is different." Sarajevo was very much a place for black humor.

In my interviews, the theme of an unhappy childhood came with many variations. "You may wish to consider prewar conditions that I am certain many journalists have," was one piece of advice given to me early by a reporter. "It is one reason why many journalists are driven to cover wars. You may note, for example, that many hardcore war journalists have few, if any, photographs of family members or loved ones anywhere in their homes." I had no way of verifying this last claim, but it does disclose one insider's perspective of a highly defended profession, some members of which are perhaps incapable of forming lasting attachments with family.

A few journalists went so far as to suggest that family malaise was virtually endemic. "In my profession, photojournalism, I would say eight out of ten of my colleagues have fairly dysfunctional backgrounds: a parent or both parents dead, divorced, stuff like that," one man told me. Six months later, in an interview on a different continent with another journalist, these observations were spontaneously repeated and the percentage endorsed.

> There was a lot of instability in my life. I remember very clearly when my parents separated, and they didn't do it very well. It was a bit messy. I remember them fighting a lot. I remember being abandoned a lot, left alone a lot. I am convinced it had something to do with the way things turned out. If you sit around a table of foreign correspondents or photographers or people who run around and do this business, I've found out that around 80 percent will have something similar, something screwed up. I think that initially, until you get that out of your system, and some people never do, that influences your later behavior.

Of the twenty-eight interviews I completed, a little more than 40 percent revealed a troubled childhood characterized by divorce or poor relationships between the nascent journalist and his parents. The most bizarre example of how distorted family relationships could become was offered by a cameraman whose parents divorced when he was a toddler. He was never told this and always assumed his stepfather was his true dad. His mother, somewhat dissolute of habits, continued to lead a chaotic life, her two priorities being a good party and a ready supply of booze. Among the many men who frequently visited the home was someone introduced to the child as his uncle. Only as an adult did this cameraman learn that the man was really his biological father.

Informative as these anecdotes are, it is important to remember that recall is often subject to bias, the events of childhood potentially colored by troubled adult lives. Furthermore, divorce is common in the societies from which I drew my sample, and while a twenty-five-year follow-up study of children from broken marriages paints a disquieting picture of lives often emotionally unfulfilled, such outcomes are not invariable. This theory is also difficult to reconcile with the personal histories of those war journalists who come from loving, intact families, in which relationships with parents are close and nurturing. These limitations aside, to some journalists, association clearly equals causality, and they consider their difficult childhoods the root cause of unsettled existences spent wandering the globe in search of conflict.

Divorced parents; aloof, dysfunctional military fathers; troubled families; rudderless young men and women in search of identity and meaning and that missing family — if I have dwelt on these factors first and at length, it is because in my interviews with war journalists, these were the issues raised most often and spontaneously by them. However, there was a group of war journalists who experienced none of this domestic turmoil. Their largely middle-class family backgrounds were uncomplicated and happy. What was their motivation? Some, to be sure, were individuals we would regard as high sensation seekers, men and women with a drive for thrill and adventure. But others expressed a strong dislike for the bang-bang: these journalists were fearful of risk and apprehensive of the many threats that lurked in zones of conflict. What beguiled them was the drama of the events they were witness to. Time and again the war journalists, when asked about motivation, would respond, "I've been around history for the past ten years, and it's a privileged ringside seat, too." Then they would smile somewhat sheepishly and apologize for the cliché. Yet bearing personal witness to the memorable events of history was only part of the story, as the more perceptive among them realized. What their status as war journalists offered was something equally heady: unheard-of access to the living rooms of citizens around the globe. It was through the imprint of their verse and image that the great mass of humanity was kept informed.

The way war journalists rose to these challenges varied considerably. For some, war became a conduit to self-aggrandizement, stoking an ego that allowed little space for competitors, be they fellow journalists or the victims of catastrophe. To others, it was simply a job, and while at times they marveled at the spectacle of it all, or were moved by it, it generally amounted to little more than a way to make a living. And then there was that small group, those Gary Knight characterized as being finely tuned to all the nuances of the conflict, who were not only alert to the broad political sweep of events, but whose antennae were able to detect, among the convulsions of a nation, those unforgettable individual cases of suffering and heroism that cloak the events of war with such pity and poignancy.

Conscious of their responsibility in bearing witness, aware of the privilege their access afforded them, these war journalists often invested their entire being, their physical strength, their emotional resources and their intellect in telling the story of war. To Janine di Giovanni, it became imperative to view personally what she wrote about: "What is this front line stuff? What has happened in this battle? I feel you cannot write about it unless you see it. You just cannot write about it. I believe it is fundamentally dishonest to take information from other journalists and write about it. Things happen to you if you are in a country at war, and that gives you a precious insight into what the war is about. A lot of journalists covered the Chechnya story from Moscow. The average reader living in London would not know this and would think the journalist was in the middle of a war. But they were not. They were sitting in a nice comfortable hotel."

Maggie O'Kane of the *Guardian* newspaper expounded on this theme; she told me that if war journalists want to write about war and the victims of war, they cannot turn their backs on these victims once the dangers start to mount.

I had this sense of mission in Baghdad, it's 1990 and the coalition was going to bomb the city. Fifteen of us decided to stay. I stayed because a colleague of mine said to me, "There are very few times that we can actually be a bit useful and this is one of them." In addition, I was too ashamed to leave. I was with a taxi driver, and we had been together for about ten or twelve days. He had ten children, and during the time he had brought me into his life. You know, I come in and his wife is cutting up the tablecloth to make masks for the gas. There was this kind of closeness and intimacy with him and I felt ashamed to leave him and say, "I'm sorry, you're going to have the shit bombed out of you and I'm off." I've got a sense of responsibility, and when I said goodbye to him, as I did initially, I got out the car and felt my face go completely red in embarrassment. I recognized that as shame. So therefore I thought I had to stay, that it would prove useful, that we should be there. And the same thing happened in Bosnia, this sense that we the press had to be there. We have to stop this madness. That's why I do this job. Otherwise, why bother.

"How do you connect with what people are going through?" asked James Nachtwey, and his answer, quietly given, revealed a steely resolve. "Through your photographs, that's how. You have to put yourself in the same space that they are in, and when you are in that same space, then you experience the same risks. So you are sharing that with the people you are photographing. But it was never for the sake of taking a risk. It was risky because it was required to get the job done. And that's how I always felt about it and that's how I still feel about it. I'm still willing to take the risk to get the job done. That hasn't changed."

Being finely tuned to the issues at stake in a particular conflict and getting a buzz from the dangers involved are not necessarily incompatible. Indeed, my impression was that the majority of committed career war journalists, those who had been doing it for a decade or more, combined both facets in varying ratios. However, only from the small ranks of the knowledgeable did I encounter those journalists who were the very antithesis of the thrill- and adventure-seeking personality. Cognizant of the myriad dangers that zones of conflict presented, they waged a constant internal battle with their fears, misgivings, and confidence when breaking news demanded they enter the front lines. Allan Little recalled:

One of the first times I felt myself to be in this position, of having to decide [was just before the Gulf War]. There were maybe twenty of us. We were from different news organizations. We were suddenly granted visas and told to be ready by midnight the next day. So we had twenty-four hours to find the trucks, load them with food and water and petrol. It was a tense and horrible day. There were a few who just seemed excited by the whole thing. I was both excited and scared. It wasn't just the physical danger — the thought that this could get you killed. I think I was also frightened by the magnitude of the story. It was the biggest thing I'd been trusted with, and I didn't know whether I'd be up to it, or just lost. I was convinced that I was surrounded by people much more sure of what they were doing than I was. So I was scared in several different ways.

We had a big meeting a few hours before our departure. There were some American TV journalists who had visas and were having cold feet about going. We would have to make the journey up the same road that the Scud missile launchers firing at Israel were coming down, so vehicles on that road were being bombed by the allies. A couple of the Americans were arguing that we shouldn't go unless we got a guarantee from the Pentagon of safe passage. I thought, well, this is just not going to happen. Forget it. You're not going to get a guarantee of safe passage from the Pentagon. I thought they were just looking for a way not to do this. There was just no way to make this journey safe. They were trying to measure the risk, asking "How safe is this?" and I thought, "You're trying to measure the unmeasurable." You just have to make a judgment about it. You have to make a pact with your own feelings. You have to make a deal with yourself. I hadn't said anything at this meeting. I was one of the youngest there and the least experienced in war zones. But I heard myself say, "You're trying to measure the unmeasurable. It can't be done. You must just decide whether you want to do it or not. If you don't want to go nobody blames you. It's a personal decision." And when I said that the meeting kind of wound up. I hadn't intended to close off the discussion, but afterwards a couple of the more gung-ho reporters there — those who had no doubts at all that they wanted to go — came up and said, "Good for you, you spoke for us all." And I thought, "Well, I didn't mean to speak for us all," and I thought, "If only you knew how stressed I am about whether to go or not!"

A bit later I bumped into a photographer I knew who was very anxious about the whole thing, and he said, "Are you going?" I said yes and he said "Why? Why?" And all I could come up with was, "Because if I don't I'll never forgive myself. I'll regret it all my life."

If there is no emotional high waiting alongside danger, if the resolve to confront the risks is not spurred by the buzz that comes with such actions, then the job presents a different set of challenges: making a pact with your own feelings, gaining mastery of fear (never truly accomplished), weighing your emotional reserves. War journalists who feel this way find their motivation primarily in two sources: their often fierce ambition and the content of the story. Ambition, of course, is often just as prevalent in the overweening narcissist as it is in the more high-minded journalist. It's just that the war journalists who are leery of risk rather than embracing it, who do not place themselves at the center of the story, have to access motivation through a different route. Still, in the end, ambition is a common denominator linking virtually all in the profession. They know that the kudos earned on the front lines are a good way of gaining recognition and advancing up the ladder. They have all seen examples of a career becalmed because a colleague lacked the "right stuff."

Commitment to the story, the desire to bear witness and keep the world informed, the drive to expose a great moral outrage, these become the issues by which a subset of journalists define themselves. The magnitude of the story to be told counterbalances the anxiety felt in zones of conflict, pushing them yet again to go down *that* road, not knowing what hazards lie around the corner. One cynical voice within the profession, however, scoffed at the moral high-mindedness of some of his colleagues.

> I think there is an altruistic motive, but I also think that a lot of people are not being entirely honest with themselves. Because you know what the answer is that people want to hear? They want to hear that you do it for the idealism and to save the world. I think it takes a rare degree of courage to say, "Well, I actually love this." It takes self-awareness to see that you do it for other reasons as well. If I had met you ten years back I probably would have avoided you like the plague. But if you had persuaded me to sit down with you and talk, I would have angrily denied that I did this work for anything other than my mission to speak on behalf of the dispossessed. It's easier to do that.

Reflecting on this observation, I wondered whether this journalist was not being too harsh in his peer assessment, holding up his colleagues to a higher set of values. Ambition, self-promotion, choosing a profession because of its rewards while espousing altruistic motives — the same could be said for many professionals. The war journalists I asked to comment on motivation all looked back on many years' cumulative experience when formulating their answers. They spoke freely about the thrill of danger, their ambition, the challenges they found stimulating, their mission as messengers of war. Many stated openly and without reservation that they loved this work. Where they differed was in defining exactly what it was they loved, and for some, the primary impetus was a need to tell a remarkable story, one whose meaning transcends conflicts of nationality, religion, and culture even as it embraces all of them. For a small clique of journalists, Bosnia in the last decade of the twentieth century was a case in point. This is how a senior BBC journalist explained it to me:

> Bosnia was many things for us. I personally felt it was Europe going back to the past. I felt it was important to understand it and not shut it out. I felt some kind of responsibility as a citizen. I grew up in the twentieth century with fine declarations, in an atmosphere in which we all believed there would never be another holocaust. We all believed that if it happened this time, the world wouldn't stand for it . . . I was burning with indignity and I saw a clear injustice. I saw my own country and most of the allies ignoring it. I felt tainted by that. I felt that I had some kind of responsibility to stand up. I couldn't bear the shame of it and in the end that is why I stopped covering Bosnia, I couldn't bear it.
>
> The war tore apart a society that closely resembled my own as a European. You could see that what happened there wasn't uniquely Balkan or a Yugoslav phenomenon. It was European. It was something that marked European history, and it seemed to me Europe was in some ways going back to its past, and I felt bound up in it, wrapped up in it. Bosnia drew us all in. Bosnia also represented clear choices, moral choices, choices about the kind of values you adhered to. At the time the Bosnian war was happening, all the Western governments except the United States, which was very much in the background at first, were saying, "It's a Balkan thing, savages, they've been killing each other for centuries. What can you do, they're all as bad as each other." Those of us who were there knew that wasn't true. We absolutely knew that was a lie those governments used to justify their own inaction. And because we knew that, it involves a kind of responsibility.
>
> There was a criminal elite running one side of the conflict. They chose to have war because it was the only way they could stay in power. They planned the ethnic cleansing, resourced it, funded it, executed it, drove it, believed in it. They believed in it ideologically, as much as they did it. They thought it was a good thing. The other side wanted multiethnicity, tolerance, human rights, membership in the European club. One side aspired to what was good about Europe and the other side wanted some kind of ethno-fascist project, which was also drawing on a certain supposedly discredited European tradition. So you have two European traditions here in conflict with each other. And if you make them morally the same, then you are

morally compromising yourself. And it seemed to all of us who were there that there was some kind of moral responsibility. It was our Spain, in a way. We had a choice to make. We could go along with the rubbish, but it wasn't true.

These are the reasons why I think you've only really got one war in you. I think you can only commit yourself in that way once in your life. And you can only believe in it once. It's like virginity, you can't lose it twice. You can only really believe that you are doing something good, you can only believe in the moral value of what you are doing once, and when the disillusionment has entered your soul, once you understand that you are not doing any good at all, you cannot commit yourself in that same way a second time. I genuinely thought — I don't think I ever articulated this because I just took it for granted — I genuinely believed that in the world I grew up in and was part of, if such a gross injustice existed, all that had to happen was for it to be made clear. For it to be spelled out. You could summon the force of international indignation. You could summon this righteousness, so to speak, and the injustice would be ended. It took me about four years to understand that this was a childish delusion, that you can't summon the force of moral indignation, because the freedom citizens are enjoying includes the freedom not to care. That terrible disillusionment fixes itself and that is why I think you can only do it once. We've all got just one in us.

This articulate voice speaks for other war journalists whose careers were also defined by events in Bosnia. And yet even this man remembers being thrilled by the sound of gunshots going off near him in Bucharest early in his career. "That was the first time I heard a gun go off in anger," he told me. "It was great. I loved it and I was good at dealing with it and I'd found something that I could do well and I was being rewarded for it." Does such a reaction lessen his conviction or invalidate his moral argument? How can we reconcile the cogent, eloquent, and passionate espousal of motivation in Bosnia with a different reaction in Bucharest? As I got to know the profession better, I came to realize that there was no contradiction, no self-deception, that all the reasons applied, each having its own validity, and that one of the most important variables that controlled which motivating factor predominated at any one point in time was age. As one war photographer said to me, "The reasons I started doing this as a young man, and the reasons I still do it, are probably largely different. There has been a readjustment, although some core features remain immutable, such as I do it well and I am able to earn a living by it. I think I was foolish at times when I was younger, but I think that is just youth. Now, I do this work because I am more empowered, I am a better photographer, a better storyteller, and I have a better conscience, a better understanding of what is right, what is wrong, what is moral, what is ethical. I didn't know black from white when I was younger."

This evolution in motivation was common to that small group of "finely tuned" war journalists. Youthful impetuousness, that thirst for adventure spiced with risk, owes much to individual biochemistry and factors that modulate dopamine. War journalism offers an outlet to assuage that innate drive. Exposed to remarkable events, privy to suffering on a grand scale, moved by the plight of war's victims, some journalists begin to realize, with time, that their job is more than a series of exotic adventures. This emotional maturation includes a heightened sensitivity to those nameless individuals left dispossessed, powerless, and grieving by war. In consort with this changing outlook, biochemical changes are occurring too; MAO levels are increasing and dopamine levels are declining, leading to a dwindling desire for those daredevil escapades that, in retrospect, invoke a shudder. It is not an all-or-nothing transformation, of course. Some frisson of excitement persists with time, just as an element of moral indignation was probably there to start with. Over the course of a decade or two, the risk-morality ratio gets re-calibrated.

For some journalists, neither risk nor morality is highly relevant — war journalism is simply a job. For others, the degree of recalibration will vary according to the individual. This model, which fits together widely disparate motivational factors, may also help explain the journalist's assertion that he was good for one war only. In support of his theory, I have encountered other war journalists who also tend to define their careers by a single major conflict. These are frequently protracted civil wars that entice foreign military intervention. Thus, the last quarter-century has seen the Vietnam Generation, the Beirut Generation, and more recently, the Bosnian Generation of war journalists. The long duration of conflict provides sufficient time for a motivational shift to occur, and given what a formative influence it has on the journalists' outlook, no subsequent conflict will ever again attain the same degree of intensity. Even for those journalists who do not follow this transformation, the simple passage of time, associated as it is with a falloff in neurotransmitter levels, may mean that when peace wearily supervenes, their love for the bang-bang has peaked. Both groups will move on to other wars, where their aptitude and skills honed in conflict will ensure the quality of their work. But some will always look back, either in bitterness or nostalgia, on that one all-embracing, career- and life-defining war.

* * *

It is understandable that, given the risks war journalists take, they should at times question their motives. This self-examination becomes particularly acute when their lives are directly threatened. When the immediate threat subsides however, and survival emerges victorious yet again, the urge to question rapidly disappears from consciousness. Paradoxically, the inten- sity of the close call may be one of the factors that draws the journalist back into the zones of conflict. But the death of a colleague and, especially, age can have great dampening effects on motivation. By the time journalists reach their forties, they are faced with new pressures: a need to settle down and have children, or the demands of a partner who, after a decade or more functioning largely as a single parent, delivers the ultimatum. And then there are the biochemical changes that occur with natural aging. We have already looked at the effects of an increase in MAO and falloff in dopamine concentration. Alongside these chemical changes comes a physical slowing down. War journalism is physically taxing. Walking up a mountainside in the heat of an African summer or the snow and ice of a Balkan winter is far easier for a journalist when he's a young man than twenty years later, par- ticularly when the intervening period has included generous quotas of alco- hol and cigarettes. If journalists want to get out into the field, if they want to be seen on the front lines, gathering their own facts, then they need to forsake their comforts. These privations were not lost on Evelyn Waugh during his brief stint as a foreign correspondent. Trapped for days on end with a large group of locals and a single lavatory between them, he com- plained somewhat bitterly to his editor back home that every time he went for a shit he vomited instead. Seventy years later the sanitation issue re- mains no less taxing. In an article entitled, "One Toilet and the World's Press Wants It," Janine di Giovanni described conditions in Khoje Bahwu- dine in northern Afghanistan: "The place has virtually no infrastructure. Water comes from the river carried by donkeys. Sleep is on the floor, if you are lucky. I have not slept three nights in the same place. Journalists were sleeping in hallways, sleeping outside the stinking hole that served as a toilet, sleeping on the concrete verandah. Confrontation began when the press corps woke up and began fighting for water and electricity. At one point one toilet was shared by everyone, but NBC bought the house temporarily and hung up a sign, This Room Is Property of NBC."

Such esprit de corps is easier to tolerate when one is young.

When plotting the reasons why war journalists chose such a hazardous profession, we can see there are few absolutes. This should not come as a surprise, for explaining the complexities of behavior demands a synthesis of many factors. A "spectrum of traits," a "continuum of responses," thresholds, ratios, and probabilities—this is the language in which etiological theories of behavior are couched. Yet despite the imprecise nature of our understanding, many strands of evidence shed light on why war journalists have taken this particular path in life. None of these factors—biochemical, environmental, political, or moral—can stand alone, but when taken together, they produce a coherent and persuasive argument. Devising a model to fit every possible permutation treats all war journalists equally, whereas from a behavioral point of view, they differ in terms of interest. By focusing on that relatively small group whose creativity in zones of conflict has shaped our impressions of war, we can distill certain core truths about motivation. That level of war journalism is seldom, if ever, achieved by those who regard their work as simply just another job. When the primary motivating factor is the paycheck at the end of the month, imagination and ingenuity languish. That is not to decry the technical skill of these journalists, but technique in the absence of passion usually leaves us unmoved. Similarly, journalists driven solely by thrill-seeking behavior will seldom sustain a career. Dismissed by their colleagues as habitual adrenaline junkies, they may be good for a quick war or two before moving on to other sources of titillation. Lastly, we can also split off those journalists whose narcissism gets in the way of the story, for by positioning themselves center stage, they deflect the spotlight away from combatants and victims. In doing so, they contaminate the news.

This leaves a group of journalists, few in number, whose mission is defined by their desire to go to the heart of a conflict and tell the story of those who wage war, those who are destroyed by it, and those who rise above it. They get a buzz from the adventure. Satisfaction comes from a job well done. There is pride in the awards that follow. But in the end, what moves these journalists to take such extraordinary risks is ultimately what moves us as human beings—tragedy unlocking the grandeur of the human spirit. Each of the war journalists I spoke to lent credence to this with a series of remarkable anecdotes. From these I have selected one haunting image with which to close this chapter. The photojournalist Jon Jones, trapped atop the Caucasus with refugees. A family's worldly possessions in a car. In Jones's honor, the wife prepared a meal with what little she had. A white tablecloth was found and spread across the car's hood. The father rummaged among the boxes. He unearthed a bottle of champagne. He had been saving it for the birth of his son. But the journalist had braved grave dangers to tell their story. His courage must be saluted.

# 4

# Depression, Drink, and Drugs

As you empty the bottles you refill them with your soul.

Gérard de Nerval

The war against the Taliban in Afghanistan provided bleak evidence of the high mortality rate that comes with telling war's story. In just over one week, eight journalists were killed. Among them was Julio Fuentes, ranked as one of the half dozen most experienced war journalists of his generation by the *Guardian*'s John Hooper. There is nothing new in war journalists dying violent deaths, but even for this hardy profession, the degree of carnage in Afghanistan was unusual. Soon after I began my study, Kurt Schork and Miguel Gil Moreno were killed, and eighteen months later, the murder of Julio Fuentes triggered the same intense sadness intertwined with bewilderment. "I still cannot believe Julio Fuentes is dead, even after seeing the crematorium curtains close silently before his coffin," grieved his friend and fellow war journalist Emma Daly in her *Observer* column. What made these particular deaths so unsettling for journalists, apart from the pain of personal loss, was that they were yet another reminder that no combination of experience, skill, intelligence, compassion, and caution could prevent some tragedies. Discussing the loss of a colleague and friend, Jerome Delay recalled, "When we were all at Miguel's funeral, we looked at each other and wondered who was going to be next." The answer was not long in coming. And as the doors of the crematorium swung closed behind Fuentes's coffin, the same thought was no doubt rekindled once more.

Bereavement can at times merge into clinically significant depression. Furthermore, one in two patients with PTSD, the quintessential trauma reaction, may also have an associated depression. For these reasons, it was important for my study to include an assessment of journalists' moods. A widely used self-report questionnaire, the Beck Depression Inventory–Revised, was therefore given to all participants. This scale lists twenty-one symptoms of depression and assesses the severity of mood change by scoring the responses as minimal, mild, moderate, or severe. When the results of the Beck scale for the 140 war journalists and the group of 107 non-war journalists were compared, the former were found to be significantly more depressed. A closer examination revealed that severe depression was uncommon in both groups of journalists, but more war journalists fell into the moderately severe group. Most of the domestic journalists had only minimal or mild depression scores. This difference was again statistically significant.

Of the twenty-one symptoms of the Beck Depression Inventory, those most often reported by the war group included sadness, a perception of past failure, loss of pleasure, guilty feelings, self-criticism, suicidal thoughts or wishes, crying, loss of interest, indecisiveness, change in sleep patterns, irritability, and loss of interest in sex. Pessimism, agitation, and change in appetite were also reported, though less frequently. There was no symptom that was more prominent in domestic journalists. The list demonstrates the extent to which those with depression experience symptoms other than sadness, and it helps explain why depression can be such a debilitating disease. While informative, the Beck self-report scale cannot be used to generate a clinical diagnosis. For that, a structured interview is required. This was completed on the random sample of twenty-eight war journalists, and it revealed a lifetime prevalence of major depression slightly less than 22 percent.* The equivalent figure for clinically meaningful major depression in the domestic journalists was significantly lower and corresponded to that noted in the general population of the United States.

Although the association between depression and loss is well documented in the psychiatric literature, some further refinement of this relationship is needed when applied to war journalists. For, as events in Afghanistan demonstrated, the profession is a special case. No experienced war journalist has been spared the violent death of a colleague. Focusing therefore on a more discrete group, those who have lost a close working partner, someone with whom they have braved the front lines and endured many shared dangers, becomes more informative. "In this business, there's a kind of forced closeness because of what you do," is how Greg Marinovich described his working relationships. The intensity of this shared existence forges strong bonds of friendship that in some cases supersede ties to

---

*One journalist's diagnosis of major depression predated his work in war zones.

family. Anthony Loyd, for example, was estranged from his father but wears a locket containing some of Kurt Schork's ashes.

For some journalists, when death takes a colleague the sense of loss is not only profound but, depending on circumstance, often stoked by guilt. What befell Allan Little during his time as one of the BBC's Balkan correspondents is such an example. He told me:

Bosnia was really tough in '92. I was absolutely committed to the story. I believed in the importance of being there. It was under my skin. In October I was in central Bosnia. There was a sudden huge refugee exodus. I called my office and said, "You should see this — it's huge. You must send me a cameraman." Well they did send me someone — a friend of mine — we'd worked together in Bosnia and in Croatia the previous year. He drove up from the coast, we spent the day filming together and then spent the night sleeping on the floor of someone's apartment. The next day we swapped cars — I took his little soft-skinned hire car and gave him the armored Land Rover. I headed back to the coast to a place where I could edit and transmit the report. He waited in central Bosnia and was due to be joined by another correspondent the next day. Half an hour after I left him he was killed. A Serb gunner fired an armor-piercing anti-aircraft round horizontally through the cab of his car.

I fell apart after that. I thought it was my fault. I couldn't imagine ever "getting over" this. I felt guilty just for being alive. I remember the moment I was told he'd been killed and I simply didn't believe it. I said, "No, you're wrong. I've just seen him. He's alive. You're mistaken." I argued with the man who broke the news to me. The next day we got up at six and drove back into Bosnia to collect his body. We took a hearse. I think the reality of what had happened hit on the way back, when we'd picked up the body. I think I wanted to swap places with him. I knew that if, at that moment, some divine authority had come down and said, "You have a choice, it could be him or you," I would have said, "Okay, me." I felt totally wretched about being alive.

Writing in the *Evening Standard* eight years later, Little noted: "I became withdrawn and moody. I couldn't sleep without nightmares. I started to fear the night. I drank too much, which made everything worse. I even grew paranoid and began to imagine that people were talking about me. I didn't realise any of this at the time — but some of my friends thought I was going mad and had become dangerously obsessed."

Like most of the journalists I interviewed, Little was difficult to pin down. When we finally met at a café in Johannesburg, we had only an hour to chat before he was off to catch a plane back to London en route to Yugoslavia. Events in the Balkans were once again moving quickly, but for a change they appeared headed in a positive direction. Thousands of demonstrators had taken to the streets of Belgrade, and Milošević was about to be toppled. During the interview, Little was by turns happy and sad, excited about the imminent fall of the Yugoslav dictator and somber as he recalled the death of his cameraman. "In the weeks that followed, I began to feel that any sort of enjoyment of life from now on was unthinkable. I thought it would be impossible ever to laugh again, ever to dance or just have a happy time or enjoy myself. I thought it would be a betrayal. I was also very angry. I wanted to kill the person who had done it. I wanted to go to the gun position, because I knew exactly where the thing had been fired from, and I really did want to go to that place and kill the guys who had done it."

Little's symptoms of loss of pleasure and guilt are typical of the grieving process. Some mourners, however, may experience more unusual symptoms, such as a transient disturbance in their perception. Examples include the bereaved hearing the voice of or catching a fleeting glimpse of the deceased. These "micro" hallucinations are extremely brief, lasting only a few seconds before reality intervenes. They also occur almost exclusively during the acute period of grief, which by definition does not last much longer than two months. The persistence of these altered perceptions beyond this period suggests bereavement merging with a more ominous depression.

I was able to document reactions such as these in a couple of journalists who had lost close colleagues. In one case, the hallucinations persisted for two years. This journalist, who had survived a particularly harrowing ordeal in the Middle East, would see a dead colleague in crowds or walking down the street towards him. He also had vivid dreams in which his friend featured prominently. What troubled him about the dreams was their lifelike intensity: many of the dead man's idiosyncrasies, mannerisms, foibles—in short, all the personality characteristics that made him such a distinctive individual—were perfectly reenacted. At times the hallucinations were so authentic that the journalist came to doubt whether his colleague had indeed been killed. These reenactments, whether during consciousness or sleep, triggered considerable guilt and depression. For relief, he turned increasingly to alcohol and cocaine, both of which can interfere with sleep, heightening the floridness of the already altered perceptions.

Jeremy Bowen was covering a story in the Middle East when he too lost
a close colleague and friend. In his case, the death was witnessed firsthand.
It was 2000, and Israel was in the process of withdrawing her army from
southern Lebanon. Bowen and his long-time Lebanese driver, Abed Tak-
koush, were following the progress of disengagement. Their car stopped in
an area they considered safe, and Bowen got out of the vehicle and moved
off to a vantage point. Then a shell hit the car.

> I spun around because I had my back to it and there was this huge fireball. I
> didn't realize it was the car to start with, then I realized it was. And then at
> that moment I saw [Takkoush] lurching out of the driver's window and he
> was just on fire. He lurched out, slumped out on the road. What went
> through my head was first to go up and see if I could help him, but my
> second thought was not to go, it would be horrible, he would be in a terrible
> state and would probably be dead. The third thought was the most sensible
> one. I had done a combat first aid course with the BBC and they said the first
> rule is don't become a casualty. So if they tried to kill him, they might try
> and kill me too. We were stuck there for about an hour and a half or so, and
> once or twice we stuck our heads out and were shot at. So I knew.

Bowen and I were in the noisy basement cafeteria of the BBC's offices in
White City, London. He was an easy person to talk to, frank in his comments and possessing a disarming warmth. The interview flowed effort-
lessly, without the awkward gaps and unspoken tensions that can at times
characterize intimate personal revelation. Seven months had passed since
the episode he described, and the memories were still raw. And like all his
colleagues, Bowen clearly displayed the emotional pain involved in retelling traumatic events. He recalled:

> No one could get to him. So I had to lay low while my colleague who
> was also a good friend, a nice guy, full of jokes, was one hundred yards
> away and I didn't know if he was alive or dead. I suspected he was dead.
> I could see what the shell had done to the car, and I know enough about
> these things to know that even if flames or shrapnel didn't get you, just being
> that close to the explosion would give you severe internal injuries which
> will do you in. And then I knew his family, you see. I had known him, in a
> sense grown up with him in Lebanon for five years. He was a good guy. He
> had three children under the age of twenty, all in their teens. I think that
> for me, the big difference about the tragedy was the personal aspect. I knew
> the guy.

For Bowen, the death triggered a cycle of rumination and doubt during which his actions and judgment were scrutinized and challenged.

I was with him, I had just got out of the car myself. If I had stayed, as I easily could have, I would have been killed by the same shell. The thing that affected me as well was that the guy was dead and we stopped there because I said stop there. And then I was not able to help him. Looking back, I don't think I was able to help him. At the time it did not seem dangerous to stop there. We thought we were away from the front line, but the tank fired over the border and so now I don't feel so bad that we stopped on that spot. On the other hand, I know that had I not said let's stop here he might be alive today. But that really is part of the risk that comes with my kind of work. I have sorted it out in my own head, I think I have replayed it in my mind many times and . . .

The sentence is left hanging in the air, unfinished, perhaps an indication that no matter how much soul searching you do, no matter how detailed the postmortem examination, guilt can never be fully erased. The tormenting question, "What if?" for which no answer can ever prove satisfactory, is a potential nidus of self-reproach, challenging the kind of decision that has been made countless times before without adverse consequences, until one day it all goes horribly wrong and one is left in a miasma of doubt and remorse. "I have never really had bad dreams," Bowen told me, "but I did after that. Successive dreams over a period of about ten days to two weeks where they were just depressing. All my friends were dying in the dreams, everyone was dying. So I went to get some counseling." In time, as the sadness, guilt, and anger began to wane, Bowen came to realize that there is no real answer to the question, "What if?" Indeed, the question itself is inherently unfair, as it implies a death that may have been preventable. In the absence of gross negligence or recklessness, such an argument is specious, an insight Bowen was able to articulate.

I went to Abed's funeral in Beirut and I was back in south Lebanon the next morning, and there someone said to me, "Have you heard about Kurt [Schork] and Miguel [Moreno]?" I knew both of them very well — they were friends of mine. I said no and was told they were killed in Sierra Leone the day before. It was the first I had heard of it. And those two days were very nasty. Some friends of mine said, you know, we always thought Kurt had this invulnerability about him. I have never thought that, not about Kurt, nor about me, not about anybody. There is no magic potion involved in this. No one person has some muti that keeps him protected. If you are there, it is dangerous. And the more you do, the greater the chance of getting it. I mean, how many lives do you have?

\*   \*   \*

Why is one journalist killed while another survives? That is one of the great imponderables of this profession. From a psychological perspective, the arbitrariness of fate, luck, or chance may also be one of the most powerful determinants of mood, for my data reveal that if loss predicts depression, survival can, in certain circumstances, be the antidote. For when a journalist pulls through after serious injury, his close colleagues are spared an agonizing self-examination that is so often the harbinger of a persistent and disabling melancholy. John Martin's account of an episode during the Yugoslav civil war illustrates this point. Martin is a veteran television cameraman, having spent more than twenty years in conflict zones. His résumé reads like a "who's who" of late-twentieth-century warfare. We met for an interview on a rainy summer's day in London, and after running through various symptom checklists, we turned the topic to one of his more harrowing near-death experiences.

No one had got to the front lines in Vukovar, where the Serbs and Croats were battling. I showed up with my soundmen and David Chater, a colleague from ITN, and we managed to use an early morning mist to go down into Vukovar. We went straight through a barrage, the shells and mortars passing across the top of our car, which frightened the life out of the sound guys, who I think had had too much to drink the night before. We managed to get through the roadblocks and get into the front lines, and then fortunately or unfortunately found ourselves tied up with some sort of renegade Serb front-line militia who had been there too long and were already on their first bottle of slivovitz at six o'clock in the morning. They were barking mad—Rambo types, with the headbands, you know what I mean. There was heavy incoming fire and we were in a maze of buildings and around the corner a tank was firing down the street. We were in really deep, to the point where you couldn't get out because the sniping was too accurate. The two front lines were very close, a few yards away from each other, and they were lugging mortars across the street. All the while I had been filming and had some great stuff, also some crazy stuff. Then the Serbs told us they were going to try a breakthrough with some tanks and did we want to film it? Well, we moved into a church to get close to the tanks, but the attack got bogged down and we found ourselves under intense fire and it became impossible to get in or out of the church because the Croats were firing rocket-propelled grenades and mortars at the church. I told the team it would be best for us to sit tight for five minutes, during which I would try and repair one of my cameras, and then we would try to head back again. I did my normal thing of getting behind the biggest wall I could and sat down. And then as I was trying to put a lens back on I looked up and just saw David Chater go up in the air and down again. He had stood up, stepped forward in front of a window and a sniper just put one straight through him.

Faced with a seriously wounded colleague, Martin's first instinct was to reach for his camera.

Well, I filmed it, I suppose it is a natural instinct, and then ran across to where he had gone down and [the militia] put out some covering fire. At this stage there were bodies all over the place and it was turning into a bloody massacre. We managed to get through the back door, a couple of guys helped us and we dragged him out. I thought David was dead. He had gone that horrible white color and was gushing blood everywhere, the bullet had gone underneath his flak and clean out the other side. Miraculously, we managed to find a front-line vehicle that was just ferrying some troops and we threw him in there, screaming and shouting. The Serbs gave us a ride and we got him back to a front lines MASH hospital where we did a considerable amount of shouting and finally got him onto a Medivac going back and forth to Belgrade. We couldn't go with him, it was a bad scene down there and the Medivac was completely full, so we had the two-and-a-half-hour drive to Belgrade, which I didn't enjoy very much — very definitely an unpleasant time because I was pretty much under the theory that when we got to Belgrade I would find a dead reporter friend. But he survived. He was in hospital for three-and-a-half weeks and the treatment he got was better than you get in the U.K. because they are much better at doing gunshot wounds, as in Belfast.

There are many remarkable aspects to this anecdote: the risks the journalists took in getting to the front lines in Vukovar; the accounts of militiamen drunk at six a.m. while waging war; the serious wounding of a colleague; the inability of a flak jacket to keep out the bullet (echoes here of Ken Oosterbroek in the townships of South Africa, where the bullet slipped under the jacket at a slightly different angle that ensured a fatal outcome); Martin's immediate reaction in filming his stricken colleague; the fortu-

itous presence of front-line transport, a nearby clearing station, and a Medivac; the skill of the trauma physicians. From a behavioral standpoint, there
is no depression, guilt, or heavy drinking, no nightmares, ruminations, or
flashbacks. The aftermath is fundamentally different from that experienced
by Jeremy Bowen and Allan Little when their friends died, because David
Chater survived, thereby sparing Martin and his colleagues the agonizing
"What if?" question. Survival: the product of a few millimeters or a couple
of seconds. Such are the vagaries confronted by war journalists when they
report for work — a confluence of innumerable details, often so routine
they hardly penetrate conscious awareness. And it is the interplay of these
details, fortuitous or adverse, that may also determine the psychological
health of the survivors.

*   *   *

Depression is but one of the conditions frequently found together with
post-traumatic stress disorder. Substance abuse is another, as Anthony
Loyd's memoir makes clear. *My War Gone By, I Miss It So* is an account of the
Bosnian war unlike any other. Loyd goes far beyond revealing the brutality
of that conflict and the hazards confronted by journalists trying to get their
story out. He also dwells at length on his addiction to heroin and alcohol.
The title itself reveals Loyd's addictive personality — the adrenaline rush of
war fueled his deep-seated psychological need, akin to a biological craving,
for excitement. Away from the front lines, the relative dullness of daily life
was insufferable and relieved only by the seductive powers of heroin.

While Loyd's book may illustrate an intemperate case of addictive behavior in a war journalist, there are many other examples of colleagues who
resort to alcohol or drugs to modulate their environment, either to relieve
the mundaneness of life in a civil society or to blunt the fear and emotional
pain that marches in tandem with conflict. One comes away from reading
the memoirs of many war journalists with a sense that their world is awash
in booze and a pharmacopoeia of illicit and prescription drugs. Tim Page,
the photographer of Vietnam fame whose behavior and battlefield exploits
bear an uncanny resemblance to the character portrayed by Dennis Hopper
in Francis Ford Coppola's *Apocalypse Now*, did not spare his reader the
details of his substance abuse problem in his autobiography. "Everyone was
walking around with fluted glass-stopped bottles of Sandoz 25, the purest
LSD on the tightening market," he wrote. "Traditionally you were given a
lump of sugar; I got mine as a splash on my hand, behind the left thumb. I
just licked it up. Endlessly." A second anecdote illustrates how a powerful

cocktail of barbiturates mixed with alcohol played havoc with his judgment: "Lots of booze, dilaudid, phenobarb, and dilantin blurred my pain and desperation. The gun was still with me. The metal glinted purposefully. I got a handful of the hollow nosed slugs out the Indian deerskin drawsack and counted out five. The cartridges snick slid home in the chambers, which clicked satisfyingly home in the breech. I spun the barrel and in one movement pointed straight between the eyes and pulled the trigger. My eyes blurred and refocused on the barrel, unsmoking, a black hole, a round in the chamber either side. I lowered the message miracle very slowly and lay back, wiped out." Page's turbulent life is, at times, an extreme example of emotions and judgment gone awry, but it is through accounts such as his and Loyd's that drink and drugs have worked their way into the mythology of the war journalist.

The medical complications of alcohol abuse are well known and legion. To assist physicians in monitoring whether their patients are drinking too much, clear guidelines as to what constitutes heavy or excessive drinking have been formulated. The upper limit of weekly intake differs for males and females, a reflection of differences in physiology and the ability of the liver to metabolize alcohol. For males, the advisable limit is fourteen units of alcohol per week; for females, nine units. A unit is defined as a glass of wine, a shot of spirits, or an average-size (330 ml) bottle of beer.*

My study compared the weekly drinking habits of the 140 war journalists with those from the control group of 107 domestic journalists. Because there are gender differences, the data from males and females were analyzed separately. Among the male journalists, those in the war group drank significantly more than the domestic journalists. In fact, the war group's average weekly alcohol consumption was fifteen units, twice that of the domestic journalists, and exceeded the medical guidelines for acceptable drinking. A total of 14 percent of this group drank more than double the weekly limit, while some prodigious individual weekly consumptions were noted, with a couple of journalists drinking in excess of two bottles of whiskey per week. None of the domestic journalists got close to this level of imbibing.

It is important not to lose sight of the broader perspective, however. While male war journalists as a group drink to excess, 59 percent drink less than fourteen units per week, and 10 percent of these are virtual teetotalers. It is the remaining 41 percent that push the average up. Also, the heavy

*These guidelines were formulated by the Canadian Medical Association.

and moderate drinkers showed no greater evidence of depression, post-traumatic stress disorder, and overall psychological distress. Thus, excessive alcohol consumption in the war group was not consistent with more extensive psychopathology. Nor was it associated with increased physical problems. A final correlate with respect to males is worth noting; those who drank to excess were significantly more likely to be single or divorced. While the causal direction of this relationship cannot be stated with certainty, the possibility exists that the most injurious effects of alcohol are in the social domain, with impaired relationships one notable example.

The drinking habits of female war journalists mirror to a degree those of their male counterparts, albeit with the contrasts between the war and domestic groups more pronounced. Their average weekly alcohol consumption of eleven units is well above the cutoff limit of nine units, and three times that of the domestic female group. Fifty-two percent of female war journalists were heavy drinkers, compared to 41 percent of males and only 7 percent of domestic female journalists. Like their male counterparts, female war journalists whose weekly intake exceeded the cutoff point were not more likely to endorse symptoms of depression, PTSD, psychological distress, or physical illness. However, the genders diverged when it came to marital status; female heavy drinkers were just as likely to be married as those who tended toward moderation.

The reactions of those in the profession to these findings were interesting. While war journalists and their news bosses listened respectfully to the PTSD and depression data, the information on alcohol and its interpretation within rigid medical orthodoxy prompted howls of laughter and occasionally outright derision. Many war journalists are hard drinking; they know it and, in a macho way, are proud of it. They certainly have little patience for a behavioral scientist with his cutoff thresholds, pedantic definitions, and measuring cup. I had a sense they greeted my empirical data with much the same enthusiasm shown by a publican for a Salvation Army prohibitionist.

Within war zones, shortages of food and water may exist alongside a thriving black market well supplied with liquor. And here alcohol fulfills many roles. Recall John Martin's account of Serb and Croat militia tanked up on slivovitz at six a.m. and fighting with a reckless abandon. Or consider the words of a bereaved journalist, mourning the death of a close colleague: "I drank a lot . . . drugs had always been part of the scene anyway . . . I was very self-destructive." Or envisage journalists hunkered down at night in a war zone, unable to venture outdoors, with nothing but a bottle to help pass the time and assist as a hypnotic. There have, of course, been circumstances in which liquor was hard to come by. Afghanistan, for example, presented the fraternity with challenges that, to some, seemed more daunting than personal safety. The rigid imposition of Islamic fundamentalism had effectively turned the country into a dry state. A month into the post–September 11 American bombing campaign, the *Times* of London ran an article by the dauntless and entertaining Anthony Loyd entitled "Death and Moonshine." Loyd speaks for many when he describes war as a combination of the "thrilling rush of excitement followed by the backwash of boredom," and while there was little he could do to influence the former in Afghanistan, addressing the latter fell well within his repertoire. "Alcohol is a very underground scene," he wrote. "There are a few networks still in place, principally among isolated pharmacists. They need alcohol to make medicine and a few diversify. [The homemade liquor they sell] tastes like grappa. If you mix the clear liquid with fruit juice imported over the passes on mule trains from Pakistan and Iran, the result isn't bad, though the joy of our first test run was spoilt by fears of imminent blindness. To work out the quality you pour a drop on wood and try to light it. If it lights with a blue flame you are in luck: if not then the grog's been cut with meat fat and you've been ripped off."

A humorous interlude, but a revealing one. For Loyd and Seamus, his freelancer photographer friend, the illicit brew offered a way of passing the slow, dark Afghan nights. Others, however, may use alcohol for different reasons. For some war journalists, the sights, smells, and sounds of war are never entirely banished; they return unexpectedly, at awkward moments, like some unwelcome guest crashing a party. Initially, alcohol may offer respite, an effective, albeit short-lived anodyne, the powerful suppressant effects of a stiff drink blotting out the intrusive, nightmarish demons of involuntary recollection. But tolerance can set in, and soon what one drink once achieved now requires two, or three, or four. Alcohol also makes a bad sleeping draft, because it disrupts the rhythms of sleep. In time, an easy solution becomes very much part of the problem.

As a reporter for the *New York Times*, Donatella Lorch covered wars in Somalia, Sudan, Afghanistan, Rwanda, and Zaire, among others. In an article entitled "Surviving the Five Ds," she recalled how her work centered on covering "the Dead, the Dying, the Diseased, the Depressing, and the Dangerous." It is a heartfelt article, describing the intense joys and deep sorrows of life as a war journalist, and it touches on many of the themes addressed thus far, including the alienation felt on returning home ("For those few months back in the United States, I struggled with an emptiness that I nursed alone at night in my darkened living room, watching the lights of New Jersey across the Hudson River, wine in hand, deeply lonely, anxious, and unhappy"); the habituation to the horrors of war ("We joked about dead bodies over sushi at a Japanese restaurant in Nairobi, much to the shock of the neighboring tables"); the unconscious re-experiencing of trauma-related memories ("If smell can trigger memories, all I need is to catch a whiff of road kill before I remember the churches of Rwanda and the hills of Burundi"); and her hypervigilance and that of colleagues ("Even living in Rome, he felt apprehension — scanning the roads around him, looking for snipers, avoiding untraveled routes. Even now I catch myself, for brief moments, looking for danger, wary of walking on unmarked trails because of landmines or just checking people out to see if anyone looked suspicious").

Insightful as her article is, I would respectfully add one more "D" to her somber list: Drink. It runs like a thread through her brief narrative, from watching the lights of the Hudson alone in her apartment, glass of wine in hand, to her observations of colleagues ("I have watched many drink heavily and at least one slip into alcoholism") and her memories of Mogadishu ("We drank heavily, many smoked dope, at least one did hard drugs"). She also takes issue with the findings of my study, writing, "According to a Freedom Forum sponsored study, female war journalists drink five times as much as their counterparts in the general journalistic population. I do drink more than before I went to Africa, but I would like to think that it would probably compare to an European male counterpart's consumption." There is an element of defiance, if not pride, in this last sentence, an iteration that her ability to knock them back is equal to any male colleague's. And to reinforce her point, she refers specifically to the European male, with the tacit understanding that liberal drinking habits in the Old World are very much part of the social fabric of society, unlike North America where such behavior comes with a pejorative label. To which I can reply that she is correct on all points, save one. Female war journalists can drink as heavily as their male colleagues, but this should be cause for consternation, not pride. When concern is expressed over alcohol consumption (for both genders), it should not be viewed as some preachy reprimand implying personal failure. There is simply no question that drinking to excess is bad for your health.

For an empiricist, the findings seem clear enough. But I'll add one final caveat that illustrates the difficulties of drawing simple conclusions. For the majority of war journalists, alcohol has not impeded their ability to write, film, televise, and produce with skill and creativity, often under extraordinarily difficult circumstances. If it is important to recognize the medical risks of heavy long-term drinking, it is also important to acknowledge that for many war journalists, the symbiosis of drink and work fits poorly with a conventional wisdom captured by Oscar Wilde's witticism that work is the curse of the drinking class.

* * *

Data were also collected with respect to other forms of substance abuse: the use of cannabis, cocaine, barbiturates, LSD, and opiates. The cannabis findings were analyzed separately because the assumption was that this type of substance abuse would be fairly common in both groups of journalists, as it is in the general population, and therefore less likely to represent socially maladaptive behavior. This hypothesis was proved correct. Twenty-four percent of war journalists and 19 percent of domestic journalists used cannabis on a regular basis, a difference that was not statistically significant. Six percent of war journalists and 2 percent of domestic journalists reported using other drugs, cocaine being the most frequently cited. These relatively small percentages reveal that hard drug abuse is not common. Chasing the dragon is confined to a small minority, and the profession as a whole is wary of highly addictive and dangerous substances.

Given that alcohol and drug abuse often go together, I looked at hard drug use among those deemed to be either "average" or "excessive" drinkers. This analysis was confined to males, as only two female journalists were hard drug users. The results showed that those males who drank to excess were also the ones using cocaine and, to a lesser extent, amphetamines, heroin, and LSD.

There is a class of medication, the benzodiazepines (of which Valium is an example), that make good sleeping pills. Most journalists are well aware of their sedating, calming effects, but they are less familiar with the problems associated with prolonged use. As with alcohol, the potential for addiction is high, and self-medicating is ill advised. However, when a journalist is far from the safety of home and circumstances fray the nerves, the temptation to dip into the bottle is hard to resist. Fergal Keane described to me the enticing pull of an anesthetic sleep amid the stench of death in Rwanda.

I'd brought some sleeping pills with me because [people] who had advice on Rwanda were telling me it was crazy. We were stuck in this place. We had almost driven into an ambush that day. We were driving down a road and we saw two men placing a mine on the road, with AK47s on their back. We managed to turn around and drive back. We then had to take a shortcut through country that was crawling with these characters. You know, we had seen what they had done and it was the thought of falling victim to them . . . We eventually arrived that night in a village that was just full of dead bodies. There was a small detachment of the guerilla army, the good guys, in the village, and we went over to say hello. They were edgy and knew they could be attacked at any moment. That night we sat around in this tiny hut, passing around pictures of our family. And I said, you know, I've got some sleeping pills, because there was no way we were going to sleep. The smell of the corpses was just overpowering. So we took sleeping pills that night and they wiped us out.

The situation is exacerbated by the fact that Valium has a street value — vast quantities often flood zones of conflict, making its procurement easy and cheap. One cameraman recalled that during his time in Sarajevo, "I was taking a lot of sedatives. I had a bag of two thousand Valium. Somebody was just handing them out. They had been given to him by the French [peace-keepers] because he had been in a TV station that had been hit by a shell. So I remember eating a lot of Valium, getting stoned, drinking. Somehow through that, I was working as well because there wasn't any down time, only a couple of hours sleep here and there. Everything was just spiraling out of control."

This quote highlights another challenge faced by journalists, one that may inadvertently lead to the abuse of a sedative such as Valium. Sleep in war zones, even during a lull in the action, may be difficult. The advent of the twenty-four-hour news channel and the geographical separation of journalists from the newsroom, often many time zones distant, can play havoc with the sleep-wake cycle. What may start out as a well-meaning attempt by a journalist to regulate his sleep pattern becomes the first step on the slippery road to addiction. Nearly all sleeping tablets are addictive and, when taken consistently over a number of months, lead to tolerance, a situation akin to alcohol dependence. Escalating dosages cannot be sustained indefinitely, and any attempt to either stop the medication altogether or scale back the dosage triggers uncomfortable symptoms of withdrawal ranging from jitteriness, sweating, palpitations, and tremor to anxiety, irritability, insomnia, and, most worrying of all, seizures. The clinical picture, analogous to the delirium tremens of alcohol withdrawal, means that, helpful as the hypnotics can be, their use has to be carefully controlled and supervised by the prescribing physician.

✳   ✳   ✳

This chapter has laid out the evidence with respect to alcohol abuse and the use of hard drugs by war journalists. It is the first attempt at providing empirical evidence to complement or counterbalance the many anecdotes that fill this profession's genre of turbulent autobiography. To what extent do these two realities match up? Are the objective findings in concordance with the personal revelations? The answer, not surprisingly, depends on who is viewing the data.

From the perspective of the behavioral scientist, the addition of a control group, in this instance domestic journalists who were carefully screened to ensure they had never so much as sniffed the winds of war, was an essential prerequisite. This provided the means to statistically interpret the data and assign clinical relevance. With this design in place, the results are unequivocal. War journalists drink more heavily and show a trend toward more illicit drug use, particularly cocaine. These are telling observations, yet when they are reduced to the objectivity of medical diagnoses they take on a disembodied quality. What this dry taxonomy translates into is this: the lives of some war journalists are, at times, clouded by nightmares, flashbacks, eidetic images of death and destruction, emotional detachment, fraught relationships, sadness, guilt, thoughts of suicide, and periods of intense loneliness. Getting drunk and getting stoned offers temporary relief. Rather than bringing succor, though, this behavior, if sustained, may introduce a fresh set of problems while aggravating old difficulties.

But we must remember that if 29 percent of war journalists develop PTSD over the course of their lifetime, that leaves more than 70 percent who do not, which goes along with the 76 percent who do not develop major depression, the 60 percent who do not drink heavily, and the 94 percent who decline the laced, fluted glass. Depression-free war journalists who drink moderately and avoid drugs are quick to point out that generalizations are frequently misleading. They can cite angst-free memoirs, like those of John Simpson and Sandy Gall, that reveal a more moderate side to the profession. This argument too has a legitimacy.

Perhaps the most accurate and fairest summation of the many variables in my data set is this: the extent to which war journalists use alcohol, heroin, and cocaine lies along a continuum; the exploits of Tim Page and Anthony Loyd at one end, the 10 percent of teetotaling, acid-free journalists at the other. Between them come the bulk of their colleagues, whose predilections nevertheless exceed those of their domestic counterparts and the general population. The war journalist data are thus out of kilter, shifted off center, away from the norms of society at large. Given the nature of their work, this is perhaps not surprising. While these findings must be cause for concern, it would be a mistake to pathologize so large a majority, for I have no evidence that their work suffers as a consequence of this behavior, and only the weakest inferential data suggesting that their relationships are adversely affected. It is these observations, empirically supported, rather than the incandescent prose of tempestuous memoirs, that most accurately reflect the profession's complex flirtation with addiction.

# 5

# Freelance War Journalists

On September 27, 2002, the *Times* of London ran an obituary titled "British TV Man Killed in Chechen Battle." The article, which angered the small community of freelance journalists, reported that "the British author of a travel guide to the world's most dangerous places has been killed as Chechen rebels fought a fierce battle against an overwhelming Russian force." The individual in question, Gervaise Roderick "Roddy" John Scott, was found dead alongside eighty Chechen fighters killed by Russian artillery and air attacks. Russian television reported that he died when a bullet pierced the lens of his camera: a picture of the shattered lens and smashed Nikon supported the claim. Roddy Scott was thirty-one years of age.

Certain of the assertions made in the *Times* obituary particularly angered Vaughan Smith, the director of the freelance agency Frontline Television News Limited. Rather than concentrating on the quality of Scott's journalism, the authors played up his contributions to an annual travel guide, *The World's Most Dangerous Places*, mentioning that he once spent time "cooling his heels in an Ethiopian jail" and that he chose to "seek out the least visited or most dangerous spots, and then manage[d] to choose the world's most dangerous people to travel with." Moving between innuendo and frank assertions of reckless and potentially self-injurious behavior, the obituarists quoted an anonymous colleague, who labeled Scott's desire to cover the war in Chechnya "practically suicidal and really crazy. There's this bandit, outlaw connection. You could be kidnapped. The Russians might shoot you. The rebels might shoot you. There's no safe side for you if you are a Western journalist in Chechnya."

Reading the faint and damning praise in the *Times*, one comes away with little sense of Roddy Scott's worth. Instead, one has an uncomfortable feeling that a combination of extreme sensation-seeking behavior and a cavalier and foolish bravado inevitably brought about his tragic end.

However, a subsequent obituary, published in the Toronto *Globe and Mail* and written by a colleague of Scott's, paints a very different picture. The man who looks out from the pages of the *Globe*, an image of his youthful, open gaze inserted beside a blurry enlarged photograph of his destroyed camera, is remembered as a charismatic figure, intrepid, enquiring, devoted to telling the story of the world's forgotten conflicts. Forsaking financial reward, undaunted by the risk of nasty infectious diseases (while reporting the civil war in Sierra Leone, Scott contracted cerebral malaria and temporarily lost his sight), he had ventured repeatedly into territory, both geographical and abstract, that many other war journalists avoided, befriending the local people and their militias, gaining their trust and respect, and in the process telling a compelling and articulate story that the world's news organizations were increasingly reluctant to hear. The tone of the article differs markedly from that expressed in the *Times*, for in the Canadian broadsheet, the obituary eulogizes Scott and is filled with affection and admiration. It celebrates a remarkable life while mourning the premature demise of a journalist whose work combined the rare attributes of courage and selflessness.

*   *   *

What to make of two such radically different perspectives on a life short lived? Such a posthumous falling out is more often the fate of a veteran politician than a little known thirty-one-year-old cameraman, killed along the border of Chechnya and Ingushetia. That the individual in question was a freelance journalist, however, hints at a fault line that runs through the profession, a divide separating the self-employed from those working on contract to the news networks.

"What is clear is that many in the media still feel uncomfortable with real freelancers," wrote Vaughan Smith, three days after his colleague's death. "Of course, the *Times* would write differently of one of their own or any journalist working for any mainstream media organisation. Did they write this when the foreign correspondent for the *Sunday Times*, Marie Colvin, lost an eye in Sri Lanka?"

What lay behind Smith's ardent defense of his colleague and freelancers in general was more than a grievance over cynical double standards. It reflected his passionate belief in the importance of reportage cut loose from the control of news organizations, with their myriad competing agendas. A credo of the freelance journalist, one of the common denominators that bind this group and give their work an added significance, is independence of spirit, which can be tethered to moral rectitude. "Roddy felt the international media was in dereliction of its duty in failing to take the necessary risks to cover Chechnya," wrote Smith. He believed that freelancers were the only ones willing to report on conflicts that the mainstream media, out of fear or political bias, wanted to ignore.

Independence, however, places its own weighty demands. James Nachtwey articulated a philosophy shared by the thirty freelancers who were part of my study: "If you really want to establish yourself and show that you mean business and you're serious about it, then you sometimes have to do an assignment on your own. You may have just enough money in the bank to make it through the trip, speculating on whether or not you'll ever recover your expenses and break even . . . I've done that a number of times . . . I continue to do that, and I think it's a mark of the fact that I am very serious about what I am doing, that it means something to me and I don't just wait for an assignment."

Certainly, the career path described by Nachtwey isn't the road to untold riches. In praising the virtues of Roddy Scott, Vaughan Smith laid out, in stark detail, the meager earnings his friend could count on: "The remarkable thing about Roddy was that he was able to get into Chechnya, having waited in Georgia for several months, on a budget of just £500. His trip was delayed for three months while he waited for a broadcaster to pay us for two minutes of Afghan footage sold for £250 per minute earlier this year. We laughed with him as we handed over the £500 before he set off, when he told us he hoped he would get film so compelling that he'd be paid enough to buy a new pair of boots."

Vaughan Smith's criticism is directed primarily at the management of the major news organizations, but he is not the only one to spell out the tensions between the different categories of journalists. Mark Pedelty is an anthropologist who went to El Salvador during that country's civil war to study the Salvadoran Foreign Press Corps Association (SPECA). A chapter in his book *War Stories: The Culture of Foreign Correspondents* offers a detailed comparison of staff journalists employed by the news networks and "stringers" (self-employed local journalists who sell articles, radio pieces,

and photos to a number of news organizations, called "strings").* He writes
that stringers harbor a great deal of animosity toward staff correspondents,
whom they call the "A Team." The litany of complaints from the "B Team"
includes the following: The A Team is physically and culturally removed
from the conflict; the A Team exploits the B Team's knowledge without
adequate compensation; the A Team is too closely linked to elite, propagan-
distic sources of information (aka the U.S. State Department) and receives
preferential treatment in return. Pedelty, whose sympathies in El Salvador
clearly lay with the stringers, contrasts the objective reporting and intellectual independence of the freelancers with the A Team's excessive obedience
to their organization, seeing their piety as akin to political toadyism.

   According to Pedelty, stringers refer to this obedience as the "*New York
Times* disease," a nefarious condition whose symptoms include journalists
defining themselves by the organization they work for, while the organization in turn defines what constitutes the news (" 'if the *Times* isn't there, it
isn't news' "). Reading Pedelty's monograph is like discovering a war within
a war. He describes the *New York Times* disease as "a virulent hubris more
common than its label implies," and while the author acknowledges that
some of the stringers' accusations are extreme and driven in part by envy, he
also paints an unattractive portrait of staff correspondents. These expo-
nents of what he calls "parachute journalism" appear crassly manipulative,
short on empathy, driven by narcissism, and almost psychopathic in their
exploitation and manipulation of people. And to cap it all, Pedelty writes
that they "participate conspicuously in prostitution." In an awful psycholo-
gist manqué attempt at insight, Pedelty explains this unsavory sexual predilection: "Following the tradition of war correspondents past, they construct their professional identities through sexual adventure. Furthermore,
through such adventures they recoup a sense of power, compensating for
that which is ceded daily to censoring (neutering?) structures. In other
words, they may not be allowed to write like Mr. Hemingway, but they can
at least attempt to live like him. Therefore, it is only natural that the world's
oldest profession would intersect with one of its most frustrating."

   It is unfortunate that the foreign correspondent that emerges from
Pedelty's pages is at times closer to caricature, for his study is the first
and most detailed social examination of the profession. Nevertheless, em-

---

*While the term "stringers" is generally reserved for individuals hired *on* location in
zones of conflict, as opposed to freelancers who are hired to go *to* a location, there may be
considerable overlap in what these journalists do and in the terms of their employment.

bedded within his distorted profile are certain truths that define the differences between staff journalists and their freelance counterparts, and these
resonate with Vaughan Smith's more composed assessment. "I wouldn't
want to give the impression that real freelancers don't have friends in the
industry," he writes.

> We have very many and are very grateful to them. You only have to look at
> the list of those who support the Rory Peck Trust — a charity to support the
> wider television freelance community, set up in the name of a real freelancer
> killed in 1993 — each year to see that we are appreciated. Indeed Roddy com-
> pleted a safety course that was part funded by trust. But few of those in our in-
> dustry who wish us well have ever quite understood us. Think awhile what
> was going through Roddy's mind as he set off with Chechen rebels. As a sin-
> gle man, he didn't worry about insurance, though he would have welcomed
> it. Nor did he miss the flak jacket he couldn't afford on his £500 budget.

Unlike agency journalists, freelancers lack support and backup should
they get into difficulties, which they often can't avoid given the nature of
their work and the places they visit. The benefits of working for a news
agency, such as life insurance, armored vehicles for transport in and out
of areas of conflict, and help on the other end of a telephone line, are
eschewed in favor of independence — the choice of deciding what to do,
where to go, and what to record, unfettered by the constraints of the news
bosses and an imposed political agenda. Gary Knight, a freelance photographer married to an agency journalist, deftly summarized their different
work conditions:

> During the war in Bosnia, my wife Fiona and I would often make our sepa-
> rate ways to the field. Fiona, a network TV producer, would leave the house
> in a silver limousine, with $10,000–$20,000 in her bag, armed with pages of
> research. She would fly in business class and be greeted upon arrival by a
> local producer, who would have arranged her onward travel and would brief
> her fully on the current situation. Fiona would work for two or three weeks
> in the field, traveling in an armored car with her crew and correspon-
> dent, communicating by satellite telephone, with practically everything she
> needed at her disposal. When she returned home, in the same elegant man-
> ner as she left, she could even get counseling and medical care, if needed.
>     I [on the other hand] was totally on my own. During the war in Yugo-
> slavia, some magazines would give freelancers only guarantees, not assign-
> ments. That way they could not be held responsible if a photographer was

killed or wounded. Guarantees never covered expenses, however. So shortly after Fiona left, I would head for the airport in the cheapest taxi available, raiding an ATM brave enough to accept my card. I would take a cheap flight and, on arrival, would hire a cheap, "soft-skinned" car and make my way to the story. If things got hot along the way, I would put the car seat in maximum recline and drive as fast as I could. If I needed to speak to the magazine client, I would first have to find a satellite phone. In Sarajevo, that meant driving down Sniper Alley in full recline. Once I got in phone contact with the magazine, I would be kept on hold for ten minutes. That cost $450. My overnight accommodation was usually on someone else's floor. By the end of some of these trips, I would arrive home having spent more money than I had earned.

The differences between these two groups belie the fact that they often need one another. The freelancers' much-cherished independence ends when it comes to getting their work before the public; while the news organizations may look to them to provide content. So begins an uneasy, enforced symbiosis amid often divergent agendas. These tensions magnify when a freelance journalist is wounded or killed. Many of the journalists I interviewed gave examples of how a news organization that had been keen to purchase their material suddenly dropped from sight when they were in trouble. When the plane in which John Liebenberg was traveling was shot down over Huambo in central Angola, he suddenly confronted just such a reality. "It was then that I got really pissed at Reuters," he told me.

Reuters never contacted my family. Reuters knew we had gone down. There was a plane flying above us and those guys in the plane saw the aircraft going down and immediately put it on the wires. We, the survivors, were stuck on the front lines for fourteen days. When I got out of that hole, I took it up with them [but] they just kept quiet. They never answered anything. I was really angry with them. Reuters has that ability to do that to people. They will warn you, "John, watch out for the dangers and the consequences, but we want the pictures." And when you are putting your ass on the line, and you get knocked out, hurt, they are going to ask you, "John, didn't you take too many chances? Are you sure it was the right decision you took?" It made me a little shaky. Because I wanted to come back to my work, I wanted to come back to my children, I wanted to be alive, and I wanted to be a father.

The photographer Greg Marinovich tells of a similar experience in his memoir *The Bang Bang Club*.

The reason for my unease about working with *Newsweek* as opposed to *Time* was one of corporate culture. I felt unsure that *Newsweek* were the right people to back me up in what was a potentially dangerous story: in Bosnia I had done work on guarantee for *Newsweek*, covering the Muslim-Croat conflict, a nasty war where a drive along a valley road saw you cross front lines several times and I came to experience the difference between *Newsweek*'s attitude and that of their great rival, *Time*. I had asked if I could hire a "hard car" — a bullet-proofed vehicle — that would dramatically increase my safety, and give me an advantage in getting pictures. *Newsweek*'s answer was no; they suggested I get a ride with someone who had a hard car. This meant asking Nachtwey, the *Time* photographer, if I could ride with him. When *Time* assigns a photographer to a war zone they make sure there is as little extra pressure put on them as possible. They spend money to get the best pictures and safeguard their photographers, even if they are just freelancers.

An assignment is an agreement to temporarily employ you on a fixed day rate, pay all your expenses and accept responsibility for you in case something happens. *Newsweek*'s method was to give freelance photographers a guarantee that would cover expenses, day rates and car hire. The guarantee system could put a few dollars more in your pocket if you stayed in cheap hotels and skimped on expenses. It was quite different to being on assignment. The system of guarantees had evolved as a hands-off way of getting photographs. The company is allegedly less liable if someone gets hurt or killed while on guarantee than if that person is on assignment. Photograph-lore has it that *Newsweek* had instituted that system after photographers working for them had been expensively hurt or killed.

Soon Marinovich had an opportunity to see for himself if the rumors about *Newsweek* were true. While covering the township violence that preceded the 1994 elections in South Africa, he was seriously wounded. "I would discover that my unease about working for that magazine was well founded," he wrote. "They did not offer one day's pay for the weeks in hospital or the months of recuperation."

When we met, six years had passed since Marinovich's shooting and his views of the news organizations remained uncompromising. "Most of them are just exploitative," he asserted. "*Time* magazine is one of the few that isn't . . . The last day *Newsweek* paid me was the day I was shot. I was on assignment for them. I was on contract. They paid my little bills. They paid no compensation. Nothing else. And they kept promising, instead of which they never delivered. And I was in such a fucked-up state I just went along with everything. I kept on asking for help and they just kept evading. Listen, it's a business. It's taken me a long time to discover that, but it's a business. Nothing more, nothing less."

Being judged exploitative and callously indifferent does not sit well with the news bosses. I asked Stephen Jukes, then the global head of news at Reuters, to clarify what had happened to Liebenberg in Angola, but he drew a blank—the episode in question had taken place too far in the past for anyone currently working at Reuters to remember the details. Jukes did, however, provide me with a list of safety procedures and policies that his organization had implemented for freelance journalists. These include providing insurance in the event of death or long-term disability. Freelancers are also sent on hostile-environment training. Furthermore, Jukes made it clear that Reuters is aware that the intense competitive pressures among freelance cameramen in war zones may push them to take greater risks. To mitigate this, Reuters and other large news networks have agreed to pool material in situations of extreme danger. Jukes also cited specific cases of the highest rungs of management in his organization intervening when tragedy and danger overtook one of their freelancers. When Kurt Schork was killed in Sierra Leone in 2000, for example, Reuters worked with his family to make the funeral arrangements, which involved repatriating his body from West Africa. Reuters also helped establish the Kurt Schork Memorial Fund.

The situation at *Newsweek* was in many respects similar. The photographer Gary Knight related that the current management was more safety conscious and had recently sent him on a nuclear, biological, and chemical warfare training course. He did, however, acknowledge that back in the early 1990s, when Marinovich and the Bang Bang Club were combing the dusty, lethal alleys of the South African townships for photographs, management was more indifferent to their fate.

In a profession in which death, injury, and illness are unavoidable, the business Marinovich refers to is a complicated one. News networks must ask themselves if, by purchasing material from freelance journalists, they are endorsing a work ethic that on occasion places the journalists in grave danger. Is there not a moral responsibility tacit in this financial transaction? If freelance journalists are the only ones prepared to risk their lives to get a particular story, and the news organizations want that story, can these organizations turn their backs when the journalists are injured or worse? "We present an ethical problem that comes to the fore when one of us is killed," wrote Vaughan Smith in his obituary for Roddy Scott. Of course, the news organizations could dispense with any moral ambiguity, and banish guilt, by refusing to buy material from freelance journalists, citing unacceptable risk-taking behavior. But that opens up another dilemma: should it be the prerogative of the news organizations to define which stories can and cannot be told, which war is important and which one can be ignored?

Dramatic war footage will always prove irresistible to news organizations. Not only are the images riveting, but they often have the additional allure of political and even historical importance. Take Roddy Scott's last video, for example. Found on the battlefield by Russian forces, it shows Chechen rebels crossing from Pankisi to north Ossetia and then into Ingushetia, providing incontrovertible evidence that Georgian territory was being used as a springboard for their attacks on Russian forces. According to the *Guardian* newspaper, the footage was shown on Russian television and outraged officials in Moscow.

The discomfort of the news organizations, enticed by the image, yet nervous of the obligations that come with ownership, is unlikely to be assuaged by Vaughan Smith's claim that freelancers "have never asked for anything more than a market to sell to." By absolving news organizations of any responsibility for the physical well-being of freelancers, he deftly usurps the moral high ground. Failing to assist a wounded journalist, or washing their hands of the corpse while simultaneously using that journalist's material, is callous. To publicly justify doing so by quoting Smith's plaintiff plea adds a caddish element to behavior that is already questionable. Smith's high-flown sentiment might clarify where freelance cameramen stand in their business dealings, but it can only add to the moral burden of those who buy their product. This may be one of the reasons why freelancers are having greater difficulty selling their work. Smith recalls "the good old days when television news rooms were inhabited by stalwarts such as the BBC's John Mahoney, who not only clearly liked dealing with colourful mavericks like Rory Peck, but also gave us a fair price for our footage. We got £700 per minute. Ten years ago, if you were good, you could match the wage of a BBC reporter. Now we are lucky to get £300 per minute and there is much more reluctance to purchase in the first place. Broadcasters are now troubled by us."

Another problem is that the interests of a freelance journalist, such as a forgotten war in Angola or conflict in the recesses of the Caucasus, may not mesh with the priorities of a large news organization. I heard this tale of frustration repeatedly in my interviews with the freelancers. "I had a really difficult trip to the Congo," the freelance camerawoman Elizabeth

Jones told me. "I spent all my own money just to get these images, and I could not find a spot for [them]." Her terse summary of her months in central Africa was echoed by similar comments from journalists who had worked in Sierra Leone, Sudan, Mozambique, the Ivory Coast, Somalia, Chechnya, Colombia — a third world montage of civil collapse and cheap death. With the attention of the developed nations and their well-resourced press corps focused firmly on Afghanistan, the Middle East, and the Balkans, it has been left to the "mavericks" to cover the world's unnoticed wars, often at their own expense.

*   *   *

Navigating solo war's fickle, lethal uncertainties adds a new dimension of stress and uncertainty for this group of journalists and begs the question of how they fare psychologically. Of the 140 war journalists I studied, thirty were freelance, and their responses on the various questionnaires were compared to those given by their salaried colleagues. My first observation was that freelance journalists are generally younger than their tenured colleagues, although there are some notable exceptions. This fits with theories already discussed linking younger age with a more adventurous and physically demanding lifestyle. Freelancers were not more likely to develop PTSD or show more prominent symptoms of the disorder. Though they travel to more inhospitable and dangerous places, this exposure does not translate into more nightmares, flashbacks, startle responses, and the like. One reason may be that the degree of violence confronted by all war journalists, whether they are freelance or not, is so extreme that teasing out various gradations of PTSD response is not possible. Another possibility is that freelancers, as a self-selected group of individuals, have an innate ability to better withstand the adverse effects of overwhelming violence. This is not to say they are immune to syndromes like PTSD but that, relatively speaking, their greater exposure to life-threatening events does not generate more severe or frequent symptoms.

There are, however, two areas where freelance journalists were found to function more poorly than staff journalists. On the General Health Questionnaire, which is a composite measure of psychological distress, they endorsed significantly more symptoms of depression and social dysfunction. The simplest explanation for this is that financial worries, anxieties over selling work, inadequate or absent life insurance, sleeping on floors, bumming lifts, scrounging satellite phones — in short, all the impediments of a stand-alone existence — exert their own toll. Freelance journalists chose this route from conviction. Principles can, however, prove costly, as these data show.

Even in death, their position as loners, operating outside established and conventional channels, can be exploited. An ignominious sequel to Roddy Scott's ending makes the point. While colleagues in London sought to counteract the tenet of the *Times* obituary, away in the Caucasus, controversy of a more ominous nature surfaced, this one also fueled by a journalist's steadfast determination to pursue a story he considered important. The director of the secret service in Ingushetia refused permission for Mr. Scott to be buried in the region. The authorities considered him a terrorist. The British Embassy was not planning to send a representative, citing security fears. Five weeks after his death, Scott's body still lay in a morgue outside the city of Nazran, denied the dignity of a decent burial. For those close to Scott, the pain of knowing the violent manner in which he lost his life had not given way to quiet grief or calm reflection. Courageous reporting may win plaudits, but it also makes for powerful enemies. The vulnerability of the freelance journalist was once again laid bare. Stripped by injury or death of a formidable self-reliance, there is little buffer against slander, imputation, and the humiliation of having malevolent apparatchiks deny them a final resting place.

Thus far I have confined my comments to freelance journalists who travel to zones of conflict on foreign soil. One thing they have in common with journalists employed by the large news networks is the opportunity to leave war behind and return home for rest. In my conversations with freelancers, it emerged that the average length of time spent in a war zone was approximately two months. At that point, the journalist's body and mind begin emitting unmistakable signs that a rest is needed. Fatigue, insomnia, irritability, and edginess take over, or it may be some vague foreboding, often nothing more tangible than a sense of having tempted fate once too often. Jon Jones described this moment as follows: "I remember waking up in the morning — I had been in Sarajevo for fourteen weeks — and thinking, I've got to go. And within ten minutes I set off in a car. I drove from Sarajevo to Vienna without a break. I got on a plane in Vienna and went home. There was this very strong intuitive feeling I had to go. The trick is to be able to do it and not regret anything you missed during the day. You need to recognize this feeling and not be bothered by the macho kind of bullshit that says, 'Well, I stayed longer than you' and all that crap. The seriously good people will just say, 'I'm going home,' and not care what anyone thinks." Sometimes it was a particular event that made Jones or one of his colleagues reach for the return ticket. "We were driving through the streets of Sarajevo. We stopped and a tank fired at us and blew the door off the car I was in. It was slightly open. Blew it off its hinges. So I thought, oh God, there's a message in this. It was time to leave. Because your time is up. You go with a big bucket of luck and the longer you stay, the more it drips out."

I never interviewed a war journalist who had not taken a break at some point and returned home for a brief period. As disconnected as many journalists often feel back in London or Madrid, a reprieve from snipers, ambushes, and ubiquitous death can settle frazzled nerves and calm the spirit. No such respite, however, is possible for those journalists who live in the zones of conflict. Occasionally, they will be hired as stringers by western news organizations. More often than not, the protracted brutality of what is most frequently a civil war rapidly outdistances the limited attention span of the news networks and their viewers. Yet, for the journalists living in these regions, the war is not forgotten. How can it be when the conflict defines their daily existence? So the task falls to them and a tiny group of freelance journalists like Roddy Scott to bring news of war to those living through it, and perhaps, with the foresight of an enlightened editor, to those in more distant affluent lands as well.

From a research perspective, a second question now presents itself. How do journalists trapped by war within their own society, and with no chance of respite, fare psychologically? Is the depression and social dysfunction exhibited by freelance journalists magnified by circumstances that hold local journalists captive? Unfortunately, this was not a question my data could answer, because there were no local stringers in my sample of 140 war journalists. An inability to attract funding had prevented me from carrying out such a study. But I was able to witness, in a less formal way, some of the many adversities confronted by two local journalists working independently in the third world. I have no empirical data from which to draw conclusions; my interactions with these two journalists were fundamentally different from those I had with the freelancers and involved intense, daily contact, instead of questionnaires and interviews. We met for breakfast, lunch, and dinner. I met one journalist's wife and got to talk with their children and siblings. I visited their offices and spoke with colleagues. Rating scales, with their inbuilt cultural and linguistic biases, would not have been appropriate in this setting. Anecdote and personal observation, therefore, inform my opinion.

In 2001, I took part in a panel discussion in Washington, D.C., with John Owen of the Freedom Forum, Chris Cramer and Mike Hanna of CNN, and Donatella Lorch of *Time*. The topic was journalists and safety. When we came to the question and answer segment, a middle-aged African man rose from his seat in the darkened auditorium and introduced himself: "Bart Kakooza, Media Plus, Uganda." He blinked into the lights, paused to collect himself, and cleared his throat. " 'Why is it, doctor," he began, directing his question to me, "that I cannot eat meat? It has been that way ever since I returned from Rwanda. I don't have a problem with other food, but when it comes to meat . . ." His question tailed off. He shrugged his shoulders and gave an awkward laugh. "I have this problem with meat."

It was one of those moments during public speaking that I have always disliked. Self-revelatory questions such as these are difficult because they divulge only part of the information required to formulate a sensible answer. The questioner, meanwhile, stands expectantly in front of hundreds of people whose attention has suddenly been seized by the dramatic disclosure. They too expect an answer. If that is not challenge enough, you have at most only a couple minutes in which to reply coherently.

My solution, when faced with such odds, has always been to acknowledge the distress implicit in the question, provide a brief, generic statement alluding to the complex nature of such phenomena, and invite the questioner to come up to me after the symposium and discuss the matter further, and in private. Which is what I did in this case. Three weeks later, I found myself on a plane to Kampala. Bart Kakooza's question, which had so riveted the audience's attention, had moved Tom Johnson, then chairman and CEO of CNN, to underwrite the cost of sending me to Uganda to come up with a treatment plan.

There was confusion on the ground at the Entebbe terminal. It was late evening and the staff was tired. Some travelers had visas, others did not and were shunted off to one side. A few tourists suddenly became aware that a vaccination against yellow fever was required. They stood anxiously in the line for passport control, whispering, wondering if they would be allowed into the country. I produced my vaccination record. The customs officer ignored it and waved me through. Bart Kakooza was not waiting for me. He had been called away to cover a story in the Sudan, and instead sent his

brother, Deus Akambikira, along with a colleague with the unlikely name of
Henry Ford.

Ford hobbled on crutches. We made our way to their parked car, and I
settled in for the ride into Kampala. It was dark, and I could make out little
of the surrounding countryside, for there were no streetlights. We ex-
changed pleasantries about my flight, and I asked Ford about his leg. I had
not noticed a cast and assumed the injury was slight: a twisted ankle, perhaps, or a bruised knee. But I was wrong. Ford began his tale of woe, a story
unlike any other I have heard. It would unfold over the course of the week I
was to spend in the verdant hills of Kampala and involved not only Ford but
also his wife, children, father, and Bart Kakooza, the man whose phobia had
precipitated my trip.

Under the murderous regimes of Milton Obote and Idi Amin, Bart
Kakooza's and Henry Ford's lifelines to a civil society had been severed. For
almost two decades, they could not step out of the fighting, take a breather,
or replenish emotional resources. They woke up to war outside their window, spent their days with war as their companion, and went to bed with
war lurking in the shadows. They did this each day without respite — for
war allows no weekend breaks — and the days became weeks, months, and
then years. And through it all, they had not only jobs to do and livings to
make but also families to care for and children to raise, nourish, and keep
safe. Such an existence taxes the hardiest of spirits. War brings not only
death and disfigurement but also shortages of food, the collapse of medical
services, and the disruption of transport, electricity, water, and sanitation. It
also blankets the traumatized civilians of a once civil society with a paralyz-
ing ennui. For journalists like Kakooza and Ford, their work environment
was also their home environment, and this blurring of margins, common to
all local freelance war journalists, added an even more ominous dimension
to the perils faced. Not surprisingly, the adverse consequences of such an
existence, both emotional and physical, can be catastrophic.

From the moment I met Ford hobbling along at Entebbe, I was aware of
his need to talk and tell me his story. He began en route from the airport
into Kampala, even though the hour was late. The following morning I
found him waiting for me. The hotel I was staying in was built by the
Yugoslav government during the cold war and later used to billet Idi Amin's
thugs. The building, perched on a hill that dominated the landscape, had
recently been resurrected as a Sheraton, and from the windowed dining
room I could look down, between gently swaying fronds of Royal Cuban

pine, on Kampala's urban sprawl. There, on a beautifully clear July morning, Ford told me the circumstances of his injury.

In the morning, before I took my children to school I told my wife that I was going to the west of the country. Some rebel soldiers had been captured, with their tattered clothing and stained teeth, and I interviewed them. That evening, around ten p.m., I was driven from the army headquarters to a local town. We were told the area had been secured, so I was not expecting trouble. I was sitting in the front seat of an army jeep when suddenly a man appeared out of the dark, pulled open the door, pushed me out and just shot me at close range. I was shot in the stomach and the hip. One of the bullets passed through my hip — it almost took off the neck of the femur — hit part of the pelvis, and became embedded in the right buttock.

I never lost consciousness and lay on the road for about twenty minutes. I only realized my leg was broken when I tried to sit up and the discomfort started. When I touched my trousers, they were all soaked in blood, and I could feel some hot stream. Soon our soldiers arrived because they had heard the shots, and I started crying out and saying who I was. "I'm a native reporter, please don't kill me, leave me alone. I'm not a soldier. Don't kill me." The soldiers recognized me, picked me up, put me in their Jeep, and that was when the real pain started.

I was taken into the hospital's examination room at one-thirty a.m. The two doctors on duty were friends of mine, one a family friend and the other went to university with me. The hospital, which serves the whole country, had only one theater in operation at the time. My operation took five hours. I would end up having five further operations and staying in hospital for five months. One of the bullets had ruptured the rectum, and I needed a colostomy. Rupturing the rectum caused an infection in part of the shattered femur, an osteomyelitis, and the bone would not heal and the whole series of operations was designed to remove parts of the infected bone. Eventually the surgeon explained that the head of the femur was getting very little blood and that he was going to cut out this bit. And I asked, "What do I remain with?" and he said, "You remain with a leg without a bone." Of course I believed that could not happen, a limb that is supported only by the flesh. And all this came about because the hospital ward is supposed to accommodate twenty patients but had 150 at that time.

Uganda had only recently returned from the abyss, and the scars are not just to be found in what Ford told me. Kampala, "the hill of antelopes," is a beautiful city, but the crumbling infrastructure presents hurdles for the disabled. Throughout the day Ford chaperoned me, hopping around on his one good leg, his crutches getting in the way of everything, slowing him down, tripping me up. Every little task was an effort—his infernal sticks interfering with the steering wheel, under the feet of waiters and porters, clattering on the marble floors of the hotel as they slid from the side of his chair, their worn padding and chipped wood attesting to their constant use. Without them, Ford would be useless: reduced to immobility and unable to leave his house. But I could see that this lifeline to the world was also tormenting him. The most basic of activities had become laborious. Getting in and out of a car required a new dexterity, polished steps were a source of anxiety, narrow doorways and passageways a constant challenge. Kampala's uneven pavements were an obstacle course that had to be carefully, deftly negotiated lest he place his stick in one of the many sidewalk potholes, risking a fall and a whole new set of medical complications.

Ford's outward demeanor was cheerful, even buoyant, at odds with the dark and morbid content of his thoughts. Those spilled out incessantly, an accumulation of eighteen months of hellish misery that he laid bare before the doctor visiting from the comfort of life in the first world. Ford wasted little time introducing this theme, and he alluded to it often, weaving it into his tale as a way of underscoring his plight: the wealth of Canada versus the poverty of Uganda, the technical expertise of the developed nations versus the bumbling incompetence of the third world ("there is always bread on the table in the first world"), the difficulty of earning money as a freelance journalist in the third world ("not like in the developed nations"). The variations were unsettling, which, whether unconsciously or with premeditation, was the desired effect. In Kakooza's absence, Ford was using every moment of the day to obliquely solicit my help in his recovery, except he did not come out and state this clearly, preferring a circuitous route, one that embraced harrowing anecdote with physical observation. I could not fault him. A confluence of circumstances had presented him with the briefest window of opportunity, one chance to be healed and get back his dignity and self-respect. Perhaps it was pride that prevented him from asking directly for help, or perhaps this elaborate pirouetting was culturally mediated. It mattered not. I was deeply moved by his plight. The discomfort I felt stemmed from compassion coupled with a sense of powerlessness. I am a researcher, not a tycoon. I did not have the means to fund this man's medical care, which would entail a visit to South Africa for surgery and a lengthy hospital stay in a private clinic. The best I could do was to bring Ford's story to the attention of the few individuals who fund my research. Where that would lead was difficult to say.

The irony of Ford's situation was that his life was falling apart at exactly the point when Uganda was beginning to rebuild. He had lost half a femur, and his one leg hung limp and useless, the muscles shortening by the month. He had no insurance, he could not earn a decent living, he had a wife and three young children to support, a mortgage, school fees, amenities, and rates and taxes to pay. He could not run and play with his kids, he could not pick them up, he could not bathe them as he did before, he could not tend to his house, he could not live a decent, fulfilling life. The pressure of it all was suffocating him with worry and guilt, and he was trapped, helpless, and powerless to do anything because there was no money. He was forty years old. What did the future hold for him? What would become of his family? All around him, people, colleagues, family friends were getting ahead. There were opportunities to be had, but they were passing him by because in Uganda, opportunity does not knock for a cripple. And a cripple was what he had become — that bitter word surfacing time and again in his speech — someone who was useless, who had let his family down, who could not provide, who was a burden, a source of worry rather than support, a useless appendage like that flail limb that had come to define in his mind who he really was.

Ford wanted to take me to the National Museum. There was a lull in his story as we went looking for the admission office. The doors to the museum stood ajar. There was no one about and the large, cavernous entrance was devoid of people and furnishings. There was no ticket office, no gift shop, no excited queues of schoolchildren milling about. We wandered in. The exhibition halls were deserted. Everything echoed: our voices, the squelch of my shoes, the clickity-clack of Ford's crutches. We moved along to some dusty display cases; the typed labels behind the glass were yellowing with age, their corners upturned in places. I wondered how much had changed since colonial times, whether the displays I viewed predated independence, which came in 1962. A melancholic air hung over the deserted museum. This was not the place to view the beauty, richness, and diversity of Ugandan culture. I reminded myself that this country — in Churchill's view the pearl of Africa — had only recently emerged from a protracted civil war. The university, the museum — these were the institutions that suffered as the military grew fat.

As we got ready to leave, I came across a gap in the drywall and stepped through into a junk-filled room. Standing in the center was a dusty Model T Ford. The sight of the vehicle led Ford to divulge the origin of his name. Family lore had it that Ford's father was born in a Model T, and local custom dictated that propitious events surrounding a birth be incorporated into a person's name. The name was passed on to the next generation, but Ford had three daughters and no sons, spelling the end of the patronymic.

We made our way back to the hotel and sat in a garden, shaded by giant palms. The lawn was immaculately clipped, and where it ended, rich soil peeked through beneath the luscious foliage and purple-pink bougainvillea. The temperature was a perfect and unyielding 75 degrees Fahrenheit, the breeze warm and without trace of humidity. I remarked to Ford that in Uganda, God had his finger on the thermostat, and he smiled gently and said it was good that way, because in the past the finger may have been on the trigger. I winced at this reply and fell silent. Ford's eyes were not open to the beauty surrounding him, or if they were, now was not the time for superficial chit-chat. Personal matters were more pressing. He confided that he was worried about his family, particularly his middle daughter.

> It was the two eldest children, whose ages are thirteen and nine years, who were most affected by my shooting, particularly Tina, the second one. In fact, when I came home from hospital, she would bring me my shoes, always ask me if I wanted something. She could not do enough for me, and when she went off to school, you could see she was not happy about it. While I was in hospital, she wrote a letter: "Dear Daddy, we are praying so much that you will recover. I also pray that the people who wanted to shoot you also be punished." My daughter now cannot write a sentence without spelling words in a strange way, and before my shooting she was an A student. And looking back, I remember that when I came out of hospital, this same girl had developed stuttering speech. She could not speak well. It was only after a month or two that she started stabilizing her speech.

Listening to Ford's account of Tina's difficulties, I recognized similarities between her symptoms and those of the war journalist who presented at my hospital with a quasi-stroke. The child too had a conversion disorder, her emotional distress finding an outlet in symptoms that resembled neurological dysfunction. What differentiated her from the war journalist was not just her age but also the fact that the stresses she endured were not directly life-threatening. It was her father's narrow escape from death and the resultant family upheaval that became the basis for her anguish, the stammer and jumbled spelling the conduit for her suppressed fears.

My heart went out to this man. Not only did he struggle daily with a useless leg, but the burden was magnified by gnawing guilt — his daughter's failure at school a constant reminder of how he had let his family down. "My children are only in their teens, why should they suffer?" he asked with quiet desperation. "My father did not make me suffer. My children are now suffering because of me. I'm crippled. I cannot walk. I cannot move to places because I am on crutches. I'm supposed to be their provider, their protector. I'm supposed to be their everything. I go to visit them at school and colleagues look at me as a cripple. So why should I keep looking like this?"

The last sentence was a direct challenge. But to whom? Me, the doctor from wealthy Canada? His profession, which had deserted him? A health care system that failed him? The answer was probably a combination of all these. Ford reminded me of a modern day Ahab, but unlike the angry mariner, his bitterness was focused not on extracting revenge, but on a fate that had abandoned him. "One of the problems we have in the third world countries," he railed, "is that there exists a very big gap between us and our counterparts, our colleagues in the developed world." He was right, of course, and this was the gist of the matter — his misfortune had been to get seriously wounded while working in a profession that makes little money, in a third world country that lacked the necessary medical expertise to restore his leg.

The shadows lengthened across the lawn. Ford reached for his sticks and hopped onto his good leg. He told me he would like me to meet his family and offer an opinion on his daughter. Could we get together that evening? He would call for me in an hour. I returned to my hotel room. I had been in the country less than twenty-four hours and felt weighed down by what I had seen and heard. While the empty, echoing halls of the National Museum dampened my spirits, it was Ford's relentless intensity that proved the biggest challenge. He had become my shadow, and his predicament was painful to observe. For Ford, there remained a single, last hope. Me. And my discomfort stemmed from the knowledge that I might not be able to help him. I rehearsed disabusing him of the notion that my arrival in the country guaranteed his salvation.

But the speech I had prepared had to wait when I saw Ford and two of his daughters in the foyer. They were the most delightful children, pretty, lively, inquisitive, beautifully turned out in their school uniforms. We made our way downtown to the Grand Imperial Hotel, where Ford's wife would join us shortly. Twilight is brief on the equator, and the darkened streets of Kampala had emptied by the time we arrived at the old colonial hotel. It was a gloomy place, although there were clues from the faded decor and grand lounge that it had not always been that way. I followed Ford down a dank corridor that led to an outdoor swimming pool surrounded on all sides by tiered hotel rooms. The area was deserted, save for a small group drinking off in a corner and a band of musicians who had their amplifiers turned up, the sound reverberating in the emptiness. There was an over-powering smell of chlorine.

It was too noisy to talk there, so we moved to the balcony, where we were soon joined by Charity, Ford's wife. Immediately the couple started discussing Tina, their middle daughter, who sat opposite me. They talked as though she was not present. They were concerned about her school performance because she had to repeat a year. They were upset by her "stupidity," and complained that shouting at her had not made one bit of difference. They were at their wits' end. What could be wrong with the child? She was never like this a few years back.

I was startled by Henry and Charity's attitude. I had assumed they understood that Tina had been traumatized by Ford's shooting. And then I realized that they had made a connection between the shooting and subsequent emotional distress but that the origins of their daughter's stuttering had been imperfectly understood. I interrupted the parents and turned my attention to Tina. She had been sitting at her father's side, impassive, seemingly inured to her parents harangue, but she livened up immediately and asked about my children, and laughed when I told her about the height of the snow in the Canadian winter. Her older sister, Lena, joined in, and we made easy small talk about school and singing in the choir and what they did for fun on weekends. There was no sign of stuttering in Tina's speech, and she came across as a lovely, bright, articulate child. I asked the sisters what they would like to be when they grew up, and Lena answered un-hesitatingly, "a lawyer." Her parents laughed. "And Tina, what do you want to be?" She hesitated and then quietly replied, "a nurse." "And why a nurse, Tina?" "So that I can care for people and help them get better." Ford was incredulous: "A nurse! You never told us, Tina! A nurse!"

I asked the children to run off and play in the lounge and then explained to Henry and Charity the principles underlying conversion disorder. They gaped. "It could not be," said Ford. I assured him that it could, and quoted the example of the female war journalist. The scales fell from their eyes. I urged them to stop the criticisms of their daughter. Of course, of course, they agreed. They looked crestfallen.

Later that evening, Bart Kakooza arrived at the hotel, straight from the Sudan. Covered in a reddish dust, buoyant and vigorous, he apologized profusely for not meeting me at Entebbe. His obvious physical vitality and high spirits were the counterpoint to Ford's labored hops, shuffles, and morbid preoccupations. The roles could so easily have been reversed. In my many interviews, I had come across similar cases of journalists simply being in the wrong place at the wrong time with serious, often catastrophic consequences. But never had the contrast between survivor and victim been so starkly illustrated than with these two friends. And the differences were heightened, given an added emotional valence, by the environment in which they lived and worked. Nowhere were the hazards of being a freelance journalist more cruelly exposed than in the third world, where no amount of scenic beauty or warmth and hospitality could camouflage the fact that a bullet through the hip spelled doom.

But I was in Uganda to answer Kakooza's dramatic question about his inability to eat meat. A plausible explanation had readily presented itself: bearing witness to the murder of men, women, and children, most of whom were hacked to death with machetes, is likely to unsettle the hardiest of appetites. Meeting with Kakooza and noting the details of what he experienced and filmed in Rwanda partially confirmed my original hypothesis. But I also learned how inadequate my imagination had proved in assembling the collective weight of his war experience.

"I will show you a video of what was happening," Kakooza told me. "I had a camera with a long zoom, so I could see what was actually happening. I witnessed the people being hacked. At one time we went to a place where the rebels had thrown a grenade inside the house and about twenty people had died in the attack and it was very fresh, happening maybe thirty or forty minutes before. Others were still alive and the place was littered with pieces of human flesh."

Kakooza had also reported on events in the Congo, where a civil war had ignited in 1998. "On one occasion there was a firefight going on and I looked up to see a soldier surrendering," he recalled. "He had put his hands up and then down again as he approached us. And then I could see why he had put his hands down because he was holding his intestines in his hands and it was terrible. I begged the rebels not to shoot him, and we could see that the bullet had gone right through him. They put him on a truck and took him away. He was still alive but I think he must have died later on."

While we talked, Kakooza and I walked along the banks of Lake Victoria while his young son Clive played off to the side. It was a bucolic Sunday. Out on the lake, fishermen cast nets from their dhows. Kampala society had flocked to the waterfront and nearby equestrian center, and my gloomy impressions of the past few days gave way before the abundant signs of a society transforming itself. But shadows from the past were everywhere. I noticed small groups of Asians, returnees of a once vibrant culture summarily expelled by Idi Amin in the 1970s. Amin himself had had a house close by, and in the bountiful waters of the lake, carp grew to enormous proportions feeding off the corpses dumped by his henchmen.

I shifted my focus back to what Kakooza was telling me, for it was Rwanda's recent history that was so troubling to him. "I saw a lot of flesh in Rwanda," he told me.

> A lot of dead people. Every time I would go to eat meat, I would look at the piece of meat and imagine the stench of some of the rotting bodies. And that would affect me. There were so many pieces of human meat rotting, it really worked on me. I gradually found I could not eat meat any more. When I look at it, it gives me bad ideas. I've tried to brush it out of my mind, but it comes back and my thoughts say, "Look here. You remember that human flesh you saw rotting? It looked like this." Recently I was in the eastern part of the Congo, where two tribes were clashing over a little matter and more than five hundred people were killed, just like that, in cold blood. The violence terrified me. You see somebody's kidneys hanging out and they are rotting, and then you go back and they bring you liver in a restaurant. I can't eat it, so you see how it has affected me.

As troubling as the symptoms were for Kakooza, his difficulties were circumscribed, the phobia well demarcated and exerting little effect on his ability to function as a journalist. It had not spilled over into a more pervasive and generalized anxiety. He was a resourceful man who had simply modified his diet to exclude meat. There were, however, circumstances he could not control, and it was during those moments that his distress, quiescent beneath a regimented lifestyle, reared up and challenged him. On his trip through the Sudan, for example, hungry after days of eating very little, he arrived at a village, where a meal was prepared for him. The villagers were poor, but whatever food they had was shared in homage and welcome. In this case, it was meat. This presented an exquisite dilemma for Kakooza, his phobia at odds with his sense of propriety and his reluctance to offend his hosts. On this occasion, he fought his nausea and ate, but there were other times when he was not so strong.

Kakooza wanted to show me some of his archival material. He had filmed a lot of death in Africa. The offices of Media Plus Limited were housed in the basement of the Nile International Conference Centre, and we gathered there the following morning, Ford in tow. The two small, windowless offices were crowded, and people squeezed past one another as they came and went. In Kakooza's private office, the press of flesh was no less intense, and the close atmosphere was made worse by the loud and excited chatter. There were photographs on the wall, including a series of Kakooza with President Museveni. Henry Ford and Kakooza were talking at the same time, gesturing excitedly to one particular five by seven image pinned loosely to the wall. I moved closer, trying to make out the content. Soldiers were dumping bodies into a grave, or so it seemed. One of the corpses had been decapitated, and it was this headless figure that they wished me to see. The sight was gruesome, the severed head hung by a tether of dark red flesh from the torso. I was startled as much by the image as by its place of prominence. Why would a man with Kakooza's phobia display an image such as this? I looked up to see him smiling, and from that smile I learned yet another lesson from this trip to Uganda. Journalists like Kakooza had seen so much death and mutilation in the course of their work that they had to a large degree become inured to its horrors. I had occasionally come across this hard-boiled attitude when interviewing war journalists in London, but lacked an opportunity to observe it firsthand. "I don't feel emotion when confronted with loads of dead bodies," a television cameraman had confided to me. "I mean, it's just things that have happened . . . I've had years of watching people getting blown to bits all over the place and you know, watching a few get shot in front of your eyes. I suppose the first time it's a bit of a shock. What's irritating, however, and it really freaks me out, are the responses of policemen in England, for example. They see one murder or one dead body and they just have to retire from stress, for the rest of their lives. [They] take an early pension. I think, 'It's just life really, isn't it?' I've dealt with that, although my ex-wife might say differently. She thinks I'm a basket case."

This habituation to unspeakable violence seems necessary if journalists are to function in war zones. Without this protective armor, it would be impossible to deflect the emotional fallout of witnessing such depraved behavior. Yet I was perplexed by an inconsistency. Phobics are, by definition, avoidant in their behavior. The claustrophobic avoids enclosed spaces, the agoraphobic open and public spaces, the arachnophobic spiders, and so on. But Kakooza, whose phobia derived directly from scenes of mutilation and dismemberment, displayed the very images he should have been avoiding.

The dividing line separating detachment from callousness is a fine one, and journalists must tread carefully. Exactly what Kakooza's motives were in immediately drawing my attention to the headless corpse were unclear, but I suspected it was a very direct way of challenging my emotional sensibilities and quickly engaging me in the nature of what he had seen and endured on the battlefields of East and Central Africa. I was also aware that no matter how composed his emotional detachment, the man's armor had been breached.

We left Kakooza's office and went into his editing room. Kakooza and Ford wanted me to view some video material from Rwanda, the Congo, and Sudan. A collection of friends, colleagues, and hangers-on were introduced, a chair was found for me center stage, in front of an array of television screens, and the first tape inserted. I was conscious of the others watching me, keenly observing my reactions to what I was about to see. The material was clearly not new to them. What was of greater interest was how the doctor from Canada would react. A picture came into view of viridescent green hills, heavily cultivated, steeply sloping and disappearing into the clouds. A road wound its way between the mountains, and in the distance two groups of people walked toward each other. The camera slowly zoomed in on the scene; the group made up of three or four women stopped, hesitant; the second group, comprising half a dozen men, kept moving toward them. They met. There appeared to be some conversation. Suddenly, the men raised their hands and started beating the women, who sank to their knees. The camera moved in. What initially appeared to be a beating became much, much worse. The men used machetes to hack at their victims. The frenzied activity was quickly over, and the men moved off in the direction from which the women came. A heap of bodies was left lying in the road.

No sound accompanied the film, for the women did not cry out. They did not try to run away or put up a fight. They died quietly, seemingly resigned to their fate, the one brief moment of hesitation on the road their only discernable sign of uncertainty and fear. The image shifted to a close-up of the massacre, showing gaping wounds, skin and muscle neatly cleaved down to the bone, and criss-crossed wounds on arms instinctively raised in self-protection. The partly severed heads and skulls were cracked open, and the bodies lay at ungainly angles, huddled together. The continuing absence of sound imparted a sense of unreality.

There was little chance to gather my thoughts or ask questions before we moved on to the next scene, a village that had just been visited by marauding rogue militia. If the massacre we'd watched was shocking, what awaited the viewer in the village beggared belief. At first glance, there was nothing unusual in the scene: a neatly tended village made up of numerous huts and a well-constructed building with the Red Cross sign denoting a medical clinic. But as the camera got closer, the bodies came into view, and they were everywhere, inside the huts, between the huts, in doorways, out on the paths, between the vegetation. Age was no protection, for some of the victims were a few months old. All bore the imprint of the machete: cleaved flesh and darkening, congealed blood. Children and babies lying in such grotesque, mutilated fashion was an overwhelming sight. I glanced up and saw Ford observing me intently. "You see, doc, you see what happens here?"

Some villagers survived and were gathered in the clinic. Their wounds were terrible: limbs virtually severed and scalps split to the bone, bathed in blood. They had been numbed into silence. There was no crying, moaning, anger, or wailing in grief. Even the surviving children were cowed, shocked beyond vocalizing their distress or crying out in pain. They stared listlessly at the camera, their small bodies checkerboards of deep, painful wounds.

The film did not end with the massacre. Kakooza had teamed up with Laurent Kabila's forces as they moved through the jungles of the western Congo, routing the army of Mobutu Sese Seko. En route there was much killing and mutilation, and looting too, for the dictator Mobutu, the king of kleptomaniacs, had amassed wealth of staggering proportions. There were astounding scenes attesting to his decadence, nowhere more so than in his birthplace, Gbadolite, where to recognize the auspicious event of his own birth the leader built several opulent palaces modeled on great European and Asian dynasties. They stood on a series of hills surrounded by the squalor of his impoverished, bilked subjects, and featured vast rooms of marble; baths the size of swimming pools; sculpted gardens; extravagant fountains; giant kitchens staffed by French gourmet chefs; gadgetry to open windows, swivel the bed, draw the drapes, and close the shutters. Most remarkable of all, Kakooza told me of a life-size sculpture of the mother of the nation cradling the baby Mobutu. The figure had been forged from bronze — all except the penis, that is. For that, the leader demanded a metal more precious, no doubt feeling the family jewels deserved special acknowledgment. Gold sated the ego. Faced with such riches, Kabila's forces enthusiastically laid waste to the palaces, Mobutu's genitals an early target.

*  *  *

Compared to the myriad difficulties presented by Henry Ford, Bart Kakooza's problem was a relatively simple one. He had a phobic disorder of moderate severity that did not affect him unduly. Such a condition is amenable to behavior therapy, and I outlined for him the principles of graded exposure. He listened attentively and readily grasped what needed to be done. To aid him in his treatment, I promised to send him one of the self-help workbooks that can easily be found in most first world bookstores.

The session over, we left the building, descending a great expanse of stairs. A few yards away, perched on some overhanging masonry, was a vulture. What was this scavenger doing there? Kakooza told me that they were first attracted by the city's abattoirs. Then he stopped and pointed to a large, overgrown field in front of the Uganda International Conference Centre. Once again, he invoked the name of Idi Amin. As with Lake Victoria, the field had been a dumping ground for those killed. The vultures, like the carp, grew fat. In time, the killing stopped. But the vultures remained, adapting to life in the midst of a million living people.

*Addendum*: Financial contributions from the Rory Peck Trust and from Chris Cramer, managing director of CNN International, eventually made it possible for Henry Ford to visit Canada. Sunnybrook and Bridgepoint hospitals in Toronto, orthopedic surgeon Hans Kreder, Gaye Walsh, and Karen Redhill Feinstein donated their services, skills, and hospitality to assist Ford, who is now walking once more.

# 6

# War, Women, Wives, and Widows

\*　\*　\*

[War creates] a barrier of indescribable experience between men
and the women they loved. Quite early I realised the possibility of
a permanent impediment to understanding.

Vera Brittain

In October 2001, just before the start of the American bombing in Afghanistan, a female journalist from the *Express* newspaper in the United Kingdom donned a full burka, hired two local stringers, and slipped across the Pakistan border astride a donkey. Beneath the billowing folds of her disguise, she carried a camera and her notebook. Yvonne Ridley was intent on viewing militant Islamic fundamentalism at first hand. In this she succeeded, although the manner in which she came by her story was neither planned nor hardly imagined. Her undoing owed everything to the capriciousness of her donkey.

"I had been in Afghanistan for two days, undercover, and I was heading back to the Pakistan border about twenty minutes away, when the beast bolted," she told me during an interview at the BBC television studios in White City, London. "As I careened past some Taliban, my camera swung into view. When the soldier pulled me off the donkey and took my camera, everything just shut down. I went totally numb. I was without any emotion. And it was as if I was watching myself. It was quite weird. I felt as though I was observing the Taliban and this other woman who was me, and I could hear my own voice, in a disconnected way, talking to them and explaining I was English, not American. I dipped in and out of that type of feeling over the course of the ten days I was in captivity."

What Ridley described to me is, in psychiatric parlance, an account of dissociation, a splitting off of part of a person's mental faculties as a response to significant stress. Taken to its most florid manifestation, dissociation can cause an individual to have a complete out-of-body experience, in

115

which she looks down on herself as a physically discrete, separate person. Lesser variants are, however, more common. When the Taliban defrocked Yvonne Ridley, she experienced one such symptom. Called depersonalization, it refers to the sensation of being cut off from an aspect of oneself, be it voice, actions, or parts of the body.

In Ridley's case, her dissociative experiences would wax and wane over the course of her ten-day ordeal. She recalled that during the drive to a holding cell in Jalalabad:

> They suddenly stopped the car and the soldier got out and placed me on this raised piece of ground. So I am standing there and the burka is off and these men started gathering around, staring at me, getting closer and closer and I just thought I was about to be stoned. They say your life flashes by when you're going to die, but all I could think of was, "I hope that when they start stoning me, the first one knocks me out. What sort of pain am I going to feel? Will my mom and dad ever find out? Will they have to identify my body? What state will my body be in? Will Daisy, my daughter, ever find out?" It's just a horrible way to die. And I am looking at these people getting closer and closer, and I can't even beg for mercy because that's just going to make everything worse. This is a barbaric regime. So I just stood there and the Taliban soldier flagged down a car. He was looking for a woman to search me. I was so relieved I was not going to be stoned, but this quickly gave way to anger that these bastards had terrified the life out of me. So I turned around and went to rip my dress as if to say, "I'm not carrying anything." I had trousers on and lifted up my dress and the men just went, "Aaagh!" and started running in the other direction. Everything suddenly spun from high drama to high farce.

From Jalalabad, Ridley was transferred to a prison in Kabul. Her labile behavior persisted as she swung between quiet periods of obedience and episodes of uncontrollable rage and frustration. Her one constant companion was fear.

> I would have repeated episodes where I would do something and say something and I'm thinking, "Where the hell is this coming from?" One day when I was up in Kabul prison, the Taliban came to see me and said, "We're going to ask you some more questions." I was in the courtyard at this point and I just said, "I'm finished with questions. I'm not going to answer any more of your questions. Just go away." They said, "We are very concerned. You're not eating, you're our guest, you're like a sister." I just exploded and I

said, "I'm not your sister, I don't have any brothers, and if I had brothers like you I'd disown them." And I also said, "I'm not your guest, I can't walk out of here. You've locked me in this horrible prison. You know you judge civilization by the quality of its prisons. Well let me tell you, you people are primitive." And I ended the conversation by saying, "Now get out of my sight," and I went and spat at them and walked back into my cell. And I was trembling like a leaf, really shaking, and the Christian Aid workers who were there said, "Yvonne, you were very robust." And I said, "I've gone too far and I'm very, very scared." I was standing there just trembling. I think it was the first time I'd actually trembled and my mouth had gone very dry, I remember that. One female came in and translated for me. She said, "You are going to be flogged because you cannot speak to high people like that." Again, I just seemed to be out of my body, watching me. I just couldn't believe the crap that I came out with. I just said, "Well, if I am flogged and I feel pain, then I will know that I am still alive." And I'm thinking, where is this shit coming from?

Ridley's story is truly remarkable. A foreign woman journalist crossed the hostile border of a fundamentalist Islamic state that treated her gender harshly. She had no documentation, was in disguise, and war between her country and this state was imminent. Soon, she was captured, but rather than show contrition, she verbally insulted her captors and spit in the faces of those who would decide her fate. History is littered with the corpses of people who have done far less to irritate the sensitivities of totalitarian regimes. As our interview progressed, I tried to make sense of Ridley's inchoate behavior. Was this journalist courageous, feisty and spirited in standing up for herself, or did she demonstrate foolhardy arrogance, ignorance, and appalling insensitivity? What made her reactions to her Taliban captors so surprising to me was that Yvonne Ridley came across as a pleasant, open, and friendly woman in interview. There was a vulnerability to her, with none of the hard-edged arrogance she displayed while in captivity. Indeed, Ridley herself was stunned by her behavior and genuinely perplexed by her inability to control it. Such was her fear at times that any conscious resolve was swamped by emotion, rendering her actions erratic and potentially self-injurious. This intermittently fevered state of arousal triggered discrete dissociative episodes, alarming because of their foreign, dysphoric, and disconnected quality. "I just seemed to be out of my body, watching myself. Where was this shit coming from?" asked Ridley incredulously. The answer is from dissociation induced by fear, anxiety, uncertainty, and helplessness. Her belated appreciation of the potentially adverse consequences of her actions further heightened her anxiety, thereby perpetuating, if not magnifying, her distress. More erratic behavior followed. This downward spiral, in which one negative emotion fed off another, ended only with her release a few days after the Americans began bombing Afghanistan.

Dissociative phenomena are not unusual following traumatic experiences. Other journalists reported them too, but unlike Yvonne Ridley's account, their episodes were nonrepetitive and brief. Furthermore, they occasionally manifested away from zones of conflict. My interview with Janine di Giovanni of the *Times* illustrates these points well. We met on a wet and chilly summer's day in a London office overlooking Hyde Park. Slanting sheets of rain smacked against the window, blurring the greenery outside, and sounds of traffic drifted up from the street below. At first, the conversation was dominated by events in Bosnia and her description of life under siege in Sarajevo. At one point in her narrative, she fell silent, took a sip from her coffee, and lay back on the settee, eyes closed. I waited silently for her thoughts to coalesce, avoiding the temptation to break the stillness with another question or observation. When di Giovanni resumed talking, she had switched continents and moved on to Africa and the civil war in Sierra Leone. Two months before our interview, not far from the capital, Freetown, in a nondescript section of bushveld known as Rogberri Junction, her colleagues Kurt Schork and Miguel Gil Moreno were ambushed and killed. She too had traveled that area.

> I had just gotten back from Sierra Leone, where I had been for a month. I had become used to seeing amputees. They are everywhere in that sad society, and they have this kind of freaky thing they do with the stumps of their severed limbs, waving them about. I had flown back to Paris, and the day after I arrived I found out that my friends had been killed. I was walking down this street and had this weird hallucination, which I have never had before. It was a very crowded street, and all these people coming towards me were amputees. I had to tell myself, Hold on, you're in Paris now, you're in Paris, it's fine. It's okay. And then, just as suddenly they were gone.

This transient, intense perceptual disturbance occurred with full insight, that is, an appreciation by the journalist that something was amiss. When reality briefly distorts, the experience is termed derealization. Di Giovanni's derealization and Ridley's depersonalization are both variants of dissociation that may occur in response to overwhelming, anxiety-provoking events. The fact that the first two cases I encountered among journalists were in women suggested, albeit tentatively, that male and female war journalists differed in the nature and extent of their psychopathology. This would not be unexpected, for a consistent medical finding in the general population is that women are twice as likely as men to report experiencing conditions such as post-traumatic stress disorder, major depression, and anxiety disorders. Possible reasons for this vary from differences in hormonal and biochemical makeup to a greater willingness on the part of females to discuss feelings and emotions.

With these facts in mind, I reanalyzed the data comparing the responses of the 110 male war journalists to their thirty female counterparts. The most immediate observation was the disparity in numbers. There were almost three male journalists for every one female. This contrast was most obvious in the area of stills photography, where only two photographers were female, and fifteen were male. It was, however, with respect to their psychological profiles that the results were most striking, for no differences were present on any measure of psychopathology. Female journalists were no more depressed, anxious, somatically preoccupied, socially dysfunctional, or suicidal than male journalists. Nor did they appear any more prone to the re-experiencing, avoidant, or arousal symptoms of PTSD. And although my data did not unearth further cases of dissociation, I did hear of other examples expressed by male journalists who were not part of my study. None was more dramatic and evocative than the account given by the BBC's Anthony Massey, who had covered the Balkan wars. He related an episode during which, on a London street and in broad daylight, the building in front of him transformed into the facade of a Sarajevo hotel and slowly began disintegrating under bombardment. Like the visual perturbation that had unsettled Janine di Giovanni, the episode was very brief and insight was retained.

This failure to identify more psychological difficulties in females suggested a possible demographic divide between the genders, but here the results once again confounded expectations. The average age of female war journalists (thirty-nine years) matched that of the males, and both groups had been working in zones of conflict for approximately fifteen years, so there was no evidence that females had reported fewer symptoms than expected because they had less exposure to danger and conflict. The one area in which there was a difference between the genders was the marital data: only 24 percent of the female journalists were married, compared with 52 percent of their male counterparts. Given that marriage is generally considered a protective factor in the development of psychopathology, this statistic could not explain my behavioral findings.

If married female war journalists are a minority, those with children are even more rare. Only three of the thirty women in my study were mothers, and each had only one child. Yvonne Ridley was one of these women. At one point in her interview with me, she began crying and seemed embarrassed by the display of emotion. "This is the first time I have wobbled when I have been out of the house," she confessed. The main source of her distress was not what had occurred in Afghanistan, but rather the criticism she faced from many of her peers on her return home. She was accused of both endangering the safety of her two local stringers and abrogating her responsibilities as the mother of an eleven-year-old daughter. The latter was particularly hurtful and resented, and it raises the question of whether the battlefields of war are uneven from a gender perspective. When aspersions are cast on the maternal competency of female war journalists while the many fathers, most with more than one child, are allowed to escape the same moral scrutiny, the charge of sexism becomes hard to refute. All the women I interviewed saw it as the perpetuation of a stereotype of the mother as the parent who is most responsible for the upbringing of a child. This leaves the dads free to go off to the office, which in this profession happens to be the caves of Tora Bora or the ruins of Kandahar. Female war journalists, in choosing voluntarily, willingly, hungrily to enter zones of conflict, shatter the stereotype of compliant domesticity. And yet, despite their fierce determination to succeed in the male-dominated domain of war, described to me by Maggie O'Kane as "boys in sleeveless jackets talking about incoming and outgoing" gunfire, most women chose assignments away from the front lines or gave up war journalism altogether when they had children. The exceptions, unlike among the men, are a very small minority.

For those few mothers working in far-off zones of conflict, weighing the risks of the job against their commitments as parents presented uncomfortable choices. How they resolved these competing agendas was a question I put to Maggie O'Kane, the mother of a young son, when we met on a blustery cold morning at a café in north London. She cited the conflict in East Timor, before the arrival of the Australian-led peacekeeping forces, as an example of the various forces that would inform her decision making. She said it was the behavior of the *Sunday Times* reporter Marie Colvin that she admired most, for Colvin had refused to join the mass evacuation during the Indonesian militia's reign of terror.

She stayed when it was really important. Everyone, including the United Nations, were preparing to abandon the East Timorese. The UN had done that before in Srebrenica, you know. And they were embarrassed by this one woman who was broadcasting relentlessly. "I'm surrounded by women and children. The younger children are crying. The militiamen are outside." That kind of stuff, you know. There were five hundred journalists hanging around in Darwin. All of them had cleared off too. Hundreds of journalists had cleared out because someone had a stone thrown at them, or got their leg broken, or got shot. The local people really needed us then. They had had a democratic election. They had put their faith in the UN, and their courage too. And these journalists had all fucked off, basically. So I ask myself, would I have stayed in East Timor if I'd been with Marie?

O'Kane grew silent, pondering her own challenge. She took a long swig from her early morning Coca-Cola before resuming, more hesitantly. "I think if I had been with Marie, I probably would have [stayed], because I would have taken my courage from her. And then I would have had this dilemma, you know. I'm a mother. What am I going to do? Maybe that thought would have made me want to leave. And then I would have looked around me and seen all the mothers with their children. The only thing that protected them was the press. I'm not being heroic about this, but I'd like somehow to be useful."

Personal courage aside, the reality is that gender does, on occasion, become an issue. For one thing, women are more vulnerable to sexual assault in war zones where civil society has crumbled and lawlessness often prevails. Genocides in Bosnia and Rwanda are just two recent examples of how, as part of organized terror, the female population was systematically and methodically brutalized.

I asked all the female journalists I interviewed how much of a threat sexual assault was. While all acknowledged it was a concern, only one had ever been directly threatened with rape. Many female war journalists also reported the converse, namely, instances of male combatants going out of their way to be protective. One photographer told me:

On a number of occasions some of the soldiers wouldn't let me go into a conflict zone. They were motivated out of a sense of protection. At times they actually held me back, physically, from going. And I refused to submit to this restriction. I think they just felt it was their duty as [men] within that society, particularly in Bosnia. They would just not allow women to go into situations that were potentially hazardous, be it sexually or physically. And while I could understand that, I could not agree with it. Women do not have a monopoly on reporting stories of civilian issues, casualties, struggles, nor do men have a monopoly on access to the combatants.

At times, when a woman was caught in a hazardous situation, the fear of a summary execution was so real that it superseded any concerns about rape. One female reporter told me of a harrowing episode that took place in Kosovo at the start of the bombing campaign.

I just wandered across the border and was picked up by Serb paramilitary. I was with two male French journalists and the soldiers marched us off into the woods and basically staged a mock execution. They kept us for about an hour and a half. They were drunk. And then they received some news, which we later found out was the capture of an American pilot, and they decided to let us go. I guess they did not need captives any more. Afterwards, the French cameramen said they were more afraid for me because they thought I was going to be raped. In truth, it had not crossed my mind. I thought they were going to kill us. A bullet in the back of the head. But not rape.

The risks are greater in Africa. In places like Sierra Leone, for example, where there are these young soldiers, children often, high on drugs. And then there is the aspect of a crowd-driven war. You are in a crowd, suddenly some incident happens, they go wild, and chaos happens very quickly. It is more savagely unpredictable. There is something very primitive about that type of reaction in Africa. I do think that Serb militia, as much as they might be brutal, would not even contemplate raping a journalist. Chechens would probably do it. [And] a bunch of African kids, stoned, what does the Geneva convention mean to them?

The one female journalist I interviewed who had been threatened with rape was on assignment in Africa, where she was taken hostage briefly by some rogue militia. Unlike her female colleagues who had never been exposed directly to such threats, this journalist did not have to draw on conjecture or her imagination when I asked for her views. Her ordeal took place when she had just completed an assignment in Southern Africa and was ready to return home.

There were seven guys waiting for me at the international airport. They knew I was leaving that day. They did not introduce themselves. They had guns and Motorola [phones]. They were quite young and they said, "You come with us." They just grabbed me and I said no. I started screaming at the top of my voice, and there was a Lufthansa crew there, you know, the stewards, and I shouted, "Somebody help me," because I knew something bad was going to happen, but nobody did. I was screaming my head off. I felt like a madwoman in this international airport, stewards not doing anything. The soldiers took me into this room downstairs and went through my bag, took my tapes and said, "You're an enemy of the people, you are a bad woman." They started to undress me and I thought I was going to be raped.

The timely intervention of a military attaché who had witnessed the abduction stopped the assault from going any further, but it had been a close call and left a lingering, troubling aftermath. "Even now, eight months later, when I see black men, they piss me off. I can't stand the smell of them. And I become fearful, because they have a certain smell, particularly in Africa, where it is so hot and humid. I was never this way before."

An episode like this was the exception, however. More common was the kind of bumbling, fumbling attempt described by Yvonne Ridley after her capture. En route to Jalalabad in a car, she was set upon by one of her guards. "This man, who was not Taliban, started touching me, groping me. I told him to stop and he didn't, so I winded him. A Taliban soldier in front had seen part of this, and he kicked the groper out the car."

At times, the threat came not from militiamen, combatants, or drunk soldiers but from a colleague, as one camerawoman recalled.

I generally work on my own, but on one of my trips to Pakistan and Afghanistan to get an interview with the one-eyed mullah Omar, leader of the Taliban, I needed the help of a local journalist. He worked for one of the main newspapers on the northern frontier that was published in English and Urdu. So we met up in Pakistan and went out for some food before going back to his office, where we shared a joint of hash. And while smoking, he asked me, "What is love like?" One minute we are talking about the Taliban and the next, "Tell me what love is like." And I said, "Well, why are you asking? You're married, you have kids, aren't you in love with your wife?" "No, she's my first cousin." I said, "You're an educated guy. Why did you marry your first cousin?" He said, "Tribal society. I had to." And then he pounced on me. He was a pretty big guy, [but] luckily I am fairly strong.

These accounts of narrow sexual escapes should not be misconstrued as evidence that female war journalists are under constant siege from predatory males. Even in civil society, sexual harassment is common across all social strata, sparing no profession or occupation. According to a University of Maryland study, 60 percent of the women accredited to the Capitol press gallery in Washington, D.C., reported that they had been sexually harassed. A different study of more than ten thousand female employees of the U.S. government revealed that in the workplace, one-third had experienced lewd sexual remarks, a quarter had been sexually touched, one in seven had been pressured for dates, one in ten had been pressed for sexual favors, and one hundred women had been sexually assaulted or raped. The surprising fact to emerge, therefore, from the interviews with the female war journalists is not that some had been propositioned, fondled, and sexually threatened, but that it occurred relatively infrequently. A plausible explanation for this may be the subjective nature of what constitutes sexual badgering. Conflict-hardened war journalists may have a different threshold than civil servants for perceiving danger, be it physical or sexual. At the same time, political correctness in war zones will never assume the Inquisition-like fervor it arouses in federal and corporate offices. What is also singular about the relative lack of perceived sexual threat reported by female war journalists is that it stands in marked contrast to the gross violations often perpetrated on the female civilian population in zones of conflict.

Still, the female journalists I interviewed were undeniably conscious of the dangers they face, even if they were reluctant to concede that their gender confers additional risk. While the infrequency of the assaults may assuage fears and embolden commitment, the psychological defenses used to shore up confidence are also not hard to detect. "If you are afraid of everything you wouldn't do it," Janine di Giovanni told me. "If you are going to analyze all these things, forget it. It's like jumping into a swimming pool. If you are going to think how cold it will be, you will never do it. You can't think too much."

My interviews showed that female war journalists have some unique characteristics. They differ from the general female population by remaining single into their late thirties and forties and showing a striking resilience to the emotional consequences of trauma. They generally refute the notion that they are particularly vulnerable to sexual assault, and they deny this potential hazard has ever been a deterrent to pursuing work in zones of conflict. Their propensity for high risk-taking appears similar to that of their male colleagues, which yet again flies in the face of gender data in general. They also hold that their behavior in zones of conflict, as women and mothers, should not be judged by a set of rules different from those applied to male journalists, especially those who are fathers.

My data did, however, reveal one area where women journalists may be uniquely vulnerable to psychological distress. In two of the three mothers that I interviewed, childbirth was the catalyst for the recrudescence of repressed traumatic memories. Before describing the details of the two cases, it is germane to point out that the criteria for post-traumatic stress disorder makes allowances for a delayed onset of symptoms. The phenomenology of the disorder remains the same, which means that some re-experiencing, avoidance, and physiological arousal symptoms must be present, but in this instance their onset is delayed by at least six months from the time of exposure to the trauma. The woman I interviewed in New York on a late winter's evening had a *forme fruste* (partial form) of PTSD, the presence of prominent re-experiencing symptoms accompanied by some autonomic disturbance (insomnia, irritability, hypervigilance) but without any avoidance features. What made her presentation unusual was the delayed onset of intrusive recollections, which did not begin until one year after she stopped work as a war journalist. Her career over the preceding decade had been stellar. Very much part of that inner sanctum of veteran, committed war journalists who regarded their work as a mission, she had, like all of them, come close to getting killed. Her response to a landmine incident demonstrated her psychological resilience to life-threatening events. "It was pretty bad," she recalled. "We were in an armored car, otherwise we would have been blown to bits, and I was in hospital several weeks. I had severe damage in both knees and ankles and this wound in the face. There was also some internal bleeding, but it absolutely did not dent my resolve or confidence." Such was her determination to witness events at first hand that her editor, while acknowledging the quality of her work, urged greater caution. Throughout an intense ten-year period in some of the world's most dangerous places, she never developed PTSD, depression, or enduring psychological distress. And when one day she realized, to her dismay, that a missed scoop had become more upsetting to her than the misery of the countless victims who made up the content of the story, she walked away from her profession.

After leaving conflict journalism, this woman could have been forgiven for thinking she had survived psychologically the horrors she had witnessed. After all, they had never bothered her while she was working, and with imminent dangers now largely behind her, she must have considered the probability of some delayed psychological reaction remote. She soon became pregnant and, two days after the birth of her child, everything changed. "I started having, and still have to a lesser degree, intrusive memories of very violent events," she confessed.

They just flash into my consciousness. People getting killed. They are very vivid recollections. Of course, after you give birth you realize that, in very simplistic terms, everyone that you ever photographed grieving over someone they lost loved their kid as much as you love your baby. Having a child promotes a higher degree of empathy with the things that we have been covering. So I'd have flashbacks that were extraordinarily vivid. I'll give you an example. One of them was an image of a woman in Bosnia crying over the grave of her second son. She had lost both her sons in the Bosnian war within months of each other. She was just crying inconsolably over the grave. These were the kinds of things that came to me. Later on I started to have intrusive thoughts and images of people doing something violent to my child. Because I've seen people being shot and murdered in front of me, and witnessed the aftermath of such outrages perpetrated on people of all ages, I often have these kinds of things flash into my mind.

This journalist offered a plausible psychological explanation for the delayed onset of PTSD-type symptoms. Becoming a parent and bonding intensely with her newborn awoke strong protective instincts. It also sensitized her to the grief of those who have lost children in conflict. To this may be added a different, but complementary, interpretation. While working as a war journalist, she may have dealt with emotionally painful events she had witnessed by successfully repressing them. The birth of her own child activated her unconscious, awakening images that were forgotten, but not quiescent. These psychodynamic theories should also be viewed in their proper biochemical and hormonal context, for the postpartum period is one of rapid and extensive physiological change. It may precipitate fluctuations in mood ranging from the common, transient, and minor postpartum "blues," to more serious and disabling episodes of depression or mania. Although in the journalist in question, it was not depression that appeared but one aspect of PTSD, the cause of the symptoms should nevertheless be considered similar.

A second case, with overlapping features, adds weight to these theories. Mixing fragments of autobiography with events witnessed as a war reporter, Maggie O'Kane recalled that "in all my years of foreign reporting, feeling the pop of a bullet beside my ear in Timor or lying under a tree trunk in Chechnya looking up at the iron belly of a Russian gunship, nothing compares to the terror of feeling someone is going to hurt your baby."

Her *Guardian* article "I Feel the Madness More" addresses head on the emotional interaction between her years as a war reporter and subsequent motherhood. "About a month after my son, Billy, was born I took a walk on London's Hampstead Heath," she wrote. "We were alone. Me, an ecstatic mother in my new camel hair Christmas coat and a small boy in an old-fashioned bouncy pram his grandmother had sent from Glasgow." It was then that O'Kane noticed a stranger emerge from the wood. "A man with his shoulders rounded up towards his ears," is how she remembers him.

He had a black V neck pullover. No shirt. He wasn't wearing a coat. He walked past us. He never looked up. I kept walking along the muddy path, never changing my pace, never turning my head to see where the man with no eyes was. I saw a bend ahead and turned it. I yanked Billy's pram behind a tree and watched the man in the black sweater. Through what was left of the winter leaves, I saw him stop. His head up now like a gun-dog scanning, turning, then creeping after us. Slow, deliberate, alert. I pulled Billy's pram tight. I heard a voice rasping in my head. I was rehearsing a primeval scream and a message for the man who was coming for my baby. My legs were weak. But I felt a dazzling strength in my body that was completely new to me. I knew that if he touched my child, I would rip his head off with my teeth. For the first time in my life, I understood real terror at being unable to protect my child.

The shabby stranger never attacked her. He approached to within ten feet and then mysteriously turned away. Was he a stalker? Was he planning on harming her newborn son? The reader is left unclear on these points. No such doubts for Maggie O'Kane. Her fevered account of events provides ample proof of her terror. What is significant about this story, however, is not so much the intent of the stranger, but rather her reaction to his odd behavior. The magnitude of her fear is crystallized by a juxtaposition of what occurred on the heath with the flood of memories culled from her decade as a war journalist. She describes a visit to Kosovo, in the wake of German NATO troops: "Suva Reka, about twenty miles from our base, was a small town on the road to somewhere else. But for Vjolica Berisha it was the place where she was born, grew up, married and became the mother of three children. In the burned-out shopping precinct past the Beni Tours travel shop, there is a coffee shop with blue barstools. Here she saw her children murdered. In my mind I still have a picture of a woman trying to hide her toddler son between her legs, then feeling the bullet thud into his body." O'Kane managed to find Vjolica Berisha and interview her in a sunny garden in Kosovo. Fifty-three people, mostly women and children from the Berisha family, had died in the attack on the coffee shop. Among the dead were Vjolica's sister Shyreta's four children. "Motherhood," writes O'Kane, "had changed the way I would look at war forever."

She gives another example of this new outlook, this time from Cambodia.

> In [the] S21 Prison, where the Pol Pot regime executed the higher cadres and their children, the condemned were photographed before execution. Staring out from the wall of the prison museum that still smelt of their blood was a young woman with her six-month-old baby stretched out on the metal bed beside her. She had number 320 pinned to her collar and she looked into the camera with what seemed like powerless acceptance of what was going to happen to her and her baby. Upstairs, somewhere in the dusty archives, were the folders of the condemned. I spent four days searching for something about her. It was an obsession. I was driven through file after dusty file, maddened by the look on her face and by her naked child beside her on the iron frame of the prison bed. I was trying to imagine her mind knowing that, in a day or two, someone would take her baby from her and smash his head open on the trees of the killing fields outside Phnom Penh. They never wasted bullets on children.

O'Kane is not yet finished picking at the raw scab of memory, for there is a third harrowing account of loss, one that unfolded in the leukemia ward of the Saddam Hussein Children's Hospital in Baghdad: "I felt the same madness. The figures of two parents stooped over their thirteen-year-old son who would die tomorrow. The drugs he needed were forbidden under sanctions. Imagine watching your child die because some politicians in France, Britain, and the U.S. can't think of a better way of getting rid of Saddam. I had sometimes felt anger in my previous trips to Baghdad, but after Billy it was different."

All these horrors have as a central theme parents mourning the loss of a child or children. Each one of these memories assumes an added poignancy for Maggie O'Kane following the birth of her son. Although she is conscious of not equating her narrow escape on Hampstead Heath with the grievous losses of war, she acknowledges that it took becoming a mother and a perceived threat to her own infant before she could begin to understand the depth of anguish she observed in those parents.

O'Kane was four weeks postpartum when she took that frightening walk on a winter's day in north London. Like her colleague, who within days of giving birth began experiencing violent intrusive memories, she had repressed emotionally troubling images from her time spent reporting war.

For both, childbirth was the key that involuntarily unlocked their unconscious. It did not deter Maggie O'Kane from returning to war, but she did so with a heightened sensitivity. Her meeting with Vjolica Berisha took place after the birth of Billy, and it was as a mother that she reacted to the magnitude of Vjolica's loss. "That is the image that haunts me most from 10 years in this job," she writes, "a mother clinging for those last seconds to the body of her two-year-old. The agony of watching your child die and not being able to protect it."

These two examples are reminders that, despite the unusual and distinct profile of female war journalists, there may be one area where their behavioral responses revert to the mean. For whether a woman is a librarian or a war journalist, her gender theoretically confers on her a heightened vulnerability to developing psychological symptoms in the days and weeks following childbirth. A final, very personal recollection from O'Kane's *Guardian* article once again illustrates the connection, although in this case it was her own miscarriage that provided the impetus for the return of traumatic memories. She had been pregnant while in Kosovo recording details of the Berisha family's tragedy: "It was a month later, on holiday in Italy, before I knew that the foetus was dead and had waited to miscarry. In the wonderful hospital near Florence, a fat cheerful gynecologist scanned my then flabby belly: "It's all gone," she said, congratulating me on the thorough job my body had done getting rid of the foetus. My husband, standing in the corner of the surgery with Billy in his arms, had tears in his eyes; I felt very little. I can't remember if it was at that moment, or during the long night that my body was rejecting the foetus, that I thought of Shyreta and her four dead children, of those final seconds when she held the body of the smallest one."

* * *

My investigation of female journalists and their experiences with childbirth led me to wonder how the partners of war journalists in general were faring emotionally. The few times I had met spouses or former spouses, they had hinted at a Pandora's box of fear, frustration, and discord. I therefore wanted to expand my study to include them, and I soon got the chance. CNN and the BBC were prepared to fund a new research protocol.

Using the 140 war journalists from the first study, I contacted a sample of partners scattered over three continents. They were given the study's Internet address and asked to fill out basic demographic data and complete the same questionnaires their partners had. By essentially replicating the original methodology, I would be able to undertake statistical comparisons between two groups. Sample size was set at thirty subjects, which represented approximately half the total number of married or cohabiting war journalists. The spousal group was predominantly female. This was anticipated, given that only seven of the journalists who were married or cohabiting were female.

The questionnaires showed that war journalists and their spouses had similar scores for depression and psychological distress, but not for PTSD. This was an important observation because the original study had already established elevated levels of psychopathology in war journalists. The new data extended this finding to their spouses and partners by demonstrating unequivocal signs of similar emotional difficulties, PTSD apart. In other words, evidence of increased psychological distress in the war journalists, be it depression, anxiety, social dysfunction, or various combinations of these signs and symptoms, was associated with depression in their partners. Association does not, however, equate with causality, so the data preclude establishing the direction of this relationship. Furthermore, the absence of detailed social data hinders etiological assumptions. It may well be that low mood in some spouses is secondary to the emotional dysfunction in their journalist partner, but until this question is directly addressed with a different methodology, such conclusions remain premature.

Informative as these initial results were, I wanted to get between the questions and flesh out more personal and detailed responses from spouses. What was it like to be married to someone who worked in such a hazardous profession? Did they ever adjust to their loved one jetting off, at short notice, into a war zone? What effects did their partner's peripatetic existence have on their relationship, social contacts, children? What had first attracted them to their partner? Did they know they were marrying a person by temperament wedded to risk taking? A blank text box was placed at the end of the questionnaires to record the spouses' responses.

Before giving details of the replies received, two cautionary points need emphasis. The first is that while male partners of war journalists completed the behavioral questionnaires, none supplied anecdotal accounts of what it was like to be married to a female war journalist. The second point is that only one-quarter of the female spouses and partners who completed the study used the text box for describing their feelings in greater detail. As such, the views expressed probably do not reflect a consensus opinion. It is quite possible there are wives and husbands who fully accept what their war journalist partners do and are not unduly distressed by the nature of their relationships. If so, I never heard from them. Similarly, none of the female respondents spontaneously praised an uxorious husband. The open-ended text box therefore may have selectively tapped into a wellspring of spousal frustration, hurt, and anxiety. The comments I received should be viewed with this limitation in mind.

All of the spouses who did use the text box wrote of difficulties in their relationships, and all but one expressed little enthusiasm for the profession of war journalism. In tones of anger, hostility, bitterness, and, for some, sadness and resignation, the replies were a litany of complaints directed against the partners. Replies ranged from the disillusioned ("I think the common answer to spouse or partner reaction might be divorce") to the cynical ("one of the constants in this game is that relationships tend not to last very long, which in turn means it's sometimes easier not to have them at all") to the apologetic ("I got a message from my husband about your research on how journalists who cover conflict zones deal psychologically with the stresses of the work and what effects it may have on their partners. I would like to help you, but I do not qualify anymore as we are getting divorced. My husband has a new partner and might be able to put you in touch with her"). No signs here of that almost transcendental buzz of excitement experienced by the journalists as they head off to yet another war. In their wake comes a house to run, kids to look after, perhaps a career on hold, a limited family budget to get by on, and the challenge of maintaining a veneer of domestic tranquility in the face of a constant undercurrent of anxiety and worry. Spouses spoke of the impossibility of planning social arrangements in advance, precipitous departures, the abdication of family responsibilities, the difficulties of staying in contact because of poor communication, and the struggles of children either bemused by a father's prolonged absences or overexcited on his return. "It is very difficult watching the pain of children whose birthdays and precious rites of passage have been ignored, forgotten, or overlooked," bemoaned one respondent.

Even the response from the one more upbeat spouse was tinged with a multiplicity of worries and a resigned sense that she had been relegated to a supporting role. She wrote, "Partners of war journalists must be independent, forgiving, mature, willing to sacrifice, feel that he or she is contributing to their spouse's ability to perform an important job, stable enough to be both the father and the mother when necessary, willing to take risks (even though we may not like it), accepting of people's differences and assets, non-egoistic (there isn't usually room for two huge egos in a long-term relationship), and feel respected by their spouse for the role they play." The sentence reads at first like a checklist of attributes that a partner of a war journalist must have in order to sustain the relationship. However, a closer inspection reveals that her last point is not something she can give. Inadvertently, she has interpolated one thing she asks in return: respect.

Notwithstanding these attributes, there's no guarantee her anxieties are kept at bay. She muses:

> I wonder how many spouses of war journalists you'll find out there? Most journalists cannot maintain a long-term relationship, for many reasons. I think I have been able to cope because I met my husband very young, was willing to sacrifice many things for our relationship to work, have a strong, stable family background, and am able to parent without a partner. You need all this to deal with the stress of "security" (money, insurance, savings, retirement, etc.). But the biggest issue for people like me is confidence in your spouse to make the correct and safe decisions—and also that your partner will remain sexually faithful. That seems to have been the breaking point for many couples that I know. Matter of fact, we are the only long-term couple still together that I personally know about (that is, where the spouse is not also a journalist).

Before signing off, she returns yet again to the issue of what she has given up for her husband. "Time away from home is one thing, but time spent when they are at home is another. My husband works almost constantly when he is here. The only down time we have is when we go off on a holiday. Even then he is still constantly being contacted for work. During our last family trip the agency wanted him to leave for Israel. This time he said no. I don't get angry about this kind of life. It is just the way it is. As for the children, they don't know any other kind of father and accept it. That basically is why I don't work—so that at least one parent is there for them."

As we saw earlier, many war journalists experience difficulties adjusting on their return home from a war zone. They're often left alienated by an ordered civil society replete with domestic chores and humdrum routine. The adverse effects of a difficult readjustment all too often spill over into relationships, and may disturb a family milieu that has already been unsettled by a hurried departure. "Partners often feel very stressed that their spouses are in such danger," one wife explained. "Family life can be difficult when the journalist comes home from a long and traumatic trip. We want them to snap back into domestic life, yet to them a case of chickenpox or a broken dishwasher seems so trivial after witnessing starving children or victims of landmines, say." To this may be added another wife's cache of pent-up irritations: "They fill the house with loads of stinking kit. Sometimes they even give you infectious, unpleasant tropical diseases. They dominate all social occasions with endless retelling of adventures at the front. Lots of voyeuristic descriptions of violence in inappropriate situations."

Mistakes are frequently made by both journalists and partners in a constant cycle of resented separation and fraught reunion. One photographer explained:

> It took a real concerted effort to understand how to readjust to life back home. It was foolish to bring the war back. It was stupid to expect people here to empathize with you; to even make the attempt was more frustrating than anything else. Not that I wouldn't tell my girlfriend what happened. [But] only people exposed to that event, and it is a location-specialized thing, could grasp the essence of it. And I think she just thought it was better not to talk to me about life at home because I wouldn't be able to relate to it. I realize now that I should have made more of an effort to talk to her about this. When you actually return home, the decompression thing was always a problem because I would just need time to readjust on my own. I did not know how to do it properly with somebody else. So I just alienated my partner.

Another recurring theme expressed by the stay-at-home partners was, understandably, safety. To offset her own anxiety, one wife reached an unusual arrangement with her journalist husband. "Before we got married," she explained, "we decided that if my husband did conflict coverage, we would go together. So far, he's been pretty good about it. However, even when he does local assignments I am a nervous wreck and often imagine the worst."

Another wife raised concerns about the safety of a family accompanying a journalist posted on long-term assignment to a dangerous region. "I feel that it is often very stressful for the partners of foreign journalists to live in an alien environment. We lived in Africa for four years. My husband was usually away and as a family we were often scared not just for my husband, but of the constant threat of violence at home. One wife always slept with her children as she was too scared to let them sleep alone."

A further cause for spousal worry is the mental state of some of the journalists on their return from the front lines. War journalists may bring back not just the detritus of war, but also the troubling behavioral manifestations of PTSD, depression, and heavy drinking. Having spent weeks fretting about the physical safety of their husbands, wives may end up doing little more than exchanging one set of concerns for another. And all the while, there are bills to pay, the heating to fix, a car to service, homework to supervise, birthday parties to organize, sleepless nights tending children with fevers, a career to manage, if it hasn't been placed on hold, and anxious in-laws to placate. The domestic situation becomes particularly unsettled when the war journalist lacks the necessary insight, not only into his own state of mind, but also into the inordinate pressures faced by his partner. Because they are faced with such a plethora of challenges in their relationships, it did not come as a surprise when I received this gratuitous piece of advice from a disheartened spouse: "Don't ever be tempted to marry one!"

Some partners of journalists live with the anticipation of tragedy. Others simply block their minds to the profession's many dangers. "When my husband went away to cover war zones, I had great (misconceived as it turned out) confidence that he would keep his head down — in effect I would deny the fact he was in danger," one wife wrote. "He in turn would blithely reassure me by claiming cowardice." The journalist partners of three women who took part in my study had been murdered. Their deaths were no accident of war, the result of a stray bullet, a missile off target, or a bomb gone awry. Each was deliberately targeted and killed. I never had an opportunity to interview these women. My understanding of their situation is based on the results from their questionnaires plus the written comments they sent to me. What they went through far exceeded bereavement. All became depressed and suicidal, and two required antidepressant medication. One woman revealed, "My grief was (and still is, five years later) compounded by the fact that at the time I was pregnant with our daughter. Caring for a small person meant so much of my own feelings had to be put on hold — in itself a 'coping' strategy, as I made her my absolute priority and she in turn became my lifeline."

"No story is worth dying for." I heard this statement repeatedly from those in the news business, and yet journalists continue to die, leaving behind their partners and children and children yet to be born. Their youth, the violent manner of their dying, the talent lost, the arbitrariness of the event, the difficulty in bringing the killers to justice, the logistics of dealing with death in a foreign, hostile land, all complicate the bereavement process, bequeathing a residue of intense sadness.

\* \* \*

My data did reveal one protective factor in a relationship. Journalists often marry journalists, a pattern of social behavior found in other professions, too. This phenomenon, referred to as *assortative mating*, cannot be accounted for by chance. When birds of a feather flock together, there is often a biochemical underpinning to this mutual attraction. Zuckerman's theories of sensation seeking behavior driven by dopamine and MAO provide the clue. Indeed, there is empirical evidence to show that should partners be incompatible when it comes to searching out new experiences, their relationship may flounder. In my data, over a quarter of the war journalists had married another journalist (not necessarily a war journalist), and it was in this group that the least psychological distress was found.

This chapter has focused on women as war journalists, domestic journalists, wives, partners, and widows. In combining these five categories, it is important not to lose sight of the fact that, from a behavioral perspective, female war journalists stand apart. Their predilection for living intensely, and often dangerously, is unique to this group. From the enclaves of Bosnia to the jungles of the Congo, from the back alleys of Gaza to the disfigured landscape of Sierra Leone, they have matched their male counterparts in confronting the perils of war to get an important story or telling picture. Indeed, Thomas de Waal, in his introduction to Anna Politkovskaya's *A Dirty War*, her book on the Chechen wars, notes that many of the best journalists in that most dangerous of conflicts have been women, including Carlotta Gall, Petra Prochazkova, Yelena Masyuk, Maria Eismont, and the late Nadezhda Chaikova (murdered in Chechnya in 1996). Though they may be fewer in number and are still faced with gender stereotypes, the kind of work they do and their psychological fortitude in the face of great adversity dispels any notion that female war journalists are interlopers in a male domain.

Single, articulate, mentally resilient, possessing an inner physical toughness, competitive, insouciant, able to drink with the boys: applicable as all of these descriptors are, they fail to convey the overarching impression created by these women. That essential, defining essence is instead best summed up by the reaction of Marie Colvin to her near-death experience while reporting on the Tamil Tigers in Sri Lanka. "I am not going to hang up my flak jacket as a result of this incident," she wrote in the *Sunday Times*. "I have been flown to New York, where doctors are going to operate on my injured eye. They have told me it is unlikely I will regain much use of it as a piece of shrapnel went right through the middle. All I can hope for is a bit of peripheral vision. Friends have been phoning to point out how many famous people are blind in one eye. They seem to do fine with only one eye, so I am not worried. But what I want most as soon as I get out of hospital, is a vodka martini and a cigarette."

# 7

# Domestic Journalists and Urban Terror: The Aftermath of September 11

## * * *

**Men never do evil so completely and cheerfully as when they do it from religious conviction.**

**Blaise Pascal**

On a bright autumnal September morning I was doing a ward round on a psychiatry unit. Situated in a crumbling wing of an old veterans hospital, the ward, like many psychiatric facilities dating from the World War II era, has a rundown, decrepit feel. A sparsely furnished room, upholstery stained and ripped, drapes that hang limp and shut unevenly, serves as a patient lounge. Messages and poems are penned on the walls, and in one corner sits that ubiquitous appliance that seldom rests, the television.

To those who have no interest in the observation and study of mental phenomena, the ward may seem a sad place, a way station for the forlorn and forgotten of society. Prey to their delusions, hallucinations, and manias, many of the patients have ceded reality to a cornucopia of fantastical beliefs that preoccupy thoughts, affect emotions, and dictate actions. How can it be otherwise, when you are convinced that your food has been poisoned by your neighbors, or you believe that the police have inserted a microchip into the recesses of your brain to control what you say, or you hold a grievance against the authorities for incarcerating you with a bunch of madmen simply because you have evidence, incontrovertible proof in fact, that you are nothing less than the messiah and all you have to do to prove it is to fast for forty days and forty nights, instead of which the bastards send around a van with a bunch of goons, and the next thing you know you wake up in this shithole where doctors, or they call themselves that anyway, ask you absurd questions like, "Do you ever hear voices?"

Overwhelmed by psychosis, these people care not one iota that inflation is up, Milošević awaits trial in the Hague, Lance Armstrong has won a seventh consecutive Tour de France. Nor does it matter that there is no money in the bank, no housing to be had, no family members who visit. Simply arrest the neighbor, get the surgeon to remove the implanted brain chip, and all will be resolved. Anything else is of no consequence. "Another routine day in state-sponsored purgatory," is how one of my patients described existence on the ward, milling around in the lounge, oblivious to each other's private torment.

On that sunlit September morning, the television was on, as usual, although the volume was muted. I was chatting to a patient, listening to his tale of how the physicist Edward Teller had stolen his ideas and claimed credit for developing the H-bomb. Out of the corner of my eye, I saw a plane drift lazily across the TV screen and sink into one of the twin towers of the World Trade Center. My patient had seen it, too.

"Crazy pilot," he muttered before resuming his complaint of dark deception.

A nurse burst into the room. "Have you heard? Have you heard? A plane has crashed into the World Trade Center. It's on the TV, look!" She pointed excitedly at the screen as colleagues joined her, obscuring the view.

Unfazed by the gathering commotion, my patient hardly broke stride. Teller was a fraud, Teller had stolen intellectual property, Teller had ruined his life, Teller was not even a real physicist, he was an imposter, a cunning charlatan who had fooled the world.

I had heard this all before, countless times, but by now my attention had been distracted by events unfolding on the television. I stood to get a better view. Teller's phantom victim stood too, not to follow the breaking story, but to continue his harangue. The drama of the moment was lost on him. I noted that the other three psychotic patients in the room were oblivious to events, too. Two sat slumped in chairs, looking vacuous, while a third shuffled around aimlessly, picking up a magazine and skimming desultorily through it. By now the TV's sound had been switched on, with the volume on high, making conversation difficult. Undeterred, my patient continued his monologue: a conspiracy among Hungarians, East European nepotism with Teller as the arch puppeteer. He made this last point just before the Pentagon was hit.

The room filled rapidly with nurses, secretaries, and physicians, all jostling for space in front of the box. I moved off toward a window, between two chairs occupied by patients lost in thought. A corridor of space there presented an acutely angled view of the screen. Smoke and flames were all I could see. Undeterred, my patient shadowed me, his back to the television, and once more my view was obscured. 1956! In 1956, Hungarian secret files were taken by the Russians when their tanks rolled into Budapest. That's where Teller gave his game away, where he revealed his true colors, his loyalty to himself only, and in the confusion of the uprising, Teller — devious, loathsome Teller — switched documents and assumed my patient's identity, and for forty-four years this man had lived with a doppelganger who had stolen his life, his brain, his ideas, his family, swindled him out of his inheritance, and as a final indignity, driven him into the asylum where Teller continued the persecution by controlling the physicians, paying them on the quiet, oh yes, on the quiet to keep him locked away where no one would believe him. Just because Teller was not a physicist did not make him any less clever. He was unbelievably clever, devious, cunning, and scheming, able to switch identities, in fact: he fooled the Russians, the Americans, the Canadians, he was so fucking clever he could turn goulash into hamburgers if he wanted to and the only person who had ever seen through him was . . .

I knew what was coming but never heard it. The collective gasps and shouts from the staff in front of the screen drowned out my patient's *idée fixe*. The second tower had been hit. I had heard enough of Edward Teller and needed to see what was going on. Maneuvering my way into position, I stared disbelievingly at the screen in a room that had become eerily silent save for the broadcaster's commentary. We stood there transfixed, our work at a standstill as we watched the second tower collapse. Belief suspended, we watched the first tower come down soon after. Little was said. We were all too stunned.

It becomes hard to gauge the passage of time when so engrossed. Perhaps twenty minutes had passed — I cannot be certain — when I became aware that the Teller tirade had abated. To my surprise, I noticed that my patient too was riveted by events unfolding on the screen. And a second man, whose schizophrenia had long rendered him aloof and disdainful of everything but his monomania, had roused himself from his stupor to follow events. Swept up in the agony of the moment, for that briefest window in time, staff and patients were united in their collective incredulity. In an environment in which the reality of physicians clashed daily with the delusions of their patients, it had taken a cataclysm to bring about this tenuous unanimity.

Those horrific images of September 11 did something that neither my verbal interventions nor medication had achieved. They distracted one psychotic patient from an all-embracing delusion and roused another from his state of profound indifference. For a brief interlude, the images brought them back into the world of sound judgment and empathy. It was, of course, no cure for their schizophrenia, but remarkable nonetheless. An outrage of startling ferocity had momentarily reawakened these patients' blighted humanity, overriding the faulty neurotransmitters, dysfunctional receptors, and altered cerebral blood flow that lay at the root of their psychosis. It remains for me a powerful, enduring memory of that fateful, beautifully clear September morn, and the paradox was striking. It had taken an act of moral insanity to restore, albeit briefly and in circumscribed fashion, part of my patients' shattered realities. "Tsk," muttered my patient, finally turning away from the hypnotic images, "you have to be really crazy to do a thing like that."

*   *   *

In earlier chapters, the emphasis has been on journalists who travel to foreign shores in search of stories and pictures of conflict. Driven by a complex set of motivations, these men and women have stood apart from their colleagues because of their unique demographic profile and higher levels of psychological distress. In contrast, the domestic journalists used as control subjects in my study have led different lives. Although called on to cover emotionally disturbing stories such as murders and traffic accidents, domestic journalists rarely confront situations of grave personal danger. This was reflected in their lower scores for depression and post-traumatic stress disorder. While they were as driven as their war counterparts to cover the news, get the scoop, and make deadlines, their desire to enter zones of conflict was conspicuously absent. War held no attraction. It was something that happened far from their civil society, and it was best left to others of different temperament to tell the public about it. War was to be avoided.

And then one morning everything changed. Suddenly, violently, events that had for generations been viewed as foreign, far-away conflagrations in godforsaken places arrived in the very heart of a great power's most populous and symbolic cities. Journalists who had, by choice, shied away from war and the accompanying slaughter, could avoid it no longer. Skyscrapers were leveled, thousands were killed, the Defense Department was on fire, and soon killer microbes would be on the loose. The public must be informed. Middle East fanaticism ceased to be a foreign affair; it was now the all-encompassing domestic story. For days on end, as the events of September 2001 unfolded, a group of journalists unaccustomed to mass destruction and death witnessed apocalyptic scenes and were confronted by the distraught and bereaved.

How would they cope psychologically with this situation? By nature more cautious and risk averse than their war colleagues, these journalists had never been tested by traumatic events of this magnitude. There were early clues that they found the aftermath of the attacks emotionally overwhelming. For some, the dispassionate objectivity sought after by many in their profession was no longer attainable. The public, accustomed to viewing journalists as the imperturbable harbinger of bad news, were now faced with reporters crying while broadcasting live. In one highly publicized incident, the veteran CBS news anchor Dan Rather broke down while on air, prompting a debate about the importance of a journalist maintaining his professional sang-froid, no matter how disturbing the content of the story. Yet if someone with the experience of Rather was reacting that way, others in the profession were likely to be affected too.

I therefore thought it would be interesting to study the psychological responses of a group of domestic journalists who had to cover the events of September 11. I approached the management of CNN with the suggestion of extending my original journalist study into the domestic domain. They were sympathetic to the request, and a list of sixty-four names of CNN journalists chosen at random from the New York, Washington, and Atlanta bureaus was forwarded to me. My methodology remained essentially the same: a website was set up with a series of questions to elicit basic demographic data, details pertaining to their coverage of September 11 and the anthrax attacks, and responses to inventories for post-traumatic stress disorder and depression. One difference, however, was that journalists were not interviewed face-to-face as they were in the war study, so no diagnosis of the full PTSD or major depression syndromes could be made.

Data collection began toward the beginning of November 2001. The forty-six journalists who agreed to take part did not differ from the eighteen who declined in age, gender, or location, three important variables that could potentially have influenced PTSD scores. This suggested that the 72 percent who said yes to the study were truly representative of all the staff involved in covering the terrorist attacks. To provide a way of interpreting the behavioral responses, two sets of control subjects were chosen from previously collected data. The first of these was a group of forty-five war journalists, and the second was a group of forty-five domestic journalists whose responses had been gathered well before September 11. None of the latter group had worked in zones of conflict. Once again, care was taken to ensure that these three groups of journalists (the war group and the two domestic groups) were well matched on four variables that could have influenced their PTSD scores: age (the average age was late thirties), gender (approximately 60 percent were male), marital status (about 50 percent were single), and the numbers of years worked as a journalist (the average was about fifteen years).

In comparing the psychological responses of war journalists and their domestic colleagues pressed into covering the aftermath of the September 11 attacks, there is a risk in blurring the margins between disparate sets of events. The Al Qaeda attacks were quickly interpreted by President Bush and many of the news organizations as "America's new war." At face value, this makes comparisons between journalists of different temperamental bents of interest. But the researcher must avoid getting swept up in the emotion of rhetoric. To the behavioral scientist, objectivity is paramount. Without this essential requirement, the interpretation of data — indeed the very collection of data — becomes tainted, and any conclusions relegated to a morass best served by propaganda. War is a small word with a multiplicity of big meanings. It is not necessary here to open a debate over semantics or whether a terrorist attack on the American mainland equates with the more conventional conflicts the United States has become involved in. What is required, however, is an attempt to differentiate between the levels of danger, the degrees of threat, faced by domestic journalists thrust involuntarily and briefly into conflict and war journalists who, by choice, have reported on foreign conflict over the course of a decade or more.

Many stressors confronted the group of domestic journalists during the latter third of 2001. September 11 saw the coordinated air attacks on New York and Washington, D.C., with another hijacked plane crashing into the Pennsylvania countryside after passengers stormed the cockpit. In the months that followed, anthrax became the new weapon of terror, with news organizations one of the selected targets. The offices of NBC in New York had to be vacated while men in space-age protective clothing probed the environment for the dreaded spores. And then in November, an American Airlines plane crashed in Queens, killing 265 people. The cause of the accident was eventually found to be pilot error, but with feelings already running high, many initially feared terrorism.

Throughout all these events, the media fulfilled an essential public service, keeping citizens informed. To do so demanded regular exposure to scenes of grief, fear, uncertainty, anger, and helplessness. To a degree, these were offset by the resilience and fortitude of survivors and rescue workers, but the overwhelming emotions associated with the attacks were pain and sorrow. The intensity of the moment, the sheer volume of news generated, the constantly evolving homeland security concerns in the United States, and the unique nature of the biological weapons targeting their profession produced a constellation of stressors unusual in the history of North American journalism. And, for the most part, it fell to the domestic correspondent, photographer, broadcaster, and cameraman to weather the threats, collate the facts, and sift through the fraught and jumbled emotions of the moment, all the while managing his own fears and feelings.

The targets chosen by the terrorists on September 11, 2001 were symbols of American financial and military power. Shocking as the events were, however, civil society in the United States did not implode along with the twin towers. Just the contrary — institutions mobilized positively and quickly to deal with trauma's aftermath. The world's richest nation activated a network of support services of mind-boggling proportions. Or so it must have seemed to those in less fortunate, long-suffering nations crushed by war and years of strife. The domestic journalists called on to cover the events of September 11 may have done so amid the detritus of shattered buildings and shattered lives, but they were also surrounded by functioning cities, water in the taps, sewage taken care of, food aplenty in an array of restaurants, the lights of Fifth Avenue undimmed, and foundations and corporations pouring in millions of dollars in relief aid to supplement the billions promised by the president.

Contrast this with the *New York Times* journalist Chris Hedges's description of life in a Balkan city:

Sarajevo in the summer of 1995 came close to Danté's inner circle of hell. The city, surrounded by Serb gunners on the heights above, was subjected to hundreds of shells a day, crashing into an area twice the size of Central Park. Multiple Katyusha rockets — whooshing overhead — burst in rapid succession; they could take down a four or five story apartment building in seconds, killing or wounding everyone inside. There was no running water or electricity and little to eat; most people were subsisting on a bowl of soup a day. It was possible to enter the besieged city only by driving down a dirt track on Mount Igman, one stretch directly in the line of Serb fire. The vehicles that had failed to make it lay twisted and upended in the ravine below, at times with the charred remains of their human cargo inside. Families lived huddled in basements, and mothers, who had to make a mad dash to the common water taps set up by the United Nations, faced an excruciating choice — whether to run through the streets with their children or leave them in a building that might be rubble when they returned. The hurling bits of iron fragmentation from exploding shells left bodies mangled, dismembered, decapitated. The other reporters and I slipped and slid in their blood and entrails thrown out by the shell blasts, heard the groans of anguish, and were for our pains in the sights of the Serb snipers, often just a few hundred yards away. The latest victims lay with gaping wounds untended in the corridors of hospitals that lacked antibiotics and painkillers. By that summer, after nearly four years of fighting, forty-five foreign reporters had been killed, scores wounded. I lived — sheltered in a side room in the Holiday Inn, its front smashed and battered by shellfire — in a world bent on self-destruction, a world where lives were snuffed out at random.

What befell New York and Sarajevo deserves closer comparison if one is to make sense of the data collected from journalists reporting each city's travails. Both occupied an elevated niche within their respective societies, Manhattan as the flagship of capitalism's triumphant ascendancy, cosmopolitan Sarajevo as a unique blend of urbanized Balkan chic and multicultural harmony that had hosted a recent winter Olympics. These superficial similarities extended to the violence visited upon them; many killed, buildings leveled, thousands bereaved and traumatized. But the manner in which this came about differed considerably between sites. The attacks on New York City were unexpected and sudden, the damage inflicted within a brief period, a morning's mayhem. Death came quickly to thousands, and the wounded were few. The physical damage was circumscribed — apart from the devastation at the site of the World Trade Center, the remainder of the city was unscathed physically. Sarajevo, on the other hand, was ravaged slowly, piecemeal over the course of years. This steady, deadly attrition claimed a daily quota of casualties and insidiously destroyed families, apartments, schools, hospitals, health care, and sanitation — the very infrastructure that had elevated the city to Olympian heights. The unrelenting destruction, on any one day less in magnitude than that inflicted on New York on September 11, continued unabated over many years. The cumulative effect on the city and its inhabitants was ruinous. By the time the Dayton Accords brought an uneasy, mistrustful peace, a bereaved populace was left to survey their blighted conurbation and wonder where and how they would find the will to rebuild their splintered lives.

Sarajevo exemplifies countless other besieged cities. The end point of any protracted warfare is predictably uniform: full cemeteries, empty stores, and apathetic, dependent survivors adrift amongst the remnants of civil society. Chechnya, Rwanda, the Congo, Sierra Leone, Lebanon, or

Afghanistan may be substituted for the Balkans, the fate of their cities analogous to that of Sarajevo. Horrific as the events of September 11 were, terrible as the fate was of those trapped in the twin towers, by the time the dust settled on that surreal day, New York away from the circumscribed, encapsulated rubble of Ground Zero bore little resemblance to those cities. Which meant that the domestic journalists who were pressed, by circumstance and necessity, into gathering the news from New York confronted a terrain both superficially similar to and fundamentally different from that faced by Hedges and colleagues as they navigated the lottery of Sniper's Alley in Sarajevo. The forty-five dead foreign journalists in the Balkans underscore this gulf. These similarities and differences in personal experiences, linked as they inextricably are to the environment in which the journalists function, will help explain the domestic journalists' psychological responses to covering the events of September 11.

Of the forty-six journalists in my study, nineteen had covered the breaking story from Ground Zero, seventeen had been in the newsroom, and ten were roving reporters, gathering news from many different sources. Two journalists had been wounded in the attack, while one-third of the group studied knew someone who had been killed or injured in it. In early January 2002, I visited the New York bureau of CNN to meet with a dozen of the study participants. No structured interviews were completed. Rather, the session provided an opportunity for journalists to ask questions and discuss the data I was collecting. A few in the group carried overt emotional scars. It was soon apparent that everyone knew who these individuals were and deferred to them when discussing and interpreting events. Those journalists who had emotional difficulties in the immediate aftermath of the attacks were surprisingly naive about the origin of their distress. In this, their responses were reminiscent of those of some war journalists. They misinterpreted the sudden sprouting of an intense dysphoria coupled with fear bordering on paranoia as a sign of incipient insanity, of losing one's mind and going crazy.

"At CNN we have a deck outside on the twenty-second floor which looks right at downtown," one journalist told me. "I was downtown and witnessed the buildings falling. And then I heard planes overhead and panicked at first, thinking we were going to be attacked as well. I was feeling very vulnerable and so was relieved to see the planes were our military. That evening I would not go home. I was not going to go into Penn Station on a train in a tunnel. I was afraid we would be trapped. I was happy my office put me up in a hotel so I could delay going through the tunnel. Even now, I still have difficulties going through tunnels or crossing a bridge."

The role of many domestic journalists had undergone a profound change. The job expectations were still there, albeit more intense and pressurized. "My office put me up in a hotel for four hours to get some sleep later that night (midnight to four a.m.)," recalled an editor. "And then I was back at work for two straight days, looking at video over and over." Some of the journalists, because of their proximity to Ground Zero and the armory, assumed the role of comforter to the thousands of relatives and friends searching for missing loved ones. The dissolution of the margins historically separating journalists from the story meant that in some cases, they themselves became the news. Some were caught in the spotlight by virtue of a miraculous escape from the crumbling towers, none more so than David Handschuh of the *Daily News*, the president of the National Press Photographers Association whose leg was shattered by falling masonry. Others found they were the focus of a story because of their inability to control their emotions while on the air. "They Can Cry If They Want To. Chris Cramer, CNN President, Salutes the Tearful Urban War Correspondent," ran a headline in a London broadsheet, the *Independent*. And then there were the journalists who simply put their humanity first. This was their city that had been scarred, their neighbors who wandered the streets in numbed bewilderment clutching photographs. They knew the children of parents whose cars had been left standing at the station long after the last commuter train had run.

Miriam Falco, senior producer for CNN medical news, gave compassionate voice to the new roles that many journalists were called upon to adopt.

I produced live shots and packages from outside the armory in New York, where families and friends gathered to find out if their loved ones were alive and later to drop off DNA evidence for identification purposes. We met with a lot of people who were in shock or beginning the grieving process and yet still hoping that their loved ones somehow miraculously survived. Was I on the front lines of the war? No. Was I at Ground Zero, where the destruction and demise of thousands of people were blatantly obvious? No. But I saw the thousands of people pouring past our live shot location, searching for their loved one, sharing their pictures and stories about those missing, hoping when there was really no way anyone could have survived. It may not sound like a difficult assignment, but it certainly was not easy hearing the accounts of those devastated people. What helped me and my correspondent get through this was knowing that simply listening to their stories, even if [they] never made the air, provided a little bit of comfort and catharsis for the individual sharing their memories of their missing/lost relative or friend. Another factor, which was reflected in our reporting but also provided some "therapeutic" balance for me, was seeing the countless kind gestures from strangers who flocked to the armory and anonymously dropped off aid, handing out flowers to the grieving, passing out Hugs candies to anyone passing by, cab drivers refusing to take payment, and so on.

To some journalists, the catastrophe that befell their fellow New Yorkers was disturbingly reminiscent of foreign events they had made a conscious decision to avoid. "I had previously been in war-reporting situations in Central America in the early 1980s and in Afghanistan under the Soviet occupation in the late 1980s," a domestic journalist wrote to me. "The Afghan experience was one that in particular had left me with some post-traumatic stress difficulties. In fact, seeing people die and being under fire led me to stop wanting to chase wars as part of my occupation. Seeing too much of man's inhumanity is corrosive to the human spirit." For this journalist the rapidity and destructive force of the events of September 11 conjured up memories of another kind of trauma. "I would say that the 9/11 events were different in a number of ways: the unexpected, shock nature of it. And also the impact it had on a wide variety of people that I knew. It reminded me more of the Kobe earthquake in Japan that I covered, an event that reverberated for months after." And yet, even here the analogy fails. Equating a natural disaster with the events of September 11 misses the central tenet of what made the attacks on the World Trade Center and the Pentagon so troubling. Unlike the Kobe earthquake, or those in Armenia and Mexico City that preceded it, what occurred on September 11 was no natural disaster, no "act of God," despite the crowing of those fundamentalists who saw it as such. Coupled with grief came the knowledge that the cataclysm was a carefully conceived and daring manifestation of unbridled and, to a naive populous, barely credible hatred. When lives are violently taken, there is no victim hierarchy. The dead are pitied equally, accorded the same degree of respect. It is, however, in the manner and the quantity of the dying that a horror differential is established. Shock and revulsion lie along a sliding scale and crescendo according to the deed: car crash, train crash, jetliner crash, the Lockerbie bombing, genocides in Srebrenica and Kigali, reaching an apogee with Auschwitz and the Holocaust. The events of September 11 belong in the upper echelons of a cabal of terror, and it fell to domestic journalists immersed in those events to tell the story as it unfolded.

"One of our journalists was downtown at the time of the World Trade Center attacks and saw people jumping out of windows," another producer recalled.

> We let her take some time off immediately, but she has had some lingering emotional trouble. And since then there have been a couple of occasions when events such as the plane crash in Queens have had a number of staffers upset and very emotional. Some of our staff folk who I would put in the "hardened New Yorker" category from time to time have tears well up, often while watching stories of victims' families and sometimes even while seeing stories not related to the attacks. I am not sure where this fits into the whole analysis of things, but it is real and it's continuing. Everybody puts on a brave face. This is CNN, after all, and the news *does* continue, but folks are more brittle overall now. And it does take a lot of my time to try and figure out ways to smooth things out for my staff.

Informative as it was to hear from individual journalists, I had no way of gauging whether those present in the room were representative of the bureau as a whole. I would have to wait for the group data before any trends became apparent. Over a period of four to five months following September 11, the data were collected.

The PTSD results provided unequivocal, empirical evidence that from a psychological perspective, domestic journalists were adversely affected by the terrorist atrocities. This was most obvious in New York–based journalists, but it was not limited to them. Domestic journalists of all types post–September 11 had significantly more PTSD symptoms than domestic journalists pre–September 11. Now their PTSD profile resembled more closely that of the war journalists. Indeed, with respect to the PTSD triad, the scores of the two groups overlapped. When the analysis was extended beyond the three subscales to the twenty-two individual symptoms of PTSD, only one statistically significant difference was found—the domestic journalists had higher hypervigilance scores than those in the war group.*

To better understand these findings, we need to revisit some of the

---

*The question posed was: Do you feel watchful and on guard? In the aftermath of the September 11 attacks, more domestic journalists answered yes.

theory underpinning PTSD. In response to a sudden and overwhelming traumatic event, an individual may develop a hitherto dormant sense of heightened personal vulnerability. The traumatic event shatters a cocoon of inviolability that has never been questioned, and in response, newfound fears and uncertainties quickly take hold. If the unthinkable could happen once, people tell themselves, what is to stop it happening again? This question holds a compelling logic. Having been exposed to, and therefore sensitized by, violence, the body's nervous system readjusts to the threat recently posed. In this state of increased arousal, pulse and respiratory rates quicken, blood pressure rises, and the senses become more acute. Sleep, a period of vulnerability when physical and emotional defenses are down, is affected. Typically, recently traumatized individuals describe difficulty falling asleep simply because their "early warning system" refuses to switch off. To do so would let the guard down. Insomnia ensues. But the body cannot maintain this state indefinitely, for sustained amplified awareness is stressful, associated with an outpouring of hormones like cortisol that are helpful in the short term but injurious thereafter. In response to this altered physiology, difficulties with concentration become apparent, and the combination of sleep-deprived nights and stress-filled waking hours produces irritability and outbursts of anger.

Nothing validates the expectation of further dangers more than a new, very real threat. In the wake of the collapse of the twin towers, these were not long in coming, and many targeted the media. "Two days after the attack, we had a bomb threat clear our building," one study participant told me. "Some journalists refused to return to the office for a week after that." This was followed by anthrax-laced mail arriving in the post. The threat had shifted from incendiary jetliners to microspores: invisible, silent, odorless, but no less lethal. A constant wariness of fresh dangers exemplifies the responses of journalists covering the September 11 attacks and their aftermath.

While the above explanation accords well with trauma theory and makes intuitive sense, the reasons for the increased PTSD scores among the domestic journalists defied such neat categorization. Difficulties with sleep and concentration, irritability, and newfound strains in relationships, while all part of PTSD, are not unique to the disorder. Other factors, *epiphenomena* or "spill over" of the attacks, also affected how the journalists responded to the questionnaires. Considerable stress was generated simply by the sheer volume of news. "Immediately after the attacks, the demands for more work were very heavy," one respondent told me. "Near around-the-clock coverage from New York meant a lot of our staffers were pressed into service on other programs." Another journalist wrote, "As with many of my colleagues, I actually enjoy the challenge of reporting/producing under pressure. This is a huge story. It's why we became journalists in the first place. I would say that most of my current stresses (less sleep, a bit more edgy) are due to the intense focus and long hours on a single story. I have cut back on outside activities, let bills pile up, and with the exception of two weekends away have spent virtually all my waking hours in the past few months focused on *the* story. But, I am aware I need a break."

Ironically, the very traits of dogged persistence and perpetual curiosity that make successful journalists may have unforeseen drawbacks. The public's hunger for news, the competition among news agencies for a dramatic story, the individual quest for a scoop, and the endless replaying of video footage before deciding what to air all combine to hold journalists captive to events that may be painful to witness or listen to. The thermostat of emotional comfort is set individually, not collectively. Like their war colleagues, the domestic journalists each respond differently to traumatic and stressful events. Apply enough pressures, and symptoms of psychological distress become frequent. And in some cases, unexplained medical symptoms arise, as with the war journalist with the quasi-stroke or the stammering speech of the young Ugandan girl whose freelance journalist father had been shot. Following September 11, domestic journalists found themselves susceptible to similar conversion symptoms. A letter from one of the participants in my study described his physical difficulties.

About 5 days after the attacks, my hours were changed to help out on other shows. A few days later I developed a horrible pain in my left shoulder. I am left handed and had just finished training hard for a triathlon. In light of the attacks, the triathlon was cancelled. Anyway, my point is this: I was at peak fitness and was ready for the competition but developed this ailment. I could not turn a doorknob or hold a pen it was so painful. I tried to make a doctor's appointment, but the earliest I could be seen was in 2 weeks. Within 3 days, the pain went away on its own. It is possible it was from over-straining, but I had stopped swimming. I feel stress was the reason for the pain.

In a similar vein, a second journalist wrote, "I've accepted the probability that my recent physical ailment could be the direct result of the events of September 11." The displacement of psychological distress into physical symptoms, the conversion of unconscious feelings and emotions into weakness, pain, and immobility, was not reported by a single domestic journalist among the 107 studied well before September 11.

Interestingly, domestic journalists after September 11 were not significantly depressed; their scores on the twenty-one-item Beck Depression Inventory were indistinguishable from their pre–September 11 colleagues and well below those of the war journalists. Here, the New York–Sarajevo comparisons are particularly germane. For journalists covering the news in New York, the threats and dangers were largely ephemeral. Apart from the anthrax attacks, which were quickly contained and for which curative treatment was available, the insecurity was linked to an anticipation of future attacks that never materialized. To be sure, this generated a prominent hypervigilance, as my data revealed, but contrast the phantom fears, whipped up in part by the Department of Homeland Security's kaleidoscopic warnings, with the situation in Sarajevo, where anxieties received daily validation in the form of fresh attacks, new casualties, and colleagues wounded and killed. For some war journalists, relentless siege had a corrosive effect on mood. These stark differences in personal safety were a product of fundamentally different environments, the one with civil society intact, rallying, supportive, restorative, the other with little but the remnants of such a society undefiled, the vestiges in daily peril, disintegrating into a racial abyss familiar to Europeans of an older generation. For some war journalists, the weeks, months, and years spent in the resurgent barbarity of Sarajevo wasted the spirit, inducing a melancholy in tune with the blighted surroundings and disconsolate populace.

It is of course possible that the signs and symptoms of psychological distress in domestic journalists post–September 11 were simply part of a collective societal angst that gripped many of those living in the greater New York area. In March 2002, an article in the *New England Journal of Medicine* described the prevalence of PTSD among the residents of Manhattan living south of 110th Street. Of more than a thousand adults interviewed, 7.5 percent reported symptoms consonant with the diagnosis, significantly higher levels than those found in the general population of the United States. Furthermore, the authors noted that the rate of PTSD tripled in those residents living south of Canal Street, the area close to the World Trade Center. This link between physical proximity to the attack and the development of PTSD symptoms was mirrored in the journalist data, in that those working in New York had significantly higher PTSD scores than those reporting from elsewhere.

While location was a powerful predictor of whether an individual developed PTSD symptoms, the psychological fallout of the Al Qaeda terror was not limited to journalists in the United States. Unforgettable images of jetliners plowing into skyscrapers, people leaping from the upper stories, and ghost-like survivors embalmed in dust staggering from the scene appeared repeatedly on television screens around the world. In deciding which pictures to run, staffers in international newsrooms sifted through untold variations on a theme of death. In the process, PTSD-like reactions by proxy were induced in journalists many thousands of kilometers removed from the scene. One European journalist described to me a plethora of stresses, emotional and physical, that followed in September 11's murky wash. The fact that the journalist had no direct exposure to the trauma does not invalidate her distress, which stemmed in large measure from the concentration of visually disturbing images to which she was subjected. News bosses should take note. Emollient assurances that all is well with journalists away from the front lines, cloistered in the hothouse shelter of a production room, may prove misleading. Repetitive exposure to images of dehumanizing acts can exert its own insidiously corrosive effect on the psyche. The journalist told me:

> For the past couple of years I have managed a team that monitors and logs all incoming TV footage. We are often confronted with horrendous scenes — which haven't really had much impact on me. Apart from one occasion when I had nightmares about seven years ago, my attitude has always been that this is part of life, and I have developed a very warped sense of humor to deal with some of the things I have seen. However, the workload has had some negative effects on my physical health.
>
> On September 11, I worked through 'til two-thirty the following morning and was back in the office by eight. I continued to work in similar fashion for the next two weeks and was totally exhausted. We were subject to nonstop pictures from a variety of sources and angles. There was no time to eat properly, take a break, see my friends or family, cry, talk it through, pray — all the usual things you do to get it out of your system. For weeks afterwards I suffered flashbacks and nightmares about people jumping out of the towers. The image seemed imprinted on my mind. I wasn't sleeping well, and I just couldn't stop working for fear I'd never be able to start again. Finally I came down with some sort of flu bug and had to stop. However, I

didn't seem able to kick it, and when I did try and go back into work, I started having panic attacks, going hot and cold and crying at the least thing. At this point my doctor told me I had to rest, gave me some medication and signed me off work for three weeks. Even then I was working from home by logging in, dealing with calls on my mobile, etc.

It was only when one of my senior managers rang me up full of concern and told me I had to stop and get some rest that I started to calm down. The hardest thing was not watching or listening to any news bulletins and trying to switch off. Eventually I went abroad for a couple of weeks to try and chill out, and I am now back at work. The nightmares and flashbacks have stopped, and I'm down to the odd panic attack every few days. Although I am feeling a lot better now I am still not 100 percent, and it does cross my mind that I will never be able to function properly in my current job. My tolerance level is very low and I'm even finding social situations hard going. Noise drives me crazy, e.g., phones ringing, TV monitors on, general chat, etc.

I know I will get better. I'm absolutely determined. I realized what was wrong with me as soon as the panic attacks started — and hopefully I'm doing the right things to get better. I do not want the rest of my life to be affected by this — especially the inability to control my body's reactions. I have several friends who have really lost the plot after a number of years working in war zones with several near misses, and they are a bag of nerves. I do wonder whether if I'd actually been sent out to cover the story I'd be okay — mainly because I'd feel I was helping in some way, rather than just having to observe.

Three months after the events of September 11, on a chilly winter's evening, I met a Serbian journalist for a drink at a favorite watering hole in Toronto. Having left her homeland during the repressive years of the Milošević regime, she now resided in England and had come to spend a brief sabbatical at the Munk Centre for International Studies at the University of Toronto. We perched on our barstools. The pub was crowded. The wood paneling, subdued lighting, and pints of Guinness invited conversation, and inevitably the topic turned to war and the dismantling of civil society in the Balkans. At first, there was nothing unusual about what we discussed, how ethnic hatred had blighted the region, leaving a legacy of anger, mistrust, and, above all, grief. For the most part, I listened while she spoke of broad, sweeping themes, widely debated in the media during the many years of civil war. But gradually, her thoughts and recollections became more focused, personal, heartfelt. She talked of Balkan journalists, the archetypal tough guys reporting on a tough war, suddenly finding it difficult to control their emotions. Haunted by memories, perplexed by a vulnerability that was somehow shameful, adrift in a society that lionized strength, they felt too guilty to express their distress when those around them, their own communities, had suffered so much more. As she spoke, this petite, courageous, lively woman was crying, silent tears coursing a gentle slalom over the high color of her cheeks. She began to tell the story of a colleague who, traveling from one ravaged Bosnian hamlet to another, came to a clearing in the woods where a local militia had set up camp. Initially, there seemed little amiss. It was a typical camp scene: smoke rising from fires, men lazing about, strips of what appeared to be meat being smoked above a flame. And then, to his stupefaction, the journalist realized that the meat was human flesh. Strips of human flesh, cut from the bones of men and women not as a descent into cannibalism, for there was food enough, but rather as one further despoliation of the dead, mocking and dehumanizing those who had so recently been neighbors.

There was a troubling incongruity in hearing a tale of such depravity while sitting in the gemütlich ambience of the pub, the barman discreetly attentive to the level in our glasses, and outside safe, silent streets and the sparkle of festive bunting on trees. After a tale of smoked human flesh, there is nowhere else for conversation to go. What is there to say? How is one to respond? My guest dabbed her eyes and apologized. I told her there was nothing to apologize for. She laughed. "It's that Balkan temperament," she joked. "Can't show signs of weakness." And then she grew serious once more. "You know, what happened in New York recently was terrible," she said, "too terrible for words. My heart goes out to those people, but maybe now, just maybe, others like the Americans and the Canadians can understand what we went through, what it is like to have such trauma, such evil in your society." There was no schadenfreude in this statement, only a lingering sense of sadness.

On the first anniversary of the September attacks, I returned to the offices of CNN in New York. The mood was somber, but quite different from that I had encountered eight months earlier. Few journalists sought me out, and those who did displayed little more than residual anxiety, now well controlled. Still, some lingering doubts and insecurities persisted, occasionally manifesting themselves as heightened concerns for the safety of their children or disturbing nightmares. One journalist, for example, dreamed of standing atop the twin towers, one foot firmly planted on each intact edifice, while below lay the devastated remains of New York City, every other building flattened exactly the way the World Trade Center had been. But for the most part, the domestic journalists were getting on with their lives. How they will continue to fare psychologically rests largely on what the future holds. Further terrorist attacks of the magnitude of September 11 will challenge some who have already been sorely tried. In the end, however, the greatest threat posed by weapons of mass terror, be they anthrax or commandeered jetliners, may not be the immediate loss of life, which can ultimately be contained, but the psychological toll of high levels of stress and the attrition wrought by an abiding sense of vulnerability, living with fear, and expectation of future calamity.

# 8

# The Iraq War:
# In Bed with the Military

\* \* \*

When you underestimate danger, it comes more quickly.

Latin proverb

The terrorist attacks of September 11 and the American-led invasion of Iraq less than two years later presented journalists with uniquely different sets of challenges. On September 11, mayhem arrived unexpectedly, the surprise was complete, and journalists averse to conflict reporting suddenly found themselves war correspondents in their own backyard. Scrambling through a chaotic entanglement of masonry and raw emotion, they were forced by unimaginable circumstances to pick up the mantle and relay news of that black day and its prolonged, somber aftermath.

The invasion of Iraq could not, in terms of timing, have been more different for journalists. The build-up to war was slow, measured, and, to all but the most naive and cynical, inexorable. Diplomatic machinations, carefully crafted U.N. resolutions, and serial ultimatums did little to camouflage the inevitability of war. They did, however, offer time enough for journalists to get their kit together, check their vaccination records, and attend hostile-environment training sessions in which, for a week, ex–Special Forces personnel taught survival techniques ranging from basic first aid to how best to respond when kidnapped. Thus, by the time the first salvo of cruise missiles was launched from warships in the Arabian gulf, a phalanx of over two thousand journalists were either already in Iraq or arrayed along its borders, primed for conflict reporting. And adding to the preparatory mix was a phenomenon not seen since the days of the Vietnam War four decades earlier: the embedded journalist.

Faced with an unprecedented number of journalists hovering on the fringes of the approaching hostilities, the American and British military decided that the best way of controlling the fourth estate's movements once battle was joined was to attach, or embed, journalists with military units. This would also, in theory, allow the military to control the flow of news — censorship in the guise of beneficence. Mainstream journalism did not need coercing when it came to embedding. After the tight restriction imposed on the media during the first Gulf war, the television networks, newspapers, and news agencies, led by their Washington bureau chiefs, readily embraced a system that offered greater access to the front lines. This chapter is not the place to debate the merits and drawbacks of this enmeshed relationship as it pertains to newsgathering. But from a psychological health perspective, it raises a number of interesting questions. Anecdotal accounts pepper this book, attesting to the hazards faced by war journalists. Confronting death, both one's own and that of others, is an inevitable component of the profession. Danger and threat in turn are the precipitants for symptoms of PTSD and depression. With the insertion of a buffer, would this relationship change? Would the protection supplied by a military unit to journalists lessen the psychologically corrosive effects of repeated exposure to grave personal threat? Or, conversely, would their proximity to a combat unit expose journalists to even greater risk, in the process potentially heightening emotional distress? Answering these questions became the focus of a new study.

Two news organizations, one American and the other British, agreed to provide a list of journalists sent to Iraq. Names were selected at random from those provided, and the individuals were approached to take part. The 85 percent response rate exceeded even that of my first study, illustrating yet again the desire of many journalists to help explore what remains a nascent area of trauma research.

The Iraq study essentially replicated the methodology of the earlier research, with a few important modifications. In addition to assessing the frequency of PTSD and depression symptoms, the amount of alcohol and other substances used, and overall levels of psychological distress, an attempt was made to quantify the number of times the journalists had been exposed to life-threatening events (or witnessed the death of civilians, combatants, or colleagues), both in the Iraq war and prior to the war. This was done using a validated instrument, the Trauma History Questionnaire, which contains twenty-four self-report questions that tally a person's exposure to "high magnitude" stressors, such as war and other violent events.

I considered it important to add this rating scale, because I anticipated that most journalists in Iraq would have been exposed to dangerous and violent events at some earlier point in their careers, well before they headed off to Baghdad, Mosul, and Tikrit. Knowing this in advance would help place the findings in context and prevent misattributing traumatic and depressive reactions solely to events experienced in Iraq.

A second important change to the methodology was my inability to complete interviews with one in five of the journalists studied. Unlike my first study, in which the data were collected during a global lull in conflicts, the Iraq data were collected as the first phase of the war ended. Although the Iraqi regime had just been overthrown, and there were sporadic celebrations of this, the country was unstable and the environment too dangerous for field work, at least according to the judgment of this researcher safely ensconced in his Toronto office. Data collection was therefore undertaken via Web-based questionnaire.

The observation that war journalists walk hand-in-hand with danger has never been more cruelly demonstrated than in Iraq. On March 22, 2005, just three days into the war, Paul Moran, an Australian freelance cameraman who was recently married and had a six-month-old daughter, became the first journalist to die. Little did his colleagues realize that the manner of his death foretold Iraq's future. Moran died in a suicide bombing. Within six weeks of his death, another fifteen journalists died. Others were more fortunate, as Kevin Sites confided to me in this harrowing account:

> Towards the final days of the war in Iraq, my team and I were captured by remnants of Saddam's Fedayeen. My translator assured us we would be killed that day. We had rounds fired at our feet, guns pointed to our heads, [and] my colleagues were kicked and punched. I was the only one to be tied up. We were forced to lie face down on the road. We believed we would be executed right there. My translator was eventually able to turn the situation to our advantage by telling our captors their village would be bombed back into the stone age as soon as coalition forces discovered our capture. We were released the same day. The event was traumatic for me, but not debilitating. We all behaved with a semblance of dignity, although we did plea for our lives. All of our equipment and personal belongings were taken, but we escaped with our lives. I harbor anger and resentment for the humiliation we were forced to endure, but perhaps the most lasting impact for me is

the understanding that when we eventually die, regardless of who surrounds us, we die alone.*

Sites's ordeal, troubling as it was, passed without much notice among his colleagues or the general public back home. Similar accounts of journalists being roughed up in this fashion only to be spared a summary roadside execution at the very last moment were not new to the profession. Conflicts in the Balkans, Chechnya, and miscellaneous African countries had all provided the precedent, and the early phase of the Iraq war was simply seeing a continuation of this trend. In addition, barely escaping execution was just one of many dangers faced. My Iraq data revealed that during the opening weeks of war, journalists by their own account confronted, on average, three events that they considered life threatening and witnessed, on average, another three events that resulted in the death of others. The responses ranged from none to ten events experienced and witnessed. Close to 20 percent of journalists confronted no danger, whereas 7 percent were exposed to ten potentially lethal threats, with similar percentages documented for witnessing death.

Drawing attention to the dangers confronted by the profession is necessary when seeking explanations for the high mortality and morbidity associated with front-line work. The nature of the job ensures journalists must seek out conflict, which often translates into finding danger, even when that was never the intent. Into this heady mix of dramatic events and high risk, the early stages of the conflict in Iraq introduced two additional factors: an extraordinarily large press corps and the twenty-four-hour news feed. Taken together, these factors made a constitutionally fraught environment that much more lethal, and they help explain why journalists began dying so quickly, and in such numbers. Yet, despite the statistics, my data showed that not one of the eighty-five journalists who took part in the study regarded the first phase of the Iraq war as their most dangerous assignment. That dubious distinction was shared by the wars in Bosnia and Chechnya.

How to explain the seeming paradox of a high mortality rate at odds with perceptions among journalists that other conflicts presented greater hazards? Two possible explanations may suffice. The first is that the opening weeks of the war saw a more or less conventional military conflict, in which two armies opposed one another. The battle lines were drawn, and

*When Sites wrote to tell me of his narrow escape, he was on assignment for CNN. Today, he has a unique position as the first journalist employed by an Internet company (Yahoo) to cover conflicts.

while the fog of war may have ensured these demarcations were often fluid or indistinct, there was still the semblance of order to what ensued on the battlefield. In this case, the overwhelming superiority of the coalition forces guaranteed not only an unequal contest, but also afforded the "coalition" journalists a degree of security. Such a set of circumstances was absent in the Balkans and the Caucasus, where lawlessness and her cousin anarchy heightened the danger. In this regard it is germane to view the results of the Trauma History Questionnaire in its entirety, for the average number of traumatic events confronted by journalists in the early days of the Iraq war (i.e., three) pales next to the more than two dozen experienced elsewhere in front-line careers that spanned well over a decade.

A second putative explanation for the paradox emerges when the cause of death in the sixteen journalists is analyzed more closely. Hostile fire from Iraqi forces accounted for a minority of fatalities, while "friendly fire" (that most terrible of euphemisms), motor vehicle accidents, and natural causes (the NBC news correspondent David Bloom died from a suspected pulmonary embolism), made up the rest. Thus, in the early phases of this war, the greatest threat was not from the Iraqi army or from the Iraqi populace, but from a miscellany of dangers that, friendly fire apart, had the most tenuous of links with war. There is bitter irony in the ferocious firepower of the allied forces affording journalists protection from Iraqi threats while spawning a more malignant menace: lethal coalition errors.

The sixteen journalists who died in the opening six weeks of war represented less than .8 percent of the assembled press corps. This places the mortality rate below that in the coalition's war against the Taliban in Afghanistan in 2001. There, fewer deaths represented a higher percentage of the total journalists in the field. Simply put, the large number of journalists who lost their lives in the opening weeks of the Iraqi invasion reflected the very large numbers of journalists on the fields of combat to begin with. In stating these bald statistics, I do not wish to diminish the tragedy of each death. For they encompass not only a whole world of sorrow for the wives, husbands, and children left behind, but also the sadness of promise lost and talent cruelly foreshortened.

✳   ✳   ✳

Researchers are always looking to validate their data. There are many ways to do this: choose a sample that is considered representative of the group or population to be studied, tighten your methodology by controlling for extraneous factors that may dilute or confound the results, choose rating scales that have been widely used and are considered the benchmark scales of measurement, and, when all this is done, select your statistical analyses carefully and interpret the results with an eye to the data's limitations. But even before the final numbers appear on the computer monitor confirming or rejecting the chosen hypotheses, a researcher can, on the basis of theoretical considerations, have a sense of what the results will be. This prescience is due to good, sound data having what is known as predictive and construct validity. Put simply, behavioral responses do not arise *de novo*, or by chance, but can be expected to obey certain principles, or constructs. In trauma research, one such construct that holds true is that if the magnitude of the stressor is increased, more individuals exposed to that stressor are likely to be adversely affected, resulting in higher rates of PTSD and depressive symptoms. The converse also applies: lesser degrees of trauma should generate fewer symptoms.

Given that none of the eighty-five journalists in my study regarded Iraq as their most stressful conflict, I anticipated that their behavioral responses would not show the same degree of distress as reported in my first study, in which journalists tapped into their Bosnian, Rwandan, and Chechen experiences. This turned out to be the case. On average, journalists reported symptoms that were approximately 20 percent less severe than did those in my previous study. But, as we are reminded by those who choose the battlefield as their station, war can never be made safe. A falloff in symptoms does not necessarily equate with acceptable levels of distress. The Iraq data showed that 15 percent of the journalists, or one in six, were troubled by unwanted, intrusive symptoms of PTSD that they considered distressing. These took the form of flashbacks, nightmares, and, most frequent of all, thoughts and images that forced their way into consciousness — unwelcome visitors all, arriving unannounced and often reluctant to leave. Almost a century earlier, during the carnage of the First World War, Sigmund Freud noted that individuals became fixated to their moments of trauma. He was alluding to the power of traumatic memory and the repetitive, insistent nature of recall. What surprises journalists on their return home would therefore not have surprised the Viennese father of psychoanalysis, for many who were in Iraq in those opening weeks of war brought home more than their word processors, cameras, and flak jackets. The BBC's Rageh Omaar gave eloquent expression to this in a *Guardian* article: "I am only just beginning to look back clearly on all the things I saw and experienced in Baghdad . . . My mind has been brimful of memories and images. Only when I return to Baghdad, I thought, will the sheer intensity of these moments come back to me in all their vivid detail. But some memories and emotions are unlocked by the things you least expect and in the most unforeseen circumstances."

Rageh Omaar was comfortable reflecting back on what he had lived through in Iraq, and the majority of his colleagues felt likewise, with only 4 percent admitting behaviors that were aimed, either consciously or unconsciously, at shying away from traumatic events experienced in Iraq. But for one journalist, simply being confronted by questions that probed recent traumas elicited such distress that his inability to provide answers spoke more eloquently than any symptom checklist. "I am sorry, but I JUST CAN'T DO THIS!!!!" he wrote. "IT IS JUST TOO PAINFUL FOR ME TO DO IT."*

Symptoms of hypervigilance and startle reactions were more common, although they too occurred with less severity than encountered in earlier conflicts. Post-traumatic stress symptoms are, however, only one way of recording the emotional fallout of conflict. It is therefore significant that, even after President Bush stood on the deck of the aircraft carrier USS *Lincoln* and declared major combat operations over, more than one in three of the journalists studied scored above the cutoff point for psychological distress as measured by the General Health Questionnaire. This measure is a composite of symptoms of depression, anxiety, social dysfunction, and physical complaints that have emotional disorder as their basis. Clearly, for some journalists, a battle of another more personal kind was being waged even as many returned home, amid a president's cheery pronouncements so at odds with Iraq's stubborn guns.

What, then, of the question posed at the beginning of this chapter? Were there any differences in the psychological responses between embedded and "unilateral" (unattached to the military) journalists to what they witnessed and experienced in Iraq? Perhaps not surprisingly, journalists saw their situations quite differently depending on their circumstances. This is how Catherine Jones of ITN described her time in Iraq to me: "I felt relatively calm and unflustered in the war zone, in large part because I was perhaps 'feeding off' the nonchalance displayed by the [British Army] troops around me, who rarely gave the impression of feeling as if they were in danger. I don't believe I was just acting tough to impress them. Instead, I genuinely felt pretty safe to be accompanying them: obviously not a position unilaterals were fortunate enough to find themselves in." And yet to Dexter Filkins of the *New York Times*, the absence of a military tether had

*The capital letters are those of the journalist.

distinct advantages, not least of which was that it afforded him easier access to the Iraqi population. "No war is a tea party," he observed, "but in that phase of the war approaching Iraqi civilians was relatively safe as well." Paul Moran's death had been the exception.

My data established that journalists, irrespective of whether they were attached to a military unit (embedded) or not (unilateral), were exposed to the same level of danger. Of the eighty-five journalists studied, thirty-eight (44.7 percent) were embedded with a military unit, and this neither afforded them protection nor exposed them to greater risk on the battlefield. It soon became clear to me that unilateral journalists, rather than passively submitting to having their access to the battlefield curtailed, used their considerable ingenuity to circumvent restrictions. One unilateral journalist cheerfully recounted how he and a colleague in Baghdad got hold of an old Jeep, painted it khaki, donned military-looking outfits, and waited by the roadside for a large American convoy to rumble past. Spotting a gap between vehicles and taking advantage of the dust whipped up by the lumbering transports, they slipped into the convoy undetected, gaining access to some action that may otherwise have been off-limits to them.

Given that embedded and unilateral journalists did not differ in their exposure to grave threat, I predicted that their behavioral responses to these hazards would be similar, too. This turned out to be the case. Their respective scores on indices of PTSD, depression, psychological distress, and alcohol consumption were almost identical.* The results thus provided an empirical answer to the question posed at the study's outset. In the first phase of the Iraq war, it did not matter from a psychological health perspective whether journalists were embedded or unilateral.

With my data newly analyzed, I paid a call on CNN's Nic Robertson in London to discuss the findings and gauge his assessment of what life was like for a journalist in Iraq. We met in London, on a perfect summer's morning, the warm, light breeze ruffling the shrubbery and shifting wispy cloudscapes high above. Saddam Hussein's regime, with its cast of killers ("Chemical Ali") and buffoons ("Comical Ali") had fallen, and news had just come in that Hussein's two sons, Uday and Qusay, had been killed in a shootout with American forces. Robertson, however, had another death on his mind. A few days earlier, Richard Wild, a twenty-four-year-old rookie journalist working for ITN, had been killed outside the National Museum

---

*Both groups also had the same average scores on the Trauma History Questionnaire, which measured their previous exposure to trauma as well.

of Baghdad. Wild, who had been in Iraq just two weeks, was murdered when an unknown assailant came up behind him on a crowded street and shot him before disappearing back into the crowd. It was unclear whether Wild had been targeted as a journalist or whether his killing was an act of anti-Western hostility. "If there are more attacks like this, or if car bombs and random violence becomes more prominent," observed Robertson, "then the cumulative stress on journalists will increase. It's already bad for the population, but this has not yet spilled over into affecting journalists on a daily basis."

For Robertson, the war in Iraq had presented some unique challenges. CNN had been expelled from the country at the beginning of hostilities, and Robertson had had to report events from the Jordanian border. "The Iraqis thought they had made [CNN] in 1991 by allowing us to be the only journalists in the country," he explained, "and this time they were unmaking us. Their culture and psychology was, we scratch your back and you scratch ours. They felt they had helped us substantially in 1991 and now we were not paying them back when they needed it. They wanted coverage that would benefit them, and that, of course, is not what we are there for. So, they felt let down and the only way they had of exerting pressure on us was to limit the number of our visas and finally to order us out [of] the country." The day after Saddam's statue was toppled and the borders became porous, Robertson returned with the marines: "We flew back to Al Numaniyah, about 130 kilometers south of Baghdad. They put us and our vehicles on a C130 transport and flew at about two hundred feet, so that was a bit nerve-racking."

Robertson's assessment of what was happening on the ground echoed that of his colleagues who had been allowed to remain during the war. "The risks appeared to come from looters and remnants of the Iraqi army acting on their own," he recalled. "I didn't feel there was such a great threat at that stage because most of my experience in Iraq had entailed driving around with relative ease and security." And yet, even as this experienced, savvy journalist reviewed recent events in Iraq, tallying up the stressors confronting journalists and drawing comparisons with earlier conflicts in Bosnia, Afghanistan, and the Congo, I became aware that he had a gimlet eye focused firmly on the future as well. Whatever conclusions he could derive from events in Iraq up to that point always came with the disclaimer that future forecasts were not so straightforward. Was there a link, he mused more than once, between the escalating number of car bombings and the assassin who emerged from the crowd to kill before melting away into anonymity? Or was it simply coincidence, random violence erupting as it so often does when repressive regimes crumble and a long-suffering populace awakens to suddenly find their shackles gone? In July 2003, the answer was by no means clear. Iraq's future hung in the balance, and with it the well-being of her people and, by extension, an armada of journalists entrained to Saddam's bloody denouement.

*   *   *

With time comes clarity. From the vantage point of the second anniversary of the war's onset, it is clear which direction Iraq has traveled in. I have been careful to make a distinction between an early and a later phase of the Iraq imbroglio. Any assessment of how journalists have fared psychologically must follow this division, for the two sets of circumstances differ greatly. Conclusions derived from the early data are not applicable to a later, more deadly period of conflict, in which the atavistic appearance of beheading as an instrument of terror forged a grisly link between today's insurgents and Tamarlane's fourteenth-century Mogul hordes.

Dexter Filkins, who has been in Iraq for much of the current conflict, believes a series of discrete markers have heralded changes in the degree and nature of the violence. The first marker was the invasion itself. Filkins, driving into Iraq from Kuwait in the intoxicating wake of an army sweeping aside all before it, likened what he saw to prying off the doors to a mental institution. "People seemed dumbfounded, uncomprehending, fear mixed with euphoria," was how he remembered it, "so different from what I had witnessed in Afghanistan where people were happy, shaving off their beards, throwing away their burkas, and so on." The Iraqis' mix of emotions may have imbued events with a lopsided, disconcerting feel at times, but hostility towards journalists was not yet part of this complex stew.

The second marker was the Ramadan offensive that took place in late 2003, with five simultaneous suicide bombings. Filkins recalls standing in the rubble of the destroyed Red Cross offices in Baghdad, the charred bodies of the suicide bombers in clear sight, the city echoing with the sounds of other bombers going about their deadly work. Twenty attacks a day jumped to fifty. Iraq was suddenly a more hostile place for journalists, who were slow to accept that the rules had changed. Soon thereafter, Filkins was attacked by a mob. He told me of an old man, face contorted with fury, yelling, "Kill, kill, kill!" as the frenzied crowd turned on the press, accusing foreigners of bringing the car bombers to Iraq. Despite these worrying signs, journalists were still traveling to get their stories, though they did begin tightening their security.

Matters reached their nadir in April 2004 with the rise of the Mahdi's army and the killing of four American contractors, whose burned remains were strung up over a bridge in Fallujah. This third marker represents the point at which journalists could no longer travel unaccompanied. Seven reporters were kidnapped that April, five more in August. The Italian journalist Enzo Baldoni was murdered by his kidnappers. It was now considered too dangerous for a journalist to travel into the Sunni Triangle except with American troops. Unilateral journalists like Filkins by necessity became embeds. Reporting was heavily curtailed, and careful planning and calculation were needed before a journalist could venture forth from a secure compound. Private security companies, generally run and staffed by ex–Special Forces soldiers, had become a ubiquitous presence, shepherding a dwindling pool of journalists to and from a day's events.

Two years after our first interview, I sat down once again with Nic Robertson, who had in the interim returned repeatedly to Iraq. "In past wars you could get caught in the crossfire," he observed. "Now you get put in the crosshairs, as a Westerner, as an infidel, as a journalist who is not telling the right story, as a pawn in a bigger political game because it could be very valuable to capture you, trade you." Robertson has, in the past decade, spent an average of nine months a year away from home, mostly as a witness to war. His assessments of risk and danger are measured, framed by the near misses of personal experience. "My sense is that [Iraq at present] is unique," he told me. "I can't think of being in a situation quite like this where I felt that we are the target, and it's very, very dangerous. Mogadishu was a worry—there was a randomness to it—you knew that you represented money and the lawlessness left you feeling uneasy about the situation. Iraq now is totally different because what you could face is being kept in a cage, paraded on television to the horror of your family and countrymen, and then having your head cut off."

What does this incremental deterioration in the security situation mean for the psychological well-being of journalists? The answer is, for the most part, speculative. Certainly, the study I completed within the first weeks of war could not be done now. Too few journalists remain in Iraq. Moreover, any group comparisons between unilateral and embedded journalists are simply impossible. As I write this in early 2006, with one or two exceptions there are no unilateral foreign journalists left. They have departed Iraq

by the hundreds. Fears of kidnapping, decapitation, and a bullet in the back
have done their job. With the promised peace as elusive as the Fata Mor-
gana, a diet of unremitting violence has challenged the hardiest in the profession. Even the option of an embedded position, embraced by more than
six hundred journalists two years earlier, has lost its allure. The French,
Italians, Spanish, and Germans have packed up and left. A few Americans
remain. Over a two-year period, a foreign press corps numbering more
than two thousand has been reduced piecemeal to a tiny fraction of their
original number. The erstwhile crowded press conferences of Paul Bremer,
the former U.S. administrator of Iraq, have given way to briefings in which
news of equally grave significance is now relayed to a handful of reporters.

What of a comparison between the psychological responses of journalists currently working in Iraq and those from two years back? Once again
this is not possible, for it would be akin to comparing apples and oranges.
Any comparison of two groups with potentially different core defining
characteristics is likely to provide misleading data. The journalists who
have remained behind in Iraq are, as a group, cut from a slightly different
characterological cloth, one that through the symbiotic process of attrition
and natural selection (to use a Darwinian metaphor), finds itself on the
front lines in Iraq, the world's most dangerous place. With each incremental turn of the terror screw, journalists have packed their bags and departed.
Iraqi journalists, of course, have not had this option. This is reflected in a
major shift in the demographics of those killed. In 2003, all but one journalist who died in Iraq was foreign. In 2004 and 2005, the situation reversed;
those dying now are overwhelmingly Iraqi. The ever-present, escalating
dangers that have whittled away the size of the foreign press corps may
therefore be seen as a series of increasingly impermeable filters. Those
foreign journalists who passed through are a small, self-selected group with
an uncommon capacity for functioning in the face of unprecedented threat.
Given the enormity of the risks confronted, managers are no longer insist-
ing that journalists take up a posting in Iraq. Assignments are now voluntary, which reinforces the assertion that those who have chosen this career
trajectory can better stomach a level of violence that has driven away most
of their hardened brethren. This self-selection suggests a certain emotional
fortitude in those who have stayed on.

Small sample size, the unique magnitude of risk, and the journalists'
skewed temperamental resilience to violence: three reasons why the emotional responses of journalists currently working in Iraq cannot be compared directly to those from the much larger pool of journalists who wit-

nessed the war's opening phase. But important behavioral data can still be gleaned from those in the field. To do so, however, the emphasis must shift from group statistics to personal anecdote and case history.

It is one thing for a behavioral scientist to write of danger and risk and to conclude, as I have done here, that the Iraqi insurgency presents journalists historically with the most dangerous environment they have had to confront. But such an approach, coolly clinical and reliant on rating scales and attempts to quantify trauma through summation of memory's imperfect recall, may fail to capture what it is like for a journalist whose workplace is the Sunni Triangle. Verbal descriptions of extreme violence usually come up short, confronted by the ineffable nature of certain human experience. But the reader can often get closest to what reality on the ground is truly like by reading firsthand accounts rather than the sanitized, disembodied statistics that pour from the researcher's sieve. Extracts from the email correspondence of freelance photographer Ashley Gilbertson, on assignment for the *New York Times* in Iraq during the height of the insurgency, provide confirmation of this, emphasizing the gulf separating the distanced objectivity of the researcher and the subjectivity of his subjects.

SAMARA: DECEMBER 7, 2003

Went up North on a story about militias to Samara, in the Sunni Triangle. A lot of things have been happening recently there, 54 Iraqis allegedly killed by American soldiers in an ambush. Foreigners have had their heads cut off there too. . . .

A car pulled up on my right. I looked inside the BMW to see that there were four men. I told Tyler to hold and said to the guys in the car "Salaam Aleychom habibi, schoolnak?" or "Peace be with you friend, how are you?" We were so close that I could smell the driver's breath. They did not reply, or even blink, all four stared with an icy glare of pure hatred. I slowly put the phone down and told Tariq that we should go.

We pulled forward and as they turned with us I watched the barrel of a Kalashnikov rise in the back seat.

Then the bullets started flying.

Tariq drove into a traffic circle quickly, purposefully veering all over the road, I am quite sure this is what saved us. Within fifteen seconds he put a vehicle between us and our pursuers who continued shooting.

We screamed ahead, putting traffic between us and them. They kept following. I'm trying to eat dirt from the bottom of the car, and Tariq is driving almost blind as he takes cover too. We approached the U.S. Special forces base at top speed.

We had no choice than try to make the open road and hope the BMW decided to stop at some point. We drove through a huge bank of traffic before hitting a checkpoint of the Iraqi Army guys. We shouted "Sahafi!" and they lowered their weapons and started shouting at us. We did not stop, though we did slow down to say black BMW chasing us, four assailants, one gun we think, trying to kill us, have a nice day friend, yes thank you, and to you too, yes good bye. peace be upon you — Arabic pleasantries can be really frustrating at times. . . .

Out of nowhere an apache attack helicopter flew over at 30 feet and circled our position. The BMW made a u-turn.

### BAGHDAD: CHRISTMAS EVE, 2003

Whoa, hotel just got hit . . . saw the whole thing and now there is a gun fight right outside. Our guards are firing. What the hell is going on? I need photos of troops and xmas trees . . . everything here safe as hell, don't worry . . . have a brandy . . .

### KARBALA: MAY 7, 2004

Today was hard. I was shooting a 7 hour-long heavy gunfight, and was narrowly missed by an RPG. we had to run past numerous unexploded roadside bombs and a lot of small arms fire. Three soldiers collapsed from heat exhaustion, and a Fox cameraman received a shrapnel wound to the hand.

### MAY 12, 2004

Dammit, under mortar fire here at the base — my drugs are kicking in and leg is feeling slightly better after being injured on that run past a sniper alley.

### MAY 14, 2004

Kid I was riding with today was shot in the hip and died a few minutes later. 25 years old. Poor kid. Only person who's name I wrote down all day too, only knew him as 'Spanky' till then . . . told the Times to hold the photo until we know the family has been informed.

BAGHDAD: JUNE 10, 2004

I am either unlucky or things in Baghdad are becoming worse. Went out this morning for pix of Iranian pilgrims in a Shrine area. While driving through a bazaar an Iraqi opened my door, and tried to sell me holy water and then angrily poured it all over my cameras. We went ahead — traffic is so bad here you can't get away even if you wanted too. A few stalls down a man started snarling at me and eventually made throat-slashing gestures as he pulled his hair up — Nick Berg style. he came close to the car with a knife and did the same thing. I laughed and joked through the window as to say, no not me ha-ha, and he solemnly nodded, meaning, yes, you . . . We inched slowly forward. Another man started doing the same thing.

NOVEMBER 9, 2004

Most intense battle I have seen in my life and lucky as hell to be alive. I ran across a road this morning with my platoon of 40 men and 5 were wounded or killed. Another couple of guys in the next room were severely injured by shrapnel when American artillery came in far too close to our position. I thought the building was going to collapse on top of us.

There's been some emotion here with some marines breaking down and crying because they were so close to being hit. I have not shot that yet as feelings are a little raw right now after so many have been wounded.

NOVEMBER 11, 2004

it is nighttime. the company we are with are further inside Fallujah than anyone other at this point and are chasing insurgents around. we are being attacked a lot.

I am in a toilet, an outdoor mud hut loo that is simply a hole in the floor and when I say it is not clean, I am going to have to ask you to trust me. It is the only place that has a door through which I can use my sat phone to file.

mortars literally coming in now as I file, and a gunship is hammering positions somewhere I can't see. To cut the light from my screen, I am under a sleeping bag too, which puts me in a literal sauna — did I mention that?

NOVEMBER 12, 2004

For some reason, this place is only good to file from toilets . . . There are guards on the windows watching artillery and RPGs come in while marines below urinate and shit in boxes. It is the only room inside the mosque from which I can safely file. We will be staying here tonight with 1st and head-quarters platoons. The other 2 platoons are pushing south during the night, but after almost being killed a dozen times last night — our platoon took 11 casualties, one KIA and one extremely serious — and not being able to make photos because of the strict darkness code, I see it fit that I stay here and wait for things to kick off at dawn . . .

NOVEMBER 16

a man was shot in the face two feet in front of me yesterday as we climbed a spiral staircase in a minaret.

have not told the desk yet. I just don't know what to say. It should have been me. Cleaned all the blood and brains off my cameras and face and arms but cant wash it out of my clothes or flak and I can smell it.

Ashley Gilbertson's description of his time in Iraq is but one variation on a theme. His colleagues give similar accounts of bullets dodged and death cheated. The visceral, searing quality of their descriptions highlights just how dangerous parts of Iraq have become. And yet, despite the magnitude of these stresses, my anecdotal evidence suggests that the journalists, with one or two exceptions, are in general coping well psychologically. Those who have chosen to remain in Iraq are not likely to pack their bags and leave each time they survive some fresh assault. They continue working effectively, creatively, despite an environment that is increasingly menacing. However, unremitting violence does not allow journalists to escape completely unscathed, even if their symptoms are not severe enough to emotionally derail their ability to work. This observation should come as no surprise. What Gilbertson and colleagues confront each day demonstrates that as the job of newsgathering proceeds, certain experiences cannot easily be blotted out. Transient, harrowing nightmares; intermittent, intrusive thoughts; and the dreaded, albeit infrequent, return of the cloying, nauseating smell of splattered brains challenge the firmest resolve. In addition, moods may fluctuate disconcertingly, from the euphoria associated with surviving an ambush to the despair that invariably accompanies incessant turmoil. In many of my conversations with journalists in Iraq and those back home for short breaks, I was asked about symptoms like these, "What do they mean?" "Should I be worried?" "Does it signify a 'nervous breakdown'?" "What can I expect in the days ahead?" These questions were cloaked in anxiety, and appropriately so. But invariably, as I charted the time course of these phenomena, all the while providing education, advice, and reassurance, I came to observe that they were essentially self-limiting. Among the small cohort of Baghdad-based foreign journalists, the re-experiencing symptoms of PTSD either stopped spontaneously within days to weeks, or else decreased to a frequency that was tolerable. Even in those rare cases in which a symptom persisted, the journalist usually habituated to it. Just another neutered horror, filed away, one among many.

Given the ubiquitous threat in Iraq, hypervigilance has become a way of life for many journalists, and it is often difficult to relinquish even when the danger has passed. "I once recall flying back home," confided Nic Robertson, "and we were driving from Heathrow to the CNN bureau in central London and I looked over at the car next to me, concentrating on the driver, to see what he was doing, trying to judge his facial expression, his general attitude and body posture. I caught myself doing this and then it dawned, well that's great, I actually don't have to look at people and I don't have to wonder what they are thinking or what they are going to do. And I don't have to wonder if they are going to blow up their car. Which was very nice."

At times, guilt looms prominently for journalists still in Iraq, particularly when a soldier or a stringer is killed and the journalists question anew their complicated relationships with the military and with local news organizations. This intense self-scrutiny is also usually transient, for as the acute distress following a death abates and the foreign journalists take stock of their circumstances with a vision less clouded by grief, old insights are quickly reaffirmed. They simply cannot function in Iraq without the assistance of both groups.

Apart from stringers and the coalition military forces, there is a third group whose activities unquestionably have had the greatest impact on how the press operates in Iraq. I refer to the insurgents. Their campaign of terror has driven the remaining foreign journalists into the military bed. Their bombs and bullets and beheadings constitute the major source of fear and distress. Their fanaticism has forced journalists to take extraordinary safety measures, effectively cutting themselves off from the main perpetrators of violence. But war perennially leads to strange permutations, odd associations, quirky liaisons. If the meager number of foreign journalists remaining in Iraq represents a highly select group with the stomach for adversity, they contain within their ranks a few who embody a further distillation of this trait. Members of this rarefied subgroup have gained access to the insurgency and can report the war from two fronts, if required. One such journalist is Michael Ware, *Time* magazine's bureau chief in Baghdad.

In the summer of 2003, Ware managed to establish contact with a group of disenchanted Sunnis, mainly former members of Saddam Hussein's security apparatus. Haifa Street and its environs, a small district of Baghdad, was one of their fiefdoms, a mini-Fallujah in the heart of the capital. The insurgency was in its infancy. Their primary aim was to rid the country of foreign invaders. With his improbable escort, Ware was able to navigate streets off-limits to his colleagues and was witness to the dethroned Baathists stockpiling weapons and manufacturing bombs. The level of support for the insurgency among the residents of the area was so high, and their enmity toward the United States so great, that even U.S. military units were leery of venturing in, estimating their chances of a firefight to be more than 80 percent.

Gradually, over the course of a year, Haifa Street underwent a transformation. With unequaled access to this hotbed of resistance, Ware observed the arrival of the foreign Jihadis who soon overran the local Iraqi fighters, displaced their commanders, islamicized the conflict, and converted a local rebellion into a holy war. The level of violence escalated sharply. All non-Muslims, including journalists, were considered legitimate targets of terror. Suicide bombings, kidnapping, and decapitation were the order of the day. Ware was taken hostage by a group led by Abu Musab al-Zarqawi, the thirty-seven-year-old Jordanian de facto leader of the Jihadis. Ware feared imminent execution and, moreover, one that would be filmed, when his Syrian captors ominously confiscated his camera and placed him under the banner of Zarqawi's group, Tawhid and Jihad. It took the speedy and forceful intervention of Ware's unlikely guardian, a supplanted Baathist commander, to save his life.

To the dismay of family, friends, and colleagues, Ware's brush with death did not deter him from working in Iraq. To be sure, the abduction did not leave him unscathed. Symptoms of an acute stress reaction were apparent in the days after his release. "I became very aware of my own mortality," he told me. "I was fearful and this hampered the way I worked. For a short while I was reluctant to leave my compound." When he did venture out, Ware was hypervigilant, intensely scanning his environment for fresh dangers. He felt more unsettled than usual when caught in traffic, concerned his reduced mobility left him vulnerable to a second hijacking. What gives this vignette a telling clinical interest is that despite the intensity and immediacy of the threat posed, these symptoms did not develop into post-traumatic stress disorder. There were no nightmares, flashbacks, intrusive images of an anxiety-provoking captivity. Furthermore, Ware's transient reluctance to venture forth from the security of his residence did not translate into persistent avoidant behavior.

But the most remarkable aspect of this account is the manner in which this dauntless journalist mastered emergent anxieties and reconstituted his emotional equilibrium. "The battle for Fallujah cleansed me," he disclosed. Michael Ware's no-nonsense, pithy explanation reveals much about the motivation and resilience of those few journalists still working in Iraq. Shortly after being released by Zarqawi's homicidal henchman, Ware seated himself in a Bradley armored fighting vehicle with an advance guard of soldiers and was among the very first to enter the besieged city. Amid the most ferocious fighting of the Iraq war, he found his footing once again, and this fortitude under fire restored his fractured confidence. This remarkable, unorthodox remedy was another high-risk rolling of the dice in an environment where work for journalists is synonymous with risk.

Ware remains in Baghdad as *Time*'s bureau chief. His unrivaled access to all aspects of the conflict has, as his history reveals, not come easily. In addition, one of his staff has been assassinated, two have been kidnapped and tortured, and two have been caught in explosions but survived. He lives day to day, still covering both sides of the conflict, conscious of the hair-trigger sensitivities of the insurgents, which translate into fresh threats from Zarqawi's brigade whenever he writes something they find objectionable. By his own admission, he now feels most at home in Iraq, where he spends approximately forty weeks a year, well beyond the duration of most other foreign journalists. Surrounded by a tightly knit and fiercely protective staff of local Iraqi stringers, he ascribes his longevity in Iraq to two factors: a belief that the Iraq conflict is an important story — "my generation's Vietnam," he calls it — and an intense loyalty to the Iraqis who take enormous risks to work alongside him, and who would be even more imperiled (and without work) should *Time* follow the course of some other news organizations and close their offices in response to the violence.

Resilience in the face of adversity is not, however, synonymous with immunity. Faced with such an extraordinary array of dangers, it is inevitable that some journalists who have survived kidnapping have fared less well. The most notorious case of an abduction ending tragically involved Giuliana

Sgrena, who works for *Il Manifesto*, one of Rome's communist daily newspapers. A confirmed pacifist, her antiwar views at odds with Prime Minister Berlusconi's support for the invasion, she had returned repeatedly to Baghdad, fueled by a desire to describe the lives of ordinary citizens caught in conflict. It was on her seventh trip to Iraq that she was kidnapped one Friday outside a mosque where she had gone to interview refugees from Fallujah. It was not long before the insurgents released one of their chilling hallmark videos showing the distraught hostage pleading for her life. A few months earlier, similar television images of a captive Margaret Hassan, the British-born Iraqi national and director of Care International's humanitarian relief in Iraq, had presaged Hassan's execution. In the face of terror, gender and altruism provided scant salvation.

Despite ominous precedents, Giuliana Sgrena was not murdered. The Italian government controversially brokered a deal that led to her release after four weeks in captivity. Freedom, however, signaled the start of a second ordeal: while she was en route to the Baghdad airport in the company of Italian secret service agent Nicola Calipari, who had been sent to escort her to safety, their car was fired upon by American soldiers. Calipari was killed and Sgrena wounded.

One of my first impressions on meeting Giuliana Sgrena was of a person whose appearance and demeanor—petite, graying, gentle, and soft-spoken—fit altogether comfortably with her beliefs. And yet, beneath the dovish exterior must surely lie a steely determination. How else to explain seven trips to a post-Saddam Iraq? A simple summer dress did little to conceal a surgically reconstructed shoulder, one legacy of the night that saw Calipari killed. We chatted in her top-floor apartment on a hot summer's afternoon. The French doors leading to a small balcony garden were open for a breeze that faltered on the threshold. A discordant symphony of protesting Vespas and Piaggios percolated up from the street. When a helicopter flew overhead, the *thwack, thwack, thwack* of the rotors caught Sgrena's attention, momentarily bringing her narrative to a stop. "Just like Baghdad," she murmured.

During her month in captivity, Sgrena was kept in an airless room in which the one window had been boarded up. Her watch was confiscated. Day and night were indistinguishable. The single, bare electric bulb was never turned off. She could only follow the passage of time from the sounds of prayer that filtered into her prison from a nearby mosque and from her brief glimpses of the sky through a small window when she was taken to the toilet. Her captors gave her food and never beat her, but her isolation was torture enough. "The days were very, very long and to spend them without anything is terrible," she told me, "so to pass the time, I tried to recall my life, starting from when I was very small, and every day I would try to keep my attention on one period of my life." At first she was accused of being a spy. There were many times she feared for her life and, much as she tried concentrating on the minutiae of the past, her thoughts would often derail, posing questions whose answers she dreaded. How would she be killed? Where would she be buried? How would her elderly parents cope with her death? Would her husband be left with guilt if he could not secure her release? When her captors demanded she be filmed for their video, she told them that if they expected the Italian forces to be withdrawn as the price of ransom, they were mistaken. "Better to kill me now," she challenged them. On another occasion, roused to anger by her helplessness and humiliation, she taunted her kidnappers: "Kill me now . . . It's easier to kill a woman because I have no defense. It's easier than to go and fight the Americans in the street." When fear took a break from numbing her thoughts, perplexity interjected. Why had the insurgents seized her, a known pacifist, someone so completely opposed to the war, and whose very aim was to bring to the attention of the outside world just how much the Iraqis were suffering? To which her captors replied, "This is war."

It was winter in Baghdad, and her airless room was bitterly cold. A kerosene heater gave off toxic fumes and could not be used. Huddled under a blanket for warmth, Giuliana Sgrena awaited her fate. As the days merged into weeks, the fear, uncertainty, sensory deprivation, loneliness, disbelief, and cold conspired to trick her perceptions in the cruelest fashion. "Sometimes I felt I was not in my body," she confided. "I was out of my body and only when I started to feel very cold in my feet, for example, did I realize I was alive." Listening to this anguished account of a classic depersonalization reaction, I recalled Yvonne Ridley and Janine di Giovanni describing variants of this symptom, the former when she was captured by the Taliban and the latter after her return from Sierra Leone.

Little did Sgrena know that the travails of her imprisonment were just the prelude to a sequence of events that epitomized the cruelty of war and the impotence of individuals to control their destinies, no matter how well meaning their intentions or indomitable their spirits. When her release came, it was sudden. A change of clothing, some cotton wool stuffed behind a pair of dark glasses, and a nighttime car ride through the deserted and dangerous streets of Baghdad. After arriving at what she presumed was the point of handover, she was left unattended in the backseat of a car. Blind to her surroundings, all she could do was sit and wait, prey once more to intense anxiety. What if she were being handed over to a new set of tormenters? What if the helicopter she could hear and presumed to be American fired at her vehicle? What if the Iraqi police did likewise? After an interminable wait, one of the kidnappers returned to reassure her that she would be free in ten more minutes. So she began counting, one, two, three, four, five, until she got to six hundred. And still nothing happened. Fighting a rising panic, she suddenly became aware of a strong light on her face. Then the car door opened once more, but this time it was an Italian voice she heard telling her she was free.

"The way [Calipari] approached me was very, very good," Sgrena recalled, "I realized immediately that he was a very good person and I could trust him." In the twenty minutes or so Nicola Calipari would spend with her, he would do what he could to put her at ease. The cotton wool and dark glasses were removed, as was the shawl in which she had been huddling. En route to the airport, Calipari put through a call to Italy, and Sgrena spoke to her partner, editor, and others responsible for her release. Finally she could accept that she was free. "I was very happy," was how she remembered the moment.

It had rained that day in Baghdad, and the streets were wet. This and the absence of streetlights meant they had to travel slowly. Sgrena remembered the driver making a joke: "Imagine, we free her from the kidnappers and now we will die in an accident." It was then that the shooting started. "No one had tried to stop us, there was no sign of a checkpoint, there was nothing there . . . my impression was that there were a lot of bullets." Calipari died protecting Sgrena, not from the scimitar of the insurgents, but from the gunfire of American soldiers. Incredulity greeted this news in Rome, Washington, London, and much farther afield. But as disbelief reluctantly gave way before the facts, what could not be expunged was a misadventure in which could be found all the heartache, stupidity, and futility of war. After the firing ceased, the soldiers came over to inspect the carnage and found Calipari slumped against Sgrena. As they tried lifting him up, she heard him breathe his last. "His death rattle," is how she described it to me. It is a sound she cannot forget. Five months after the death of the man sent to bring her to freedom, the memory of that night haunted her. Although she was badly injured, it was not the punctured lung or the shattered shoulder that remained her most troubling symptom. Rather, it was the physical and emotional imprint of Calipari and the recurring sound of his final breath that stalked her waking moments. "It is something on my body that I cannot forget," she told me through silent tears.

Given the enormity of what this woman endured, it was not surprising to learn that other prominent symptoms of PTSD were present at the time of our meeting. For the first time in her career, she had no work plan. Overwhelmed by the recent past, she could not contemplate the future. "Just to live in Rome without any plans to travel is something that has never before happened in my life," she confided. "Also, I cannot read a novel or a book," she went on. "If I start, after one page I start to think of other things." Additional difficulties included a newfound fear of the dark and the need to keep the light on when she slept, and a sense of insecurity in her home city that was heightened when she had to cross a street, this simple act now preceded by the rituals of carefully looking around and scanning her environment for imagined threats. She even feared opening mail, because she viewed it as yet another potential source of danger. The limitations imposed by these symptoms were considerable. Cut off from her former life by persistent anxieties, Sgrena's world closed in on her. This constricted existence in turn exacerbated her dysphoria and left her feeling cheated of her freedom. Having survived four weeks of the most hazardous captivity, she had her moment of liberation forever blighted. The joy of homecoming was displaced by the death rattle of a good man who died on her shoulder, protecting her. The ongoing investigation into what went wrong with her release, the national outpouring of grief for the Italian secret service agent, the accusations of some right-wing politicians in Italy who blame her for Calipari's death, all meant there was no closure to her ordeal. It is also salient to note that although her collapsed lung healed and a shattered shoulder was put together again, Sgrena had not received psychological help. The advice she was given was that writing about her ordeal would be therapy enough. Five months later, it was troubling to witness the failure of that ill-informed counsel.

Recently, a young man who had never been to Iraq asked to see me. He was a video editor, someone who occupied a safe seat at a large news organization in the heart of an orderly city far removed from the mayhem of Baghdad. He met with me not as part of my research, but as a patient. His story attests to the reach of war and the risks conflict poses for journalists. In the previous chapter, details were given of a journalist who, after watching hundreds of hours of videotape showing the collapse of the World Trade Center and victims jumping to their deaths, developed disabling symptoms of emotional distress. PTSD-type reactions by proxy, as it were, are exceedingly rare, but the war in Iraq, with its unrelenting barrage of violent images, has induced a similar clinical situation, albeit with a particularly macabre twist befitting the country's agony.

Happily married with a young son, earning a good living, and physically well, the young video editor had lived an uncomplicated, if nondescript, life. Then one morning he arrived at work and found the way to his console of television monitors impeded by a throng of colleagues. They had their backs to him and were so engrossed in what they were doing that no one even noticed his arrival. Maneuvering between them, he quickly realized what it was that held their attention.

"There was this grainy image on the television screen," he recalled, "but the figures could be made out clearly enough. A young man was seated, wearing orange overalls, and behind him stood a group of masked men, one of whom was ranting in Arabic. I had seen stills and video like this before, so the sight was not unfamiliar. But a crowd watching such a scene was absolutely unfamiliar, and in a flash I knew instinctively what was coming next." He paused in his narrative and looked away, out my office window to a cherry tree that was coming into pink blossom, shedding petals that lay scattered atop the freshly cut grass. "I had always promised myself I would never watch one of those scenes if it came my way," he intoned, voice expressionless. "I mean, who wants to fill up their head with that kind of shit." He fell silent once more and his gaze drifted back to the open window and beyond. When he started up again, the monotone had given way to agitation, his phrases staccato short, telegrammatic, effortful, as though even giving tremulous voice to his thoughts was painful: "Masked man . . . a large knife . . . struggle . . . I looked away . . . try to back off, the press of people . . . could not get away in time . . . saw very little . . . but . . ."

And there he stopped. The sentence hung unfinished, tensely suspended between what had been confided and what was to come. I said nothing and waited, reluctant to hurry the narrative along. The man needed time to marshal the emotions that threatened to career uncontrolled ahead of his troubled thoughts. On a couple of occasions he looked up at me, only to quickly avert his eyes. He shuffled uncomfortably in his chair, cleared his throat, removed a speck of dust from his jacket, blew his nose, sank back into lethargy, fidgeted a little more. All the while I waited for him to finish what he needed to tell me.

His voice was hoarse when he finally found it again. Initially, I had difficulty following the gist of what he was trying to convey. "I never saw the actual beheading," he confided, "I was determined not to look because I was scared I would never get rid of those images. So, I never saw it." An embarrassed smile quickly melded into a grimace that fixed itself on his face. "But what I had not anticipated was the sound. And now it will not leave me."

Four weeks had elapsed since this man stumbled upon a group of colleagues in the newsroom casually watching the beheading of a western captive. The TV's volume had been turned up high. No image had seared itself into his consciousness, for his vigilance and resolve had largely thwarted any morbid fascination to watch what was unfolding on the screen. But he underestimated the threat to his psyche. Avoiding disturbing visual imagery did not suffice; instead, sound seeped into that mental recess he had resolutely defended. He could not forget the screams of the man being beheaded, that ghastly piercing cry a distillation of fear so pure and intense it relayed the horror just as powerfully as any image could. A month after he first heard it, my patient could not shake that sound. At times it was there when he woke from a fitful night's sleep, and on occasion it shadowed him to bed at the end of the day. Initially the intrusions were intermittent. By distracting himself with work and socializing he got the shrieks to subside, but gradually that antidote weakened. He would hear the screams while playing with his child in the evening, while having dinner with his wife. To shut the sound off he purchased an iPod and stuffed his ears with headphones and the thudding beats of his favorite rock stars. For a while this gave some relief, but in the pauses between the songs the tormenting cries occasionally popped up, and eventually they began discordantly accompanying the music. Soon no decibel level could blot out the cries, for, as he realized, they emanated from within his head, while the remedy of music came from without. The struggle was unequal. The more he resisted the more he fixated on the sounds. Soon he began embellishing them with imagery of his own, filling in the visual blanks with the most lurid pictures. From there it was a short step to putting himself in the condemned man's place, imagining what must have gone through his mind in those frantic final minutes, knowing full well he was about to be decapitated in front of the video camera, one more lurid episode of reality TV, Iraq style. By the time this journalist decided to seek help, only alcohol was bringing relief from it all. His consumption of half a bottle of whisky at night was hurting his relationship. He had taken some time off from work.

*   *   *

Therapy provided this journalist with a way out of his obsessional ruminations, and he was able to return to work. But if this young man's future now seems brighter, the same cannot yet be said of Iraq. As I write this chapter, more than sixty journalists have been killed in Iraq in a little over two years. The hordes of foreign press have left, and it is the Iraqi journalists, with few exceptions, who are now the ones dying. Forty-two have been shot, decapitated, or blown up trying to keep their countrymen informed.* Again, comparisons across place and time are often misleading. But a brief review of journalist fatalities during major twentieth-century conflagrations places the present Iraqi situation in a historical context. During the four years of World War I, two journalists were killed, and sixty-nine died in the six-year period of World War II. Seventeen journalists died in the Korean conflict, while the Vietnam War (which lasted twenty years if one includes the conflict that spilled over into Cambodia), left sixty-three journalists dead. With more than sixty correspondents, photographers, producers, and cameramen dead in Iraq in a little over two years, the pace of dying there has outstripped all its predecessors. Iraq today, in the grip of the insurgents, represents the most hazardous quagmire for journalists since they first became a feature of war's landscape in the Crimea of 1854.

What this all means for the psychological health of journalists is only partly understood. Anecdotes and case histories show that some journalists have been deeply scarred by the war in Iraq. But many more of their colleagues appear to be weathering the terror without succumbing to posttraumatic stress disorder and depression. Perhaps the paradox of heightened danger coexisting with lower levels of emotional distress can be explained by the fact that the journalists still in Iraq are a small, self-selecting, resilient group surrounded by extraordinary levels of security. However, my behavioral conclusions are preliminary. The final chapter in Iraq's turbulent history is still to be written. With the foreseeable future clogged by violence, it is unclear whether the present group of battle-hardened journalists will remain in Iraq indefinitely or ask for a breather. Should they

---

*No study has yet looked at the psychological health of Iraqi journalists reporting on the war in their country.

decide to leave as the country drifts into outright civil war, who will replace them, and how will this new cohort fare? And what of those who choose to stay? For how long can they keep their emotional buffers in place amid the havoc of a failed state, if that is to be the country's fate? These are questions future research will need to address. But Iraq's bleak future and the uncertainty it entails for journalists should not obscure what has been learned already. There always will be fine journalists who, *in extremis*, find their emotions sorely challenged. The extraordinary efforts of news organizations to improve the physical safety of their staff in Iraq come up short if this simple truth is overlooked.

# Afterword

My interview with a defensive Maggie O'Kane started on a difficult note. "I don't necessarily buy your theory that we are all traumatized," she told me. I assured her that was not my view. And indeed, the results of my studies proved us correct. After a decade or more of confronting extremely hazardous situations, some journalists do develop psychological problems such as post-traumatic stress disorder and depression. They are a minority, albeit a substantial one. This should not be surprising, given the nature of what front-line journalists do. The more remarkable observation, perhaps, is that most emerge relatively unscathed. Through a complex interplay of factors that determine motivation, a self-selection process is at work, ensuring that most journalists who choose conflict as their area enjoy what they do, are very good at it, and keep the life-threatening hazards from undermining their psychological health. Many experience distressing residual symptoms such as troubling dreams, flashbacks, and startle responses, but these by themselves do not constitute evidence of formal psychiatric illness.

There is, however, one clinically relevant statistic I have not yet given: the journalists who developed a disorder such as PTSD or became seriously depressed seldom received treatment. This neglect, at times approaching disdain, was part of a wider, macho culture of silence that historically enveloped the profession when it came to the question of psychological health and other emotive issues such as divorce and dysfunctional relationships, heavy drinking habits, and the effects of work on spouses and children. It helps explain not only the failure of news organizations to provide treatment for their employees, but also why a study such as mine had not been

182

done earlier. While the management of news organizations was partly to blame for this, journalists themselves also played a part, through a combination of naiveté, embarrassment, and concern that future career prospects would suffer if word of their emotional distress reached their news bosses. Only in the past few years have attitudes become more enlightened and informed. Research and education are the means to strip away remaining taboos and misconceptions.

Conscious of the sensitivities of journalists and their managers to questions that probed their psyches, I was at pains throughout my studies to emphasize that my aim was not to pathologize a profession. But it has never been more important to ask the types of questions I did of those who chose war as their workplace. I never encountered a war journalist who did not view his profession as highly dangerous. And now there is evidence that these hazards are multiplying. Even before the 2003 invasion of Iraq, one event in particular sent a chill through the ranks and put journalists on notice of ominous new threats lying in wait. The *Wall Street Journal* reporter Daniel Pearl was murdered. While opinion among journalists is divided on whether Pearl miscalculated the risks attached to his story, one respected colleague, Scott Anderson, noted in his *New York Times* article that Daniel Pearl was a careful man who looked out for his safety. "What is haunting to the rest of us," wrote Anderson, "is that there appears no cautionary lesson to be derived from his death, nothing we would have done differently." In the past, journalists had been killed accidentally by stray bullets or artillery shells, or deliberately, because they were mistaken for combatants or because a warlord wanted some unsavory truths suppressed. But the death of Pearl, as Janine di Giovanni pointed out in her London *Times* article, added a new, horrifying dimension to these threats — a journalist was decapitated because of his Jewish religion.

In a post–September 11 world seething with religious and ethnic hatred, nationality has joined religion as a new risk factor for journalists. A visit to Jerusalem and the embattled news bureaus at the height of the second intifada provided me with sad and dispiriting evidence of this. Just off the Old Jaffa road, sat a nondescript three-story building, home to many of the major television news organizations. Even before I made it up to the CNN offices, I was repeatedly given well-meaning, but nevertheless alarming, advice by the journalists I met: never take a bus ride; if your taxi stops behind a bus, instruct the driver to move and, if he refuses, get out and walk; make sure your taxi stays away from the main bus routes; and so on. Foreign journalists may be able to avoid the vehicles that have become symbols of

danger and mass death, but escaping altogether from a ubiquitous terror is
not possible. CBC's Neil MacDonald told me that when a suicide bomber
blew himself up outside a private, secluded school attended by many of the
foreign press corps' children, his severed head catapulted into the school
courtyard, coming to rest in front of the horrified pupils. Personal safety
and that of dependents is, however, only part of the stress confronted daily
by the journalists. Many found themselves vilified by Israelis and Palestin-
ians alike, this hatred a product of fevered emotions that ensured both sides
regarded the news organizations as biased. CNN journalists were derided
by the Israelis for their perceived insensitivity in covering the aftermath of
suicide bombings, but the Arab world took the opposite view, mockingly
referring to the organization as the "Zionist News Network." As for the
local Israeli and Palestinian journalists, they have increasingly gone their
separate ways, reflecting the deep schisms that divide their two societies.

The problems confronted by journalists in Israel and the Occupied
Territories pale, however, when placed alongside the current situation in
Iraq. So extreme are the dangers now confronted there that news organizations are shying away from sending journalists who do not want to go. If
this principle of voluntary assignment represents a sea change for the profession, not every journalist believes his management wholeheartedly sub-
scribes to it. A case in point is former ABC news correspondent Richard
Gizbert. After working for ABC for eleven years, Gizbert alleges he was
fired for refusing a posting to Iraq. At the time of this writing, he is suing his
employer for £2.3 million. ABC denies Gizbert's charge. Notwithstanding
this very public squabble, few on either side of the argument would deny
that news organizations in general have become more safety conscious.
Here the work of the Dart Center, the brainchild of Michigan-based psychiatrist Frank Ochberg, deserves credit. The center coordinates a global
network of journalists, journalism educators, and health professionals dedi-
cated to improving media coverage of trauma, conflict, and tragedy. It also
addresses the consequences of such coverage for those working in journalism.* The center's work has resulted in a tangible change in corporate

---

*The Dart Center's mandate is broad and recognizes that many situations other than war
can present journalists with challenges similar to those described in this book. Natural
disaster like the 2004 tsunami and Hurricane Katrina and man-made disasters like the
Oklahoma City bombing and the Columbine High School massacre are examples of
high-profile news stories that journalists have found traumatic. However, whether this
type of trauma can lead to the frequency and intensity of psychological distress described
in this book remains unclear. This question deserves future study.

culture, particularly in broadcast journalism, where a discussion of topics such as depression and PTSD has finally emerged from the closet. Hostile-environment training is now mandatory for journalists who choose to work in zones of conflict. Lectures on post-traumatic stress disorder are part of this curriculum. In addition, confidential counseling, first pioneered by CNN and the BBC, is becoming more widely available for journalists traumatized in the field. Management is deliberately kept out of this process to protect the journalist's right to privacy. Much still needs to be done though, particularly by the newspaper companies, whose efforts lag well behind broadcasting.

Any innovative developments that promote increased awareness of psychological issues should be welcomed, although here too I must add a cautionary note: journalists cannot be forced or coerced into therapy. Indeed, there is evidence suggesting that mass debriefing of individuals who have experienced traumatic stressors may do more harm than good by infecting the resilient with the angst of the symptomatic. In a profession that is not for the fainthearted, such facts take on added salience. But potential pitfalls of therapy must be viewed alongside the considerable body of research demonstrating the effectiveness of certain forms of psychotherapy and medication in treating PTSD and depression.

The way forward should ideally combine an awareness of individual psychological vulnerability with accurate and confidential mechanisms for detecting those in distress. The methodology described in my studies is one way of doing this. Once identified, journalists should be offered the option of a voluntary treatment plan tailored to their individual need. It is important to reiterate that disorders such as PTSD and depression exert a heavy toll on those affected, with untreated symptoms usually worsening over time. Conversely, the prognosis improves with timely and appropriate interventions. A few discreet questions as part of an annual medical checkup may be enough to bring potential problems to light. A referral for treatment can follow quickly, as most news organizations have a roster of appropriate specialists to call upon.

It is imperative for news organizations to look after the health of their journalists, be it physical or emotional. "The reporter is the last bastion of truth," noted the veteran war journalist Jon Swain on the eve of the American-led invasion to topple Saddam Hussein. If that situation is to endure, every effort should be made to ensure the facts are not distorted by a journalist's depression, anxiety, substance abuse, or post-traumatic stress disorder, for all these conditions may act as a biased filter through which a particular event, emotional in itself, is viewed. To Mark Brayne, formerly of the BBC and now the director of the Dart Center's European office, emotions, trauma, and good journalism are inseparable, the quality and credibility of any story or image of war directly dependent on the journalist's state of mind. This should not be misconstrued as an appeal for passion- or anger-free journalism; these emotions can often generate powerful reportage. But when a journalist is overwhelmed by his or her emotions, when subjective distress clouds judgment and alters perceptions, inaccurate, misleading work may be the result. The last bastion becomes corrupted. The public is misinformed. For a journalist, there can be no greater indictment.

"Man should not try to avoid stress any more than he would shun food, love or exercise," wrote the celebrated stress researcher Hans Selye. War journalists would no doubt loudly concur. Their profession provides ample opportunity to confront and master stressful situations. War journalism will never be made safe. Risk can be reduced, but never removed. Good war journalists understand this, work to mitigate it, and in some cases, may even welcome it. But as they navigate a path through war's many hazards, they would do well to reflect on what else Selye had to say: "Don't be afraid to enjoy the stress of a full life nor too naive to think you can do without some intelligent thinking and planning."

It is in a similar light, and with an eye on journalists' psychological well-being, that I hope my book has been read.

# Suggested Reading

American Psychiatric Association. *Diagnostic and Statistical Manual of Mental Disorders.* 4th ed. Washington, D.C.: APA, 1994.

Anon. *The Love of an Unknown Soldier.* London: Bodley Head, 1918.

Arnett, P. *Live from the Battlefield: From Vietnam to Baghdad, Thirty-Five Years in the World's War Zones.* New York: Simon & Schuster, 1994.

Ayres, C. *War Reporting for Cowards.* New York: Atlantic Monthly Press, 2005.

Baxter, J., and Downing, M. *The BBC Reports.* New York: Overlook Press, 2002.

Bell, M. *In Harm's Way: Reflections of a War-Zone Thug.* London: Penguin, 1996.

Bourke, J. *An Intimate History of Killing: Face to Face Killing in Twentieth Century Warfare.* London: Granta Books, 1999.

Buell, H. *Moments: Pulitzer Prize–Winning Photographs.* New York: Black Dog & Leventhal, 2002.

Burton, R. *The Anatomy of Melancholy.* New York: New York Review of Books Classics, 2001.

Capa, R. *Slightly Out of Focus.* New York: Modern Library, 1999.

Carroll, A. *War Letters.* New York: Washington Square Press, 2001.

Challoner, J. *The Brain.* London: Channel 4 Books, 2000.

Chatwin, B. *Anatomy of Restlessness: Selected Writings, 1969–1989.* New York: Viking, 1996.

Coté, W., and Simpson, R. *Covering Violence: A Guide to Ethical Reporting about Victims and Trauma.* New York: Columbia University Press, 2000.

Cramer, C. and Owen, J. *Dying to Tell the Story. The Iraq War and the Media: A Tribute.* Brussels: International News Safety Institute, 2003.

di Giovanni, J. *The Quick and the Dead: Under Siege in Sarajevo.* London: Phoenix House, 1994.

Faas, H., and Page, T. *Requiem: By the Photographers Who Died in Vietnam and Indochina.* New York: Random House, 1997.

Feinstein, A., and Nicolson, D. "The Iraq war: are embedded journalists at greater psychological risk?" *Journal of Traumatic Stress Studies* 18 (2005): 129–32.

Feinstein, A., Owen, J., and Blair, N. "A hazardous profession: War, journalists and psychopathology." *American Journal of Psychiatry* 159 (2002): 1570–75.

Fialka, J. J. *Hotel Warriors: Covering the Gulf War.* Washington, D.C.: Woodrow Wilson Center Press, 1991.

Gall, S. *Don't Worry about the Money Now.* London: Hamish Hamilton, 1983.

Gellhorn, M. *The Face of War.* New York: Atlantic Monthly Press, 1998.

Gellhorn, M. *Travels with Myself and Another: A Memoir.* New York: Tarcher Putnam, 2001.

Gourevitch, P. *We Wish to Inform You That Tomorrow We Will Be Killed with Our Families.* London: Picador, 2000.

Gutman, R. *A Witness to Genocide.* Dorset, U.K.: Element Books, 1993.

Hedges, L. *War Is a Force That Gives Us Meaning.* New York: Public Affairs, 2002.

Herr, M. *Dispatches.* New York: Vintage International, 1991.

Holmes, R. *Acts of War: The Behavior of Men in Battle.* New York: Free Press, 1985.

Howard, M. *The Invention of Peace.* New Haven: Yale University Press, 2000.

Howe, P. *Shooting under Fire.* New York: Artisan, 2002.

Hudson, M., and Stanier, J. *War and the Media.* Gloucestershire, U.K.: Sutton, 1997.

Kapuściński, R. *Another Day of Life.* New York: Vintage, 2001.

Kapuściński, R. *Imperium.* New York: Vintage, 1995.

Kapuściński, R. *The Shadow of the Sun.* New York: Knopf, 2001.

Keane, F. *Letter to Daniel: Despatches from the Heart.* London: Penguin, 1996.

Keane, F. *Seasons of Blood: A Rwandan Journey.* London: Penguin, 1996.

Keegan, J. *War and Our World.* New York: Vintage, 1998.

Kershaw, A. *Blood and Champagne: The Life and Times of Robert Capa.* New York: St. Martin's Press, 2002.

Knightley, P. *The First Casualty: The War Correspondent as Hero and Myth Maker from the Crimea to Iraq.* 3rd ed. Baltimore: Johns Hopkins University Press, 2004.

Kogan, D. C. *Shutterbabe: Adventures in Love and War.* New York: Villard, 2000.

Loyd, A. *My War Gone by, I Miss It So.* New York: Atlantic Monthly Press, 1999.

Marinovich, G., and Silva, J. *The Bang Bang Club: Snapshots from a Hidden War.* New York: Basic Books, 2000.

May, A. *Witness to War: A Biography of Marguerite Higgins.* New York: Beaufort Books, 1983.

McCullin, D. *Sleeping with Ghosts: A Life's Work in Photography.* New York: Aperture, 1996.

McCullin, D. *Unreasonable Behaviour: An Autobiography.* New York: Alfred Knopf, 1992.

Micale, M. S., and Lerner, P. *Traumatic Pasts: History, Psychiatry, and Trauma in the Modern Age, 1870–1930.* Cambridge: Cambridge University Press, 2001.

Miller, W. I. *The Mystery of Courage.* Cambridge, Mass.: Harvard University Press, 2000.

Moran, D. *Wars of National Liberation.* London: Cassell, 2002.

New Yorker. *The New Yorker Book of War Pieces: London 1939 to Hiroshima 1945.* New York: Schocken, 1947.

Nordstrom, C., and Robben, A. C. G. M. *Fieldwork under Fire: Contemporary Studies of Violence and Survival.* Berkeley: University of California Press, 1995.

Page, T. *Page after Page: Memoirs of a War-Torn Photographer.* New York: Atheneum, 1988.

Pearl, D. *At Home in the World: Collected Writings from the Wall Street Journal.* Edited by H. Cooper. New York: *Wall Street Journal* Books, 2002.

Pedelty, M. *War Stories: The Culture of Foreign Correspondents.* New York: Routledge, 1995.

Peterson, S. *Me Against My Brother: At War in Somalia, Sudan, and Rwanda.* New York: Routledge, 2000.

Politkovskaya, A. *A Dirty War: A Russian Reporter in Chechnya.* London: Harvill Press, 2001.

Roth, M. P. *A Historical Dictionary of War Journalism.* Westport, Conn.: Greenwood Press, 1997.

Russell, A. *Big Men, Little People: Encounters in Africa.* London: Pan, 2000.

Shawcross, W. *Deliver Us from Evil: Peacekeepers, Warlords, and a World of Endless Conflict.* New York: Simon & Schuster, 2000.

Shephard, B. *A War of Nerves: Soldiers and Psychiatrists, 1914–1994.* London: Jonathan Cape, 2000.

Silber, L., and Little, A. *Yugoslavia: Death of a Nation.* New York: Penguin, 1997.

Simpson, J. *A Mad World, My Masters: Tales from a Traveller's Life.* London: Pan, 2001.

Simpson, J. *Strange Places, Questionable People.* London: Pan, 1998.

Smith, W. E. *Let Truth Be the Prejudice.* New York: Aperture, 1985.

Sorel, N. C. *The Women Who Wrote the War.* New York: Perennial, 2000.

Spinner, J. *Tell Them I Didn't Cry.* New York: Scribner, 2006.

Steele, J. *War Junkie: One Man's Addiction to the Worst Places on Earth.* London: Bantam Press, 2002.

Stewart, I. *Freetown Ambush: A Reporter's Year in Africa.* Toronto: Penguin, 2002.

Sudetic, C. *Blood and Vengeance: One Family's Story of the War in Bosnia.* New York: Penguin, 1998.

Sweeney, M. S. *From the Front: The Story of War.* Washington, D.C.: National Geographic Books, 2002.

Wallerstein, J. S., Blakeslee, S., and Lewis, J. M. *The Unexpected Legacy of Divorce: A Twenty-Five Year Landmark Study.* New York: Hyperion, 2001.

Waugh, E. *Scoop.* New York: Back Bay Books, 1999.

Whelan, E. *Robert Capa: A Biography.* New York: Alfred A. Knopf, 1985.

Whelan, E. *Robert Capa: The Definitive Collection.* London: Phaidon, 2001.

Wolff, T. *In Pharoah's Army: Memories of the Lost War.* New York: Vintage, 1995.

Zuckerman, M. *Behavioral Expressions and Biosocial Bases of Sensation Seeking.* Cambridge: Cambridge University Press, 1994.

# Index

ANTHONY FEINSTEIN is a professor of psychiatry at the University of Toronto. He received his medical degree from the University of the Witwatersrand in South Africa and his psychiatric training at the Royal Free Hospital in London. Thereafter, he trained as a neuropsychiatrist at the Institute of Neurology, Queen Square, in London, and earned a Master of Philosophy and a Ph.D. from the University of London.

After receiving a Guggenheim Fellowship to study mental health issues in post-apartheid Namibia, Dr. Feinstein developed that nation's first mental illness rating scale; he is involved in a similar project in Botswana today. His research on how war affects the psychological well-being of journalists earned him accolades from the Dart Center for Journalism and Trauma and led international news organizations to adopt education and treatment programs for their staff members who cover wars, natural disasters, and other tragedies.

Dr. Feinstein's neuropsychiatric research focuses on brain imaging correlates of behavioral disorders. He is also engaged in the ongoing study of what motivates war journalists and how working in a war zone affects them emotionally.

He is the author of two recent books, *Michael Rabin: America's Virtuoso Violinist* (Amadeus Press, 2005) and *The Clinical Neuropsychiatry of Multiple Sclerosis*, second edition (Cambridge University Press, 2007), and an autobiographical account of his time as a medical officer during the Angolan and Namibian wars, *In Conflict* (New Namibia Books, 1998). He lives in Toronto with his wife and three children.